GREEK FICTION

Greek fiction has been attracting greater attention in the last ten years as a result of the new approach associated with gender studies, narrative theory and the social analysis of ancient literature; in addition, courses in Greek literature in translation have made the novel an attractive, because apparently familiar, genre to study.

Recent work on the novel, or 'romance', has concentrated on the so-called canon of Greek fiction: Xenophon of Ephesus, Heliodorus, Longus, Chariton and Achilles Tatius. Much attention has been focused on the definition of the genre and its possible origins. The purpose of this volume is to widen the terms of the debate while providing the student with a synoptic treatment of the most important works of Greek fiction.

Greeks began writing prose fiction in the fourth century BCE and the tradition continued for a millennium and a half. Fictional modes were used not only for entertaining romances like those mentioned but as a framework for Christian and Jewish religious literature and for quasi-historical works or 'historical novels'.

The contributors to this volume have collaborated to map this extensive terrain on a larger scale than has been done up until now, and to enable the student to see the full extent of Greek fictional writing. This book sets new parameters for the study of Greek fiction.

John Morgan is Lecturer in Classics at University College, Swansea. He has published extensively on Greek fiction, and is currently preparing books on Heliodorus and Longus.

Richard Stoneman is a writer and editor specializing in Greek history, culture and travel. He is the author of the Penguin translation of *The Greek Alexander Romance*. His most recent book is *Palmyra and its Empire* (1993). He is a Senior Editor at Routledge.

GREEK FICTION

The Greek Novel in Context

Edited by
J. R. Morgan and
Richard Stoneman

ROUTLEDGE
London and New York

First published 1994
by Routledge
11 New Fetter Lane, London EC4P 4EE

Simultaneously published in the USA and Canada
by Routledge
29 West 35th Street, New York, NY 10001

Typeset in Garamond by
Intype, London
Printed and bound in Great Britain by
T J Press (Padstow) Ltd, Padstow, Cornwall

British Library Cataloguing in Publication Data
A catalogue record for this book is available from the British Library.

Library of Congress Cataloging in Publication Data
Applied for

ISBN 0-415-08506-3 (hbk)
ISBN 0-415-08507-1 (pbk)

CONTENTS

Part III The Greek context

Part IV Other traditions

Part V Aftermath

NOTES ON CONTRIBUTORS

Ewen Bowie is a Fellow and Tutor at Corpus Christi College, Oxford. He is the author of several important studies of the Greek novel and in particular of Philostratus.

Brigitte Egger is a Professor in the Department of Classics and Archaeology at Rutgers University. She has made a special study of Chariton.

David Konstan is Professor of Classics at Brown University. He is the author of *Sexual Symmetry: Love in the Ancient Novel* (Princeton, 1994).

Suzanne MacAlister is Lecturer in Greek at the University of Sydney. Her study of Greek fiction, *Dreams and Suicides*, will be published by Routledge in 1995.

John Morgan is Lecturer in Classics at University College, Swansea. He has published extensively on the Greek novel, especially Heliodorus, and is the author of the translation of Heliodorus in *The Collected Ancient Greek Novels* edited by Bryan Reardon (California, 1989).

Judith Perkins is a Professor at St Joseph College, West Hartford, and is working towards a book on suffering in early Christianity.

Richard I. Pervo is Professor of New Testament and Patristics at Seabury-Western Theological Seminary, Illinois, and is the author of *Profit with Delight: The Literary Genre of the Acts of the Apostles* (Minneapolis, 1987).

Bryan Reardon is Professor of Classics at the University of

California at Irvine. His most recent book on Greek fiction is *The Form of Greek Romance* (Princeton, 1991).

Patricia Rosenmeyer is Professor of Classics at Yale University.

Gerald Sandy is Professor of Classics at the University of British Columbia, and has made a special study of the fragmentary remains of ancient novels.

Richard Stoneman is a Senior Editor at Routledge and the author of the Penguin translation of *The Greek Alexander Romance* (Harmondsworth, 1991).

Simon Swain is a Fellow of All Soul's College, Oxford.

James Tatum is Professor of Classics at Dartmouth College, New Hampshire, and author of *Xenophon's Imperial Fiction: On the Education of Cyrus* (Princeton, 1989).

John Tait is a Lecturer in the Department of Egyptology at University College, London.

Lawrence M. Wills is Professor at the Harvard Divinity School and author of *The Jew in the Court of the Foreign King* (Minneapolis, 1990).

ABBREVIATIONS

A&A	*Antike und Abendland*
ABD	*Anchor Bible Dictionary*
AJAH	*American Journal of Ancient History*
AJP	*American Journal of Philology*
ANRW	*Aufstieg und Niedergang der römischen Welt*
BASP	*Bulletin of the American Society of Papyrologists*
BIFAO	*Bulletin de l'Institut français d'Archeologie Orientale*
Cd'E	*Chronique d'Egypte*
C&M	*Classica et Medievalia*
CP	*Classical Philology*
CQ	*Classical Quarterly*
CRIPEL	*Cahiers de Recherches de l'Institut de Papyrologie et d'Egyptologie de Lille*
EVO	*Egitto e Vicino Oriente*
GCN	*Groningen Colloquia on the Novel*
GRBS	*Greek Roman and Byzantine Studies*
JAC	*Jahrbuch für Antike und Christentum*
JEA	*Journal of Egyptian Archaeology*
JHS	*Journal of Hellenic Studies*
JRS	*Journal of Roman Studies*
JSSEA	*Journal of the Society for the Study of Egyptian Antiquities*
LCM	*Liverpool Classical Monthly*
PCPS	*Proceedings of the Cambridge Philological Society*
PMLA	*Proceedings of the Modern Language Association*
POxy	Papyri Oxyrhynchenses
PSI	*Papiri della Società Italiana*
PTebt	Papyrus Tebtunis
RA	*Revue Archéologique*

RE	*Paulys Realenzyklopädie*
REG	*Revue des Etudes Grecques*
RhM	*Rheinisches Museum*
TAPhA	*Transactions of the American Philological Association*
WUNT	Wissenschaftliche Untersuchungen zum neuen Testament
YCS	*Yale Classical Studies*
ZDMG	*Zeitschrift der deutschen morgenländischen Gesellschaft*
ZPE	*Zeitschrift für Papyrologie und Epigraphik*

INTRODUCTION

J. R. Morgan

Not so long ago, study of the Greek novels tended to be a specialist and slightly furtive business. The general estimation of their literary merit was low, and there was little sympathy with their repetitive and artificial plots, or with their idealistic and sentimental values. But now they have begun to enter the classical mainstream, partly because the modern theoretical interest in narrative has pointed scholars in their direction, with a new set of critical tools that can be fruitfully applied to them, partly also because our own taste in fiction has outgrown the realistic imperatives of the nineteenth century. With the publication of B. P. Reardon's volume of translations,[1] these works are more accessible to a wider readership than ever before, and their rehabilitation is accelerating. They have even begun to infiltrate university curricula, both within the classical disciplines, and as a component in interdisciplinary courses on the novel. The present collection of essays is intended to provide help to the newcomer to the field of Greek fiction in two ways. Some present readings of the extant novels: these are not meant to be exhaustive, so much as to suggest directions, and exemplify possible methodologies. Others offer a succinct introduction to neighbouring forms and parallel traditions, both to provide a literary context for the canonical romances of Chariton, Xenophon of Ephesos, Longus, Achilleus Tatius and Heliodoros, and also, we hope, to promote a wider definition of the canon itself, and to induce specialist and student alike to read and think more broadly in the general area of Greek fiction. There is every reason why study of Chariton and Heliodoros should not be fenced off from that of the *Alexander Romance* and the Apocryphal Acts of the Apostles. Points of comparison and contrast are illuminating in both directions.

The question of context is, we think, an important but neglected one for a proper understanding of Greek fiction. The five extant romances form a tight corpus, with recurrent plot structures and thematic repertoires. Archetypically, a supremely handsome young man and a supremely beautiful young woman fall in love at first sight. Somehow they are separated and launched into a series of adventures which take them all over the Mediterranean world. They undergo shipwreck, meet pirates and bandits, attract the unwanted sexual attentions of third parties, and believe one another dead. But through everything they remain true to one another and are eventually reunited to pass the rest of their lives in wedded bliss.

This scheme is so stereotyped in our five texts (in Longus rather less than in the others) that there has been an understandable tendency to think of them in isolation as a homogeneous and exclusive category. Only comparatively recently has due recognition been given to the range of variation within the canon. For a long time the question that aroused most interest was that of the origins of this stereotyped form. A number of answers were given, all of which assumed that the novel somehow spontaneously generated itself out of one or more pre-existing genres. So, for example, Erwin Rohde's magisterial *Der griechische Roman und seine Vorläufer*, first published in 1876, argued that the novel began as an amalgam of Hellenistic narrative erotic poetry with paradoxographical narratives of travel and adventure. This was rapidly undermined by the discovery of papyrus fragments of the so-called *Ninos Romance*, which demonstrated that a fully developed love romance was in existence too early for Rohde's evolutionary chronology to work. The response, however, was simply to look elsewhere for the novel's parents: in epic poetry, imaginative historiography, the fictitious plots of Attic New Comedy, obscure local legends or rhetorical exercises and, most recently, in oriental traditions of story-telling.[2]

These theories shared the premiss that literary similarities are to be explained in terms of causal derivation. But the production of literature is not such a mechanical and predetermined business. Resemblances to other, more established, genres should be seen not as signs of parentage so much as of deliberate self-location by individual writers of fiction within the pre-existing frameworks of Greek literature. Traditional questions of origins might be better rephrased as questions of function, context and relationship.

We might argue, for example, that fiction in general answers to a universal human need for narrative pleasure. Specific fictional forms are generated in response to changing tastes and needs, which are themselves reflections of changing social, economic and historical circumstances. The canonical romances must have been written in response to a demand not simply for fiction but for a particular type of fiction, which constitutes their social and political context.[3] The very fact that their plots are so similar suggests that the authors of romances knew they had a winning formula, that is, one which met the needs of their readers. In this case, it is difficult not to see the centrality of the individual and concern with his or her emotions as a response to the conditions of the post-classical world, when the replacement of the city-state by vast, centralized kingdoms and empires deprived the individual of a whole nexus of functioning social relationships that had given his or her life a sense of place and purpose. The romantic love of one individual for another, within a framework of domestic rather than civic values, represented a new way to assert and justify selfhood. Perry and Reardon[4] have argued that the Greek romance is a Hellenistic myth, and like most myths it contrived to function on several levels simultaneously. Thus, at one level, the protagonists of novels are focuses for narcissistic identification which allow their readers to be for a while in imagination as they would like to be in life. At another, the relentless accumulation of perilous adventures which they undergo is a sort of literary Disneyland offering a compensation in fantasy for the routine security of urbanized reality. But at the same time they also enact a spiritual unease and sense of powerlessness by casting the protagonists as noble but passive victims of a contingent and malevolent universe, except that, unlike real life, the novels hold out the implication that everything is actually under control, guided by a shaping intelligence and ultimately meaningful. This use of romantic fantasy to redeem both the boredom of material security and the concomitant feeling of having no control over one's own life is, of course, familiar to us from the popular cinema, another purveyor of powerful mythologies.

But to see the creative impulse of Greek fiction as a response to specific social and political factors is only half an answer to a possibly misconceived question. These factors governed at most the shape of a particular form of fiction – the love romance. They do not explain the more general need for fiction or the existence of other types of fiction in classical antiquity. They do not even account for every aspect of the individuation of the putative mythic stereotype in the Greek novels. Literature also has its own dynamic. It feeds off itself and is its own explanation. Individual writers were no doubt happily unaware of larger, historical forces shaping their genre. They drew both their inspiration and the material to build their stories from other literature, including other novels. There is admittedly something slightly incestuous about the way successive novelists recycled the same themes, but this can hardly be unconscious and should be interpreted not as a failure of the imagination but as alignment to and emulation within a perceived tradition. It would, however, be a mistake to imagine that the novel was somehow sealed off from literature at large. Not only does the romance draw on other genres, like epic or historiography, for story patterns and modes of presentation, but its own repertoire of themes, situations and imagery could infiltrate works which were working to a different agenda and answering to other needs, like the *Alexander Romance*, Philostratos' biography of Apollonios of Tyana or Christian hagiography.

The question of who read ancient fiction is clearly an important one. It was long assumed that the novel was an exclusively popular form, created in response to a downward spread of literacy in the Hellenistic period, and that its readership was thus distinct from that of more recognized literature. This view now seems untenable. Mass literacy never existed in the ancient world, and those capable of tackling a long continuous text were always a small minority of the population. Papyrus remains suggest that, as physical objects, novels were no different from 'normal' literature, running the same spectrum from lavish calligraphy to scruffy work on recycled papyrus. Nor do these fragments bear out the idea that the romance enjoyed any sort of mass circulation. Their numbers are dwarfed by those of the standard authors, and we can be sure that many more homes owned a copy of Homer than any work of fiction. Furthermore, scenes illustrating novels occur in mosaic pavements from the district of Antioch, in houses whose wealth is palpable.[5] The canonical novels and most of the other types of fiction discussed in this book clearly took themselves seriously as literature, and imply a high standard of literary competence among their readers, for example in the matters of allusion and stylistic awareness. There is nothing to support the idea that they were targeted solely or primarily at those of few means, low taste and poor education. No doubt the audience for Greek fiction was not monolithic and was stratified to some degree by taste and social class. The *Alexander Romance*, for instance, was clearly a fluid *texte vivant* catering, perhaps orally, to less sophisticated tastes. But, with due allowance for a wide spectrum of function and pretension, we must conclude that the audience of fiction overlapped with that of other literature. The related question of whether and to what extent that audience included women is addressed by Brigitte Egger in her essay on Chariton in this volume.

If the same people were reading fiction as other literature, there is no reason to suppose that they read their fiction in a hermetically sealed mental compartment. There clearly was interaction, and sometimes confrontation, in the reception of the novel and other literary production. Xenophon's *Education of Kyros*, discussed here by James Tatum, written in the fourth century BCE, strictly stands outside the corpus of Greek novels, but it was obviously felt to constitute a precedent of a kind. We know of three later novelists called Xenophon, which is two too many to be a coincidence.[6] We seem to be dealing with a pseudonym, exploiting a knowledge of other literature to stake out an ancestry and value-set. It cannot be an accident that some of the earliest novels we know of, the *Ninos Romance*, Chariton's *Kallirhoe* and the fragmentary *Metiochos and Parthenope*, are historiographical parasites, fictions occupying empty corners of real history.

Later novels, however, emancipate themselves from history and come into the orbit of the intellectual movement known as the Second Sophistic.[7] This phenomenon centred on the professional display by rhetoricians or sophists, whose heyday in the second century coincides with the most prolific period of novel-writing. Finding its original functions of deliberation and persuasion foreclosed by the political circumstances of the Roman Empire, oratory (which formed the backbone of the ancient educational system) turned instead to self-regarding virtuosity. Its practitioners flourished in an environment half-way between university and theatre, and its products are marked by acute self-awareness, unrepentant artificiality, the pursuit of stylistic effect and a withdrawal into the past and the imagination. The novels of Longus, Achilleus Tatius and Heliodoros are generally reckoned to show the influence of this intellectual climate, in the sophistication of both their language and their content. The novelist Iamblichos, whose work is summarized in the *Bibliotheke* of Photios, apparently referred to himself as a *rhetor*,[8] and Achilleus Tatius is said by the *Souda*, a Byzantine encyclopedia, also to have written works on astronomy and etymology. If this is to be believed, the combination of recherché interests, paralleled by the display of erudition within the novel itself, is suggestive. And from the other side of the fence, we know of an incident when a work called *Araspes and Pantheia*, which sounds suspiciously like a romantic novel, was maliciously misattributed to the leading sophist Dionysios of Miletos (Philostratos, *Lives of the Sophists*, 1.524). Fiction, if not precisely novels, comes to us from the pens of the sophists Dio of Prousa, Lucian and Philostratos, and is discussed in the essays by Simon Swain and Ewen Bowie.

Here we face problems of definition. Because the five extant romances stand so close to one another, it is easy to assume that we are dealing with a narrow and extremely rigid genre. However, recent papyrus discoveries, discussed by Gerald Sandy, suggest that the range of tone and theme in Greek fiction was very much wider than had been suspected. The *Phoinikika* of Lollianus, for example, includes, within a couple of pages, the defloration of a man by a woman, group sex, human sacrifice and cannibalism, vomit and farts and some sensational bandits in disguise; another fragment, apparently from the same work, features a ghost. The author and his readers are obviously enjoying flouting all conventional notions of decency and good taste. Other fictional fragments, such as the *Iolaos* fragment, deal in the sleazy and comic, and suggest that the distinction which used to be drawn between Greek ideal romance and Roman comic fiction, as exemplified by Petronius' *Satyricon*, was a false one. It looks rather as if our sample of texts is not wholly representative of the total output of fictional narrative, but reflects the tastes of the Byzantine Christians on whose choice we rely for the preservation of classical Greek literature. Chastity and noble ideals were obviously more agreeable to them than semi-pornographic sensationalism and the pagan supernatural, but the novel was capable of playing host to either.

We have no way of knowing whether an ancient novel-reader would have thought of the category 'novel' broadly or narrowly,[9] though the similarity of the title of Lollianus' *Phoinikika* to that of canonical romances like the *Ephesiaka*, *Babyloniaka*, or *Aithiopika* suggests that they might have been viewed as closely related, if not identical, forms. Although ancient thinkers did to some extent engage with the problem of fiction in the abstract, the novel and its relatives remained seriously undertheorized in antiquity, to the point where there is not even a single Greek word we can translate as 'novel'. Where the novels are recognized at all, they are summarily dismissed. The novel in general is a form characterized by its elasticity, its ability to enter into dialogue with and absorb virtually any other literature. This makes it very difficult to draw firm lines of demarcation: all novels are fictions, but not all fictions are novels. But whether the unarticulated ancient perception was that the ideal romance was a self-sufficient entity, or just a point on a wider continuum of fiction, it is clearly wrong for us today to divorce study of the ideal romance from other forms of fiction. Not only did osmosis occur in both directions, but the romance owes its generic identity as much to its difference from neighbouring forms as to its internal coherence. So in this volume fictional epistolography and fictionalized biography (as represented by the *Alexander Romance* and Philostratos' *Life of Apollonios of Tyana*) and religious fiction are included alongside the romances.

The environment in which the novels developed was a multiracial one. Greeks were not the only inhabitants of the eastern Roman Empire who produced fiction: of the novelists whose work survives, Heliodoros, Lucian and Iamblichos were Syrians, while Achilleus Tatius was a native of Alexandria. The possibility of oriental origins for Greek fiction has been widely canvassed, particularly in the case of Egypt.[10] Some interaction almost certainly took place between Greek and Egyptian traditions, and the papyrus finds from Egypt include a proportion of texts in Greek with a clear local interest, evidenced by Egyptian names and themes of magic.[11] The precise nature and extent of the influence of Egyptian story-telling on Greek fiction at large remains problematic, but John Tait's survey of the relevant demotic texts makes clear the points of contact and difference between the two traditions. That we can discern this local interest is, of course, due to the accidental preservation of papyrus in Egypt. A similar archive from Syria, for instance, might well have shown different but parallel influences. Likewise the Jewish novellas treated by Lawrence Wills constitute an independent tradition, which makes an interesting comparison in itself but also produced one clear hybrid with the Greek romance in *Joseph and Asenath*.

As far as we can tell, the idealistic novel had a limited production run. The *Ninos Romance* dates probably from the first century

BCE; the last of the extant novels, Heliodoros' *Aithiopika*, at the latest from the fourth century. Within this span there is a definite bulge in the second century. However, the appetite for romances did not end with the apparent end of their production: papyri show that they were still being copied, and presumably bought and read, in Egypt as late as the seventh century. Part of the creative impulse of narrative fiction seems to have been diverted into Christian writings, where typical romance motifs occur in new systems of meaning. The influence of the Jewish tradition is also clearly discernible. The relevant texts are expounded by Richard Pervo (the Apocryphal Acts) and Judith Perkins (*Saints' Lives*). The relationship between fiction and religion is a highly significant and suggestive one. In a sense, they cater to the same need to reassure the individual of his personal worth and discover meaning in the tangled web of his daily experience. Classicists have sometimes tried to make connections between the novels and the mystery cults of the Roman empire, religious movements offering personal salvation to the initiated. Reinhold Merkelbach's *Roman und Mysterium in der Antike* is the most thorough exposition of this idea, but the general view is that he goes too far in tracing specific reference to initiatory rites in the plots of the novels and suggesting that they were coded texts whose true sense was available only to initiates. But we do not need to follow Merkelbach all the way to allow that novel and cult were operating in the same general market. Given this background, it is not surprising that Christianity, ultimately the most successful of the eastern mystery cults, also exploited the repertory of the romances, despite the very clear differences in its fundamental message. The barrier which academic disciplines have erected between the study of 'classical' and 'Christian' literature produced in the same culture is one that urgently needs to be broken down, and we hope that in a small way the inclusion of essays on Christian fiction in this volume will contribute to that end.

Finally, it must be admitted that although our coverage of the literary contexts of the novels ranges widely, it is not complete. This was inevitable if the scale of this book was not to get out of hand. Sadly, there was no room for a separate treatment of Antonius Diogenes' intriguing *Wonders beyond Thoule*, although Simon Swain and Gerald Sandy both have something to say about it. Another novel summarized by Photios was the *Babyloniaka (Babylonian Story)* of Iamblichos, clearly a complex and eccentrically sensational work, with ghosts, magic and a heroine prone to homicidal jealousy. The Latin *Historia Apollonii Regis Tyri* (the original of Shakepeare's *Pericles*) seems to be a Christian redaction of a lost Greek original, to which some papyrus fragments have been speculatively ascribed.[12]

Of marginal fictional forms, mention must be made of the notorious *Milesian Tales*, humorous short stories on bawdy themes, associated with the name of Aristeides of Miletos. The lost Greek original of Apuleius' *Golden Ass*, ascribed by Photios to Lucius of Patrai, might have been an example. Another short story type was the tale of the supernatural. The fragments of the paradoxographer Phlegon of Tralleis include a fine ghost story, which inspired Goethe's *Bride of Corinth*, and similar material has turned up on papyrus.[13] Photios had read a collection of such tales by one Damaskios but gives no details. Other related texts include the imaginative records of events at Troy, attributed to Dares of Phrygia and Diktys of Crete; these purport to be authentic documents (compare supposititious letters discussed by Patricia Rosenmeyer) and are equipped with elaborate provenances. Our texts are in Latin, but fragments of the Greek original of Diktys at least have been confidently identified.[14]

And so the list goes on: the Utopian travel narratives of people like Euemeros, Hekataios of Abdera, Iamboulos and Antiphanes of Berge represent an interesting, but neglected fusion of fiction, history and philosophy.[15] Reconstructed biographies, particularly of literary figures, readily played host to invention, and could develop into something not too far distant from a novel, though not of the canonical type, as in the anonymous *Aesop Romance*.[16] Fables, religious aretalogies (miracle tales), even jokes, can also be regarded as subtypes of fictional narrative. The point is clear, I think, that the ideal love romance should be seen as a member of a large and various family of fictional genres, in relation to and difference from which its generic identity is formed. If we want to locate the novels precisely on the literary map, which we must do if we are to understand the preconceptions that were, at any period, brought to the reading of them, it is necessary to see them against a literary as well as a social context. This book, we hope, will contribute to just such an enterprise.

NOTES

1 B. P. Reardon (ed.), *Collected Ancient Greek Novels*, Berkeley: University of California Press, 1989.

2 G. Anderson, *Ancient Fiction: The Novel in the Graeco-Roman World*, London and Sydney: Croom Helm, 1984.

3 See J. R. Morgan, 'The Greek novel: towards a sociology of production and reception', forthcoming in A. Powell (ed.), *The Greek World*, London: Routledge, 1994.

4 B. E. Perry, *The Ancient Romances*, Berkeley and Los Angeles: University of California Press, 1967; B. P. Reardon, *The Form of Greek Romance*, Princeton: Princeton University Press, 1991.

5 Illustrating the *Ninos Romance* and *Metiochos and Parthenope*; see D. Levi, *Antioch Mosaic Pavements*, Princeton: Princeton University Press, 1947, vol. 1, 117–19; id. 'The novel of Ninus and Semiramis', *Proceedings of the American Philosophical Society* 87 (1944), 420–8; H. Maehler, 'Der Metiochos-Parthenope Roman', *ZPE* 23 (1976), 1–20.

6 Apart from Xenophon of Ephesos, these are Xenophon of Cyprus, whose *Kypriaka* is described by the Souda as 'another erotic history', and Xenophon of Antioch, whose *Babyloniaka* is perhaps to be identified with the *Ninos Romance*. The work's apparent enduring popularity in the area of Antioch, evidenced by the mosaics, could be easily understood if it were a local production.

7 On the Second Sophistic, see G. Anderson, *The Second Sophistic: A Cultural Phenomenon in the Roman Empire*, London, Routledge, 1993; S. Bartsch, *Decoding the Ancient Novel*, Princeton: Princeton University Press, 1989, sets Achilleus and Heliodoros against sophistic practice.

8 Phot.*Bibl*.cod.94.10, on p. 32 of Habrich's edition of Iambl.; also the marginal note to Photios, p. 2 Habr.

9 On this whole question, see J. R. Morgan, 'Make-believe and make believe: the fictionality of the Greek novels', in C. Gill and T. P. Wiseman (eds), *Lies and Fiction in the Ancient World*, Exeter and Austin: Exeter University Press and Texas University Press, 1993, 175–229.

10 See J. W. B. Barns, 'Egypt and the Greek Romance', in *Akten des VIII Int. Kongr. für Papyrologie, Mitteilungen aus der Papyrussammlung der Österreichischen Nationalbibliothek* 5 (1956), 29–36. Note also the influence of the Ahikar story, which survives in several versions in several languages, on Greek works such as the *Aesop Romance*; see R. Stoneman, 'Oriental motifs in the *Alexander Romance*', *Antichthon*, forthcoming.

11 Apart from the obvious examples of the Sesonchosis and Amenophis fragments discussed by Tait, Lollianus' *Phoinikika* seems connected with events in Egypt in 172, and was possibly written to cash in on public interest. See also P. Mich.inv.3378, which has magic, ghosts and a character called Seueris; and P. Turner 8, the so-called *Tinouphis Romance*, apparently a tale of trickery and magic with an Egyptian cast list.

12 PSI 151 and P.Mil.Vogl.260; see R. Kussl, *Papyrusfragmente griechischer Romane*, Tübingen: Narr, 1991, 141–59. See also G. A. A. Kortekaas, *Historia Apollonii Regis Tyri*, Groningen: Bouma, 1984.

13 P.Mich.inv.5 + P.Pal.Rib.152; P.Mich.inv.3378; POxy.1368. For fuller discussion and bibliography on these, see J. R. Morgan, 'On the fringes of the canon: a survey of the fragments of ancient Greek fiction', forthcoming in *Aufstieg und Niedergang der römischen Welt*.

14 P.Tebt.268 and POxy.2539. For discussion of these works see S. Merkle, *Die Ephemeris belli Troiani des Diktys von Kreta*, Frankfurt and Berne: Lang, 1989; A. Beschorner, *Untersuchungen zu Dares Phrygius*, Tübingen: Narr, 1992.

15 See J. Ferguson, *Utopias of the Classical World*, London: Thames & Hudson, 1975; J. Romm, *The Edges of the Earth in Ancient Thought*, Princeton: Princeton University Press, 1992; B. Kytzler, 'Zum utopischen Roman der klassischen Antike', *Groningen Colloquia on the Novel* 1 (1988), 7–16; and the forthcoming article by R. Stoneman on cynic aspects in Palladios' account of Alexander's meeting with the Brahmans of India.

16 For full discussion and bibliography see N. Holzberg (ed.), *Der Äsop-Roman: Motivgeschichte und Erzählstruktur*, Tübingen: Narr, 1992. Also 'The *Aesop Romance* and its influence', *Groningen Colloquia on the Novel* 5 (1993), 1–16.

GENERAL BIBLIOGRAPHY

Anderson, G., *Eros Sophistes: Ancient Novelists at Play* (American Classical Studies 9), Chico, CA: Scholars, 1982.

Anderson, G., *Ancient Fiction: The Novel in the Graeco-Roman World*, London & Sydney: Croom Helm, 1984.

Bakhtin, M., *The Dialogic Imagination* (University of Texas Slavic Series 1), Austin and London: University of Texas Press, 1981, esp. 84ff.

Bartsch, S., *Decoding the Ancient Novel: The Reader and the Role of Description in Heliodorus and Achilles Tatius*, Princeton: Princeton University Press, 1989.

Billault, A., *La création romanesque dans la littérature grecque à l'époque impériale*, Paris: Presses Universitaires de France, 1991.

Bowie, E., 'The Greek novel', in P. E. Easterling and B. M. W. Knox (eds), *The Cambridge History of Classical Literature. I: Greek Literature*, Cambridge: Cambridge University Press, 1985, 683–99.

Fusillo, M., *Il romanzo greco: Polifonia ed Eros*, Venice: Marsilio, 1989; translated into French as *Naissance du roman*, Paris: Seuil, 1991.

García Gual, C., *Los orígenes de la novela* (Collección Fundamentos 16), Madrid: ISTMO, 1972.

Gärtner, H. (ed.), *Beiträge zum griechischen Liebesroman* (Olms Studien 20), Hildesheim: Olms, 1984.

Hägg, T., *Narrative Technique in Ancient Greek Romances: Studies of Chariton, Xenophon Ephesius and Achilles Tatius*, Stockholm: Svenska Institutet i Athen, 1971.

Hägg, T., *The Novel in Antiquity*, Oxford: Blackwell, 1983.
Heiserman, A., *The Novel before the Novel: Essays and Discussions about the Beginning of Prose Fiction in the West*, Chicago and London: University of Chicago Press, 1977.
Holzberg, N., *Der antike Roman* (Artemis Einführungen 25), Munich and Zurich: Artemis, 1986.
Kuch, H. (ed.), *Der antike Roman: Untersuchungen zur literarischen Kommunikation und Gattungsgeschichte*, Berlin: Akademie-Verlag, 1989.
Létoublon, F., *Les lieux communs du roman: stéréotypes grecs d'aventure et d'amour* (Mnemosyne Suppl. 123), Leiden: Brill, 1993.
Merkelbach, R., *Roman und Mysterium in der Antike*, Munich and Berlin: Beck, 1962.
Miralles, C., *La novela en la antigüedad clásica*, Barcelona: Labor, 1968.
Morgan, J. R., 'Make-believe and make believe: the fictionality of the Greek novels', in C. Gill and T. P. Wiseman (eds), *Lies and Fiction in the Ancient World*, Exeter: Exeter University Press, 1993, 175–229.
Morgan, J. R., 'The Greek novel: towards a sociology of production and reception', in A. Powell (ed.), *The Greek World*, London: Routledge, 1994.
Müller, C. W., 'Der griechische Roman', in E. Vogt (ed.), *Griechischer Literatur*, Wiesbaden: Winter, 1981, 377–412.
Perry, B. E., *The Ancient Romances: A Literary-Historical Account of their Origins* (Sather Classical Lectures 37), Berkeley and Los Angeles: University of California Press, 1967.
Reardon, B. P., 'The Greek novel', *Phoenix* 23 (1969), 291–309.
Reardon, B. P., *Courants littéraires grecs des IIe et IIIe siècles après J.-C.* (Annales Littéraires de l'Université de Nantes 3), Paris: Les Belles Lettres, 1971.
Reardon, B. P., *The Form of Greek Romance*, Princeton: Princeton University Press, 1991.
Rohde, E., *Der griechische Roman und seine Vorläufer*, 3rd edn, revised by W. Schmid, Leipzig: Breitkopf & Härtel, 1914.
Weinreich, O., *Der griechische Liebesroman*, Zurich: Artemis, 1950.
Wolff, S. L., *The Greek Romances in Elizabethan Prose Fiction*, New York: Columbia University Press, 1912.

Part I

THE BEGINNINGS OF GREEK FICTION

1

THE EDUCATION OF CYRUS

James Tatum

IN THE BEGINNING

Human beings are not the only creation that inspires a book of genesis. Once one kind of literature is established and familiar, it is tempting to read backwards to discover earlier versions of that kind, if not indeed the source where it all began. Sometimes these predecessors are said to be directly linked to their offspring, like branches in the family tree that Aristotle drew when he observed that the tragic poets learned how to make tragedy from Homer. It is this same genealogical impulse that has more recently led readers to construe the *Odyssey* and the *Argonautica* as early chapters in what the theorist Mikhail Bakhtin terms the prehistory of the novel, and the critic Arthur Heiserman, the novel before the novel.

Reading backwards, critics of ancient Greek fiction have been able to see just such an anticipation of the prose fiction of later antiquity in *The Education of Cyrus*, written by Xenophon the Athenian about 360 BCE, some three hundred years before the earliest proper examples of the form, like the fragmentary *Ninus Romance*. They have been forging this particular link with *The Education* since the organized study of ancient fiction began, and for a number of reasons.

First and foremost, they had the authority of some of the novelists themselves: Chariton of Aphrodisias knew and imitated certain parts of Xenophon's work. Then at least one ancient novelist drew the connection even more explicitly and created his own literary patrimony by naming himself 'Xenophon', of Ephesus. To judge from a similar move by Arrian, the ancient biographer of Alexander, the name 'Xenophon' must have automatically conferred prestige. Most persuasive of all, modern searchers for the origins of the ancient novel were encouraged to connect *The Education* with later fiction because of their own developing typologies of the form. From the perspective of the five extant, complete Greek romances, this early work from Xenophon the Athenian seemed to anticipate much that would later be typical of the genre B. E. Perry constructed in his historical-literary account of ancient romance's origins. It was an early version of 'the ideal Greek romance'.

Thus did a genre and its early history arise, through an inductive reading of texts. *The Education of Cyrus* is both idealistic and romantic, and that particular combination of idealism and romanticism does seem to anticipate Chariton, Xenophon of Ephesus and other romancers by centuries. Some measure of the limitations of this kind of inductive reasoning is that *The Education* has also been identified as a 'romantic biography', occupying an ambiguous position between historiography and imaginative fiction, which Arnaldo Momigliano sees as characteristic of Greek biography in the fourth century BCE.

Not that *The Education of Cyrus* was precocious for Xenophon himself; in many important respects it was not innovative at all. He wrote it near the end of his life, very obviously looking backwards. It is a long, unhurried summing up, drawing on philosophical and political themes developed independently and much more substantially in other philosophical, technical and political works. Its political dimensions will have an important bearing on our estimation of *The Education*'s relation to the less overtly political fiction of later antiquity.

This essay will discuss *The Education* in the terms by which it is chiefly visible today, as one of our earliest versions of ancient Greek fiction; at the same time, we shall try to read it the way Xenophon himself implies it should be read, as a dedicated political education. Both lines of inquiry will lead to something of a dead end, so far as *The Education* is concerned; both ways invite us to reconsider other ways it could also be perceived. For in the candid opinion of many readers now, even when read these ways, *The Education of Cyrus* is uncommonly dull. This, too, is a topic worth exploring.

GREEK MONARCHY IN A PERSIAN SETTING

In *The Education of Cyrus* we discern the kind of utopianism reminiscent of a good deal of later ancient fiction, that curious quality of being in a Nevernever Land that seems to link Xenophon's work more with forms that were to come (the ancient novel) than ones that had already been (ancient history). The exigencies of good story-telling are what define *The Education*'s beginning, its middle course and its end. Neither author nor reader faces the kind of problems that actual experience and troublesome, incontrovertible facts tend to create, as they do in the Persia of Xenophon's *Anabasis* or *Hellenica*.

The turn to Cyrus and Persia for this project is particularly worth noting, since any narrative set there would acquire a particularly significant meaning for the Greeks. Beginning with Hecataeus of Miletus and Herodotus of Halicarnassus, who both lived within the sphere of Persian power, early Greek historians had a constant concern with Persian customs and peoples. Herodotus had defined history's characteristic concerns by focusing on an important, single event, which he identified as the conflict between the Persians and the Greeks. Xenophon's contemporary, the historian Ctesias of Cnidus, was obsessed with discrediting Herodotus and claimed to be engaged in careful researches in his Persian history. Unlike Xenophon, his reputation is not mixed. He has been labelled from antiquity to the present as a liar – neither a novelist nor historian.

Thucydides created a major interruption in this Greek impulse to relate *Persica*, Persian stories. His redirection to the study of contemporary events was decisive for the future course of history, and played an important role in Xenophon's *Hellenica*, which in some sense is a continuation of history where Thucydides' *Peloponnesian War* breaks off. Thucydides left no impression on the surface of the writing of *The Education of Cyrus*, though, as we shall see, he offers a splendid perspective on the kind of political forces that created it.

Aside from the general interaction of Persian and Greek that continued throughout his lifetime, Xenophon had had his own particular experience with the Persian empire in his service with the Ten Thousand Greeks under Cyrus the Younger. Comparison of the *Anabasis* and the *Cyropaedia* has been a convenient way to define *The Education*, if in negative terms; one is fact, the other fiction. Since the *Anabasis* begins with a defeat at the hands of the Persians and the death of Cyrus the Younger, who is said to be the worthiest Persian since Cyrus the Great, it is easy to see the *Cyropaedia* as a wistful fantasy that corrects history, at least in the imagination.

But *The Education* does far more than rewrite one book or one man's experience. By focusing on Cyrus and Persia, remote in time and distant in space, Xenophon found a way to write his way around the inconvenient realities of present-day Greece, where the very kinds of frustrations detailed so vividly for us in his *Hellenica* were inescapable.

There would be many such moves to establish intellectual authority over Persia in western culture, the kind of construction of an alien 'orient' that Edward Saïd has analysed so powerfully and so well. Before Xenophon, there had been Aeschylus, in *The Persians*, and, of course, Herodotus. Now Xenophon displaced present political reality and created an imaginary Persia that knows nothing of the destabilizing forces that tend to disrupt actual history, and experience. If problems ever occur, and they often do, they arise only to be solved. The abiding, unreal ease with which Cyrus goes about life is the antithesis of what Herodotus or Thucydides sought to contend with in writing history.

Unlike most histories, and certainly unlike most human experience, *The Education* is a narrative of fearless symmetry. The story begins with the boyhood of Cyrus in the court of his doting grandfather, Astyages, King of the Medes. It traces his rise to power, first over members of his own family, then over adjacent kingdoms (Books 1–7). He concludes his education by defeating an evil Assyrian king – so evil, as in a fairy tale, that he need not be named – returning home to acknowledge the father whose son he remains (Book 7) and establishing his own court and empire (Book 8). The entire cast of intervening characters is conceived in dialectical relation to the character of Cyrus. Good and bad, clever or stupid, family, friend or foe, each of them adds a facet to the character of the prince, sometimes with great charm, but it is Cyrus who is always in primary focus. Although time passes and locations change, there is not so much a development in time or space as a static exposition of Cyrus' evolving powers of manipulation and control. The narrative telescopes from that moment of triumph to an equally triumphant death scene (Book 8,

Chapter 7). Everywhere, from beginning to end, Cyrus is his father Cambyses' child.

The Education of Cyrus is patriarchal fantasy of the first order, perhaps the most fully developed the ancient Greek world would ever know. None of the challenges to a father's rule that tend to make life interesting or believable are here, no Oedipal struggle between father and son, no rage of Achilles, nor a lover's complaint, so far as Cyrus is concerned; nothing but a calm unfolding of the progress of an exemplary life.

One strand in particular seems to anticipate later fiction, what is customarily termed the 'novella' of Pantheia and Abradatas, a loyal husband-and-wife team who start out as Cyrus' enemies and eventually die in his service. (Pantheia's name is mentioned at this point for convenience's sake; typically for this kind of narrative, she is not actually named until a suitably climactic moment in the story.)

Even here, however, we begin to face the problematic aspects of reading Xenophon through the lens of later fiction. Formally, the episodes of Pantheia and Abradatas no more constitute a 'novella' like the *novelle* of Boccaccio's *Decameron* than do the appearances of Hector and Andromache in the *Iliad*, the famous pair whom Xenophon borrowed pretty much wholesale as his model for a poignant arming scene and an ominous farewell (Book 6, Chapter 4). They reappear at several moments in the course of Cyrus' war against the evil Assyrian king and lend a kind of tragic grace note to what is otherwise an unqualified success story (Books 4–7). But Pantheia and her husband have an unreality about them that makes them far less compelling than either Hector and Andromache, or, for that matter, any characters in Boccaccio's hundred *novelle*, chiefly because Pantheia and Abradatas acquire their identities as human beings only in relation to Cyrus and his imperial agenda.

A crucial turn early in their story will exemplify both the strengths and the weaknesses of reading *The Education of Cyrus* as romantic fiction. Pantheia, the wife of Cyrus' enemy Abradatas, is captured and comes under the power of his lieutenant Araspas (Book 5). He is captivated by her beauty:

> 'I tell you, Cyrus, I myself, and all who looked on her, felt that there never was, and never had been, in broad Asia a mortal woman half so fair as she. No, but you must see her yourself.'

> 'Say, rather, I must not,' answered Cyrus, 'if she be such as you describe.'
>
> 'And why not?' asked the young man.
>
> 'Because,' said he, 'if the mere report of her beauty could persuade me to go and gaze on her today, when I have not a moment to spare, I fear she would win me back again and perhaps I should neglect all I have to do, and sit and gaze at her for ever.'

By comparison with most of his perceived successors in fiction, Xenophon must appear curiously weak. Moralizing overwhelms romance. Xenophon has blocked what is usually an exquisite moment, the first encounter of lovers that leads instantly to love – it is the beginning of Chariton's novel, for example. Here the lovers' first gaze is still-born, dissected and examined, all for the reader's moral instruction.

> Afterwards, after the young man saw from day to day how marvellously fair the woman was, and how noble and gracious in herself, after he took care of her, and fancied that she was not insensible to what he did, after she set herself, through her attendants, to care for his wants and see that all things were ready for him when he came in, and that he should lack for nothing if ever he were sick, after all this, love entered his heart and took possession, and it may be there was nothing surprising in his fate.

Xenophon's main concern is to construct exemplary figures that will teach us a lesson. Araspas exemplifies the power of Eros by succumbing to its powers, Cyrus enhances his status as an exemplary figure by refusing to be tempted. This is but one moment of dozens that exemplify an admirable, imitable character.

But Pantheia, 'she who is altogether divine', reveals something more about the self-imposed limitations of this moral fiction. Both her name and the moment of her naming signal her unique status in *The Education*. She is the only character who has a Greek name, and her naming is postponed until Cyrus mentions her, when he asks her would-be suitor Araspas, 'Then you can really bring yourself to leave the beautiful Pantheia?' (Book 6). He has woven her into the tapestry of his story with care. What comes first to our minds, however, is the author's obvious desire to create an image of a chaste wife, moving loyally and unthreateningly within the orbit of a moral education. Even judged by the often stereotypical patterns of women in later fiction she seems little more than an abstraction of the feminine other, as abstract, in fact, as the 'Persia' in which she appears. When the time comes for Cyrus himself to marry (Book 8), his future wife and marriage will tellingly be disposed of in a sentence. The wife has no name, not only because it would customarily be omitted from mention in polite Greek society, but because none is needed in what seems the rigorously de-eroticized world of *The Education of Cyrus*.

Only Araspas feels the lure of romance as it would later be practised by a writer like Longus in *Daphnis and Chloe*, who can say of his story that it

> will cure the sick, comfort the distressed, stir the memory of those who have loved, and educate those who haven't. For certainly no one has ever avoided Love (*Eros*), and no one will, as long as beauty exists, and eyes can see.

The story of Pantheia and Abradatas is curiously stilted, with neither the tragic intensity of the scenes in the *Iliad* that inspired it nor the erotic power of the works that were to follow. It is an authoritarian, patriarchal denial, not of the possibility of erotic fiction – as we can see from Araspas and Cyrus, Xenophon knows how to assemble a conventional love story – but of its desirability. He wants something else.

LONGING FOR EMPIRE

An erotic energy drives the hero of *The Education of Cyrus*, one that is revealed by what results. Cyrus' realization of his desire to rule comes through an apprenticeship of being ruled, in order that he may rule others: a typically Greek polarity of *to archein* and *to archesthai*. And the *Cyropaedia* itself constitutes a realization of its author's desire to give an account of such a ruler and his achievement. The object of Cyrus' desire is what he does not have, power over others, and he spends the story seeking and acquiring it. The object of Xenophon's desire is the fulfilment of his own designs as a writer, and he achieves those as well. For both author and his creation, the narrative arc consists in identifying an object of desire, longing for it, striving to gain it and finally achieving it. Everything in *The Education* is a construction in harmony with that desired end.

This erotic conception of empire is a familiar theme in Athenian literature, in Thucydides' analysis of the *tyrannis polis* or tyrant city of the Athenian Empire, and in the divine burlesque of empire-building of Aristophanes' *Birds*. The drive to serve whatever Eros one has chosen explains why the narrative line of Cyrus' education is at once so similar to the typical pattern of the romances of later antiquity, and at the same time so different.

It also explains why the appeal of Xenophon's fiction is so restricted. When Longus can speak to those who have loved and those who have not, only those free of Eros are exempt from his theme. Who would they be?

The restricted scope of Xenophon's erotic project is perhaps no more easily measured than by posing the same question of him. Of how many people can it be said that they wanted to be ruled in order to learn to rule, that they pondered *to archein* in relation to *to archesthai*? In an age of Alexander or Louis XIV there is an obvious answer. To the present democratic imagination, only a politician or corporate careerist would come to mind.

If Cyrus can look past Araspas and Pantheia so masterfully, that is because he already has a strong desire he has been pursuing from the beginning of his life. He can resist this temptation to gaze, because he has already seen what he most desires with greater clarity than anyone else in his world has – more precisely, than anyone in this utopian, fictive world is permitted to have. Only one other person comes close, a jealous uncle named Cyaxares, and he is comically incapable of stopping him.

Later readers' reception of *The Education* can help us see its political dimension – readers of antiquity and the Renaissance, however, not of the eighteenth century or later. As a Greek's Persian mirror for would-be princes, *The Education of Cyrus* could provide an education for Julius Caesar, Elizabeth I of England, Augustus, Alexander and anyone else who wished to consult an authority on the establishment of authoritarian rule. It could be useful too for those who, like Cicero, Machiavelli and Elizabeth's tutor Roger Ascham, would instruct them. Its reputation in classical political philosophy and western European history has been unquestioned for some time, though the degree to which monarchs ancient and modern followed its programme remains a story yet to be told.

Whatever it might look like from the perspective of later literature, *The Education of Cyrus* begins and ends as Cicero, Caesar and Alexander's book, an account of the education (*paideia*) of Cyrus the Great of Persia, the founder of the Achaemenid dynasty and its empire. The project is as utopian as his fellow Socratic Plato's *Republic*, the other work with which, beginning in antiquity and continuing to the present, it has been most often and most unfavourably compared. Xenophon wants to show how a single person can impose command over all other human beings, who are conceived as uniting 'against none so readily as against those whom they see attempting to rule over them' (Book 1, Chapter 1). Though he does not use the term itself – even a disenchanted Athenian had his limits – monarchy turns out to be the ideal solution to the twin problems of political instability and popular resistance to another's rule. These are the central faults of all human societies, at least as Xenophon's frankly authoritarian prologue represents them.

The appeal to one who would be an Alexander or a Caesar is manifest and the primary focus of this text. Never was there a longer lead into such a simple answer to such a complex subject than we find in the preface to the *Cyropaedia*:

> Man is by nature fitted to govern all creatures, except his fellow man. But when we came to realize the character of Cyrus the Persian, we were led to a change of mind: here is a man, we said, who won for himself obedience from thousands of his fellows, from cities and tribes innumerable: we must ask ourselves whether the government of men is after all impossible or even a difficult task, provided one set about it in the right way.

Never a clearer inaugural delimitation of authorial purpose and theme:

> For ourselves, considering his title to our admiration proved, we set ourselves to inquire what his parentage might have been and his natural parts, and how he was trained and brought up to attain so high a pitch of excellence in the government of men. All we could learn from others about him or felt we might infer for ourselves we will here endeavour to set forth.

Xenophon's Cyrus is a cultural hero whose virtues are unlimited, who is conceived in terms far simpler than any political leader in actual experience ever could be. He is dazzlingly simpler than the kings of Herodotus (so reminiscent of a Sophoclean hero) or the Athenians and Spartans of Thucydides. Herodotus' Cyrus in particular is as flawed as he is gifted, a sobering portrait of the limits of power for even the greatest of kings. Xenophon's is extravagantly successful, perfectly content. He dies peacefully in bed, surrounded by his sons, the avatar of the ideal ruler celebrated by Cicero and the princes of the Renaissance. Herodotus' Cyrus is tragic, his career thought-provoking: slain in battle with Queen Tomyris of the Massagetae, decapitated and mutilated, his grisly end foretells somehow the momentous collision of Greece and Persia that is the ultimate goal of Herodotus' *historiai* or inquiries.

There is nothing of any comparable moment in *The Education of Cyrus*, not even when the time comes in war for a hero to die. Typically, it is Abradatas rather than Cyrus who has to do it. The theme is always how everything will all work out for the best, rather than what will happen next. And everything always does turn out for the best. Cyrus' education provides undisputed guidance and coherent patterns, with no space anywhere save at the very end for the inconvenient intrusion of contradictory facts or disappointments. Even then the main structure stands complete.

The sources of these alleged investigations are far narrower than a historian's research. Although a number of Persian institutions founded by Cyrus and still in force at the time Xenophon was writing are repeatedly noted, via a stylistic tic of maintaining that they continue 'even to the present' (*eti kai nun*), no one has ever been deluded about the essentially bookish, dreamy qualities of this story. Herodotus is there, and at a greater distance the *Iliad* and the tragic poets, and everywhere, above all, reworkings and adaptations of Xenophon's own works. Cyrus the Younger redies his death at the Battle of Cunaxa in Book 1 of the *Anabasis* all over again, as Abradatas, with Cyrus himself the princely survivor and spectator (Book 7); an Armenian sophist is executed by a father for corrupting the young, a finale to the Socratic life treated with remarkable insouciance for the author of the *Memorabilia* of Socrates (Book 3). Xenophon is Nestor-like: compendious, using his past life and work for the purpose of shaping a lesson to instruct – and manipulate – the young. The moral seems to be that princes must be philosophical and brave, but not so heroic as to make the mistake of dying to establish an empire, or a principle.

AUTHORITARIAN FICTION

Ah! Think not, Mistress! more Dullness lies
In Folly's Cap, than Wisdom's grave Disguise.
(*The Dunciad*)

In spite of Pope's epic, dullness remains an under-utilized instrument in most critical discussions. Fortunately we now have theoretical support to help this kind of inquiry, so central to the rescue of a neglected classic like *The Education of Cyrus*. Xenophon's politically erotic drive created something like the authoritarian fiction described in Susan Suleiman's recent structural analysis of the modern *roman à thèse* (1983). She argues that such fiction presents us with a text which interprets and re-enacts its central meaning over and over again, out of the author's strong desire to make sure that the desired lesson is conveyed unmistakably to the reader.

Like many an author of the later ideological novel, Xenophon came to the task of writing Cyrus' *paideia* to further an ideological agenda already firmly established. Much of his creative energy is directed not so much to exploring an education he wants to discover – as Socrates does in the *Republic*, for example – as revealing an education and its ideal exponent already fully-formed. Hence his clearly articulated theme of the difficulty of ruling human beings (*to archein anthropōn*) and his ideal solution to that problem (Cyrus) are exemplified again and again. Nearly every encounter in *The Education* could be summed up as exemplifying that simple theme. Since the key to an ideological novel is its redundancy, a prerequisite for reading it without falling under the spell of the goddess Dullness is, at a minimum, a desire to participate in the author's ideological agenda.

Since *The Education of Cyrus* proceeds from and is directed towards the training of an authoritarian imagination, its appeal is by its own designs already so fully-formed, the object of its desire so sharply focused, the profile of its intended readers so firmly drawn, that there is no room whatever for the desires of any of its characters to develop, or for its readers to dissent. There is only space to fulfil the desires of Xenophon, of Cyrus and of the reader who agrees to follow. In the biology of this hierarchy, the love of one person directed towards another, like the passion of Araspas the would-be lover for Pantheia, is simply an amusing aberration, off the point. Unnatural as it at first seems, *The*

Education had to be profoundly opposed to the view of love and life that Longus and the later novelists would seem to epitomize. It could and did serve as the perfect foil for later, more liberated engagements with Eros the Bittersweet.

Cyrus' restraint and circumspection, like all his other good qualities, could be said to be virtues that are displayed for the reader to admire, and learn from, and indeed this has often been the response of readers who wished to learn from moral fiction. Linked by hindsight with the novels of later antiquity, as being innovative in literary form, Xenophon's *Education* is also a profoundly reactionary work, not only when compared to the contemporary *Republic*, but when compared to those same novels, whose worldview it anticipates and just as clearly rejects, yet whose way of telling a story it also shares.

In its innovative turn to what we term fiction, *The Education* was a turn backwards, to the imagined freedom of poetry rather than history. And it was only an imagined freedom, not a real one, because it replaced the constraints of recording experience and writing history in the *Anabasis* and the *Hellenica* with an equally hard challenge to create in a way that was new for Xenophon: in short, the way of a poet. The turn from history and experience strained his talents beyond what the author of the *Anabasis* could supply. Characters and events fell into place in delightful symmetry with the initial design, each scene contributing to the education of Cyrus and the reader, the basic lesson taught again and again, with great redundancy.

A controversial epilogue (Book 8, Chapter 8) to *The Education* addresses just this strain between present reality and an imagined perfection, though Xenophon is no self-conscious artist or poet and conceives of the problem in political rather than artistic terms. (The actual term 'epilogue' is of course an interpretative rubric of modern translators and commentators, not Xenophon's word.) Whatever the artistic innovation might have been, his politically regressive fantasy of an ideal hierarchy of values ideally presented and ideally carried out would not bear the strain of historical realities.

> I venture to think I have shown the truth of the statement that I made. I asserted that the Persians of today and their allies are less religious than they were of old, less dutiful to their kindred, less just and righteous towards other men, and

> less valiant in war. And if any man doubts me, let him examine their actions for himself, and he will find full confirmation of all I say.

Thus *The Education* ends twice: first with the death of Cyrus, seemingly the end to the story, then with an epilogue about the failures and iniquities of contemporary Persia that seems to call into question the political wisdom of the whole preceding project. This makes for an incoherent text, an incoherence reflected in the curiously split, traditional reception of *The Education*: at once a novel before the novel, and an early version of what would later be the mirror for princes.

Should we continue to conceive of *The Education of Cyrus* as a place in which Xenophon intertwined the political and the fictional in a single text, and attempt to engage it in a single reading? Possibly. But this most politicized of ancient Greek fiction has something important in common with the novels of later antiquity: it is at heart a deeply erotic text. Somehow that seems a more compelling reason to read it now than the one we have known for so very long, that what Xenophon and his successors created was in some sense made up, the image but not the reality of true history.

SELECT BIBLIOGRAPHY

Anderson, J. K., *Military Theory and Practice in the Age of Xenophon*, Berkeley and Los Angeles, 1970.

Carson, Anne, *Eros the Bittersweet*, Princeton, 1986.

Connor, W. R., 'Tyrannis polis', in J. H. D'Arms and J. W. Eadie (eds), *Ancient and Modern: Essays in Honour of G. F. Else*, Ann Arbor, 1977, 95–103.

Dakyns, H. G. (trans.), *The Education of Cyrus*, introduction and notes by Richard Stoneman, London and Rutland, VT, 1992 (1st edn 1914).

Due, Bodil, *The Cyropaedia*, Aarhus, 1989.

Farber, Joel, 'The *Cyropaedia* and Hellenistic kingship', *AJP* 100 (1979), 497–514.

Fisher, Helen E., *Anatomy of Love: The Natural History of Monogamy, Adultery, and Divorce*, New York, 1992.

Freud, Sigmund, *Civilization and its Discontents*, New York, 1959.

Greenblatt, Stephen, *Renaissance Self-Fashioning from More to Shakespeare*, Chicago and London, 1980.

Hägg, Tomas, review of *Xenophon's Imperial Fiction* (J. Tatum) and *The Cyropaedia* (B. Due), *CP* 86 (1991), 147–52.

Higgins, William E., *Xenophon the Athenian: The Problem of the Individual and Society of the Polis*, Albany, 1977.
Hirsch, Stephen, W., *The Friendship of the Barbarians: Xenophon and the Persian Empire*, Hanover, NH and London, 1985.
Momigliano, Arnaldo, *The Development of Greek Biography*, Cambridge, MA, 1971; revised edn, Princeton, 1993.
Murray, Oswyn, '*Peri Basileias*: studies in the justification of monarchic power in the Hellenistic world', unpublished D. Phil. thesis, Oxford University, 1971.
Pomeroy, Sarah B., 'The Persian king and the Queen Bee', *AJAH* 9 (1984), 98–108.
Rosmarin, Adena, *The Power of Genre*, Minneapolis, 1985.
Saïd, Edward W., *Orientalism*, New York, 1979.
Sancisi-Weerdenburg, Heleen, 'Cyrus in Italy: from Dante to Machiavelli', in *Achaemenid History V: The Roots of the European Tradition*, Leiden, 1990, 31ff.
Selden, Daniel L., 'Genre of genre', in James Tatum (ed.), *The Search for the Ancient Novel*, Baltimore and London, 1994, 39–64.
Springborg, Patricia, *Western Republicanism and the Oriental Prince*, Cambridge, 1991.
Stadter, Philip A., 'Fictional narrative in the *Cyropaedeia*', *AJP* 112 (1992), 461–91.
Suleiman, Susan Rubin, *Authoritarian Fictions: The Ideological Novel as Literary Genre*, New York, 1983.
Tatum, James, *Xenophon's Imperial Fiction: On The Education of Cyrus*, Princeton, 1989.
Todorov, Tzvetan, 'The origin of genres', in *Genres in Discourse*, Cambridge, 1990.
Zeitlin, Froma I., 'Gardens of desire in Longus' *Daphnis and Chloe*: nature, art, and imitation', in James Tatum (ed.), *The Search for the Ancient Novel*, Baltimore and London, 1994, 148–70.

Part II

THE LOVE ROMANCES

2

LOOKING AT CHARITON'S CALLIRHOE

Brigitte Egger

Chariton's *Callirhoe* is the earliest of the five Greek romances that have survived entire, and thus our first European novel.[1] Although he was imitated by later novelists, notably Xenophon of Ephesus, it is questionable whether there were many previous examples of fully developed romance that could have served Chariton as models. How typical *Callirhoe* is for the early stage of Hellenistic romantic fiction we can only surmise from the scanty remains of other examples such as *Ninus* or *Parthenope*. Chariton's role is hardly that of 'inventor' of the Greek novel, but his work may have marked an important step in the development of the genre and the establishment of its conventions.[2]

Apart from the narrator's introduction of himself as 'Chariton of Aphrodisias, secretary to the lawyer Athenagoras', we possess no biographical data about the author, and little information about his audience either, since evidence of reception is sparse and generally unsympathetic.[3] Therefore any assessment of the novel's original literary status must start from the internal evidence of its composition and subject-matter. Scholarly opinions of the genre as a whole have tended to be low since nineteenth-century philologists dismissed it as popular and trivial, and *Callirhoe* was seen as a simple book aimed at 'the poor in spirit' (Perry 1967: 177). In the last twenty years, however, Chariton has not only met with the approval of some readers, but has also been credited with a modicum of erudition and technique. There has been a distinct reappraisal of the artistic merits of his novel. In a recent study R. Hunter argues persuasively that the narrative profile (and thus the readership it implies) is more sophisticated than so far realized. He shows that by exploiting a range of traditions as intertexts and deliberately working with diegetic modes drawn from historiography, epic, drama, rhetoric, myth and even medical textbooks, Chariton demonstrates considerable understanding of the potential of the new genre. The interplay of frames evoked implies that the novel was targeted, on one level, at the tastes of an educated and well-read audience, since the aesthetics of intertextuality demands a high degree of literacy.

Scholarly impatience with a subject matter seen as sentimental and plots viewed as insipid and repetitive raised the question of who these books were written for long before audience-oriented criticism reached the classics. The tendency was to postulate for them a readership different from that of more established literature: women, along with the immature and frivolous, were cast in the role of the 'other'. This assumption of a female audience resulted from the gendering of what was considered culturally non-authentic as feminine, reinforced by the modern association of women with romantic fiction. The central roles played by women in the stories and a set of textual values that struck scholars as 'female' acted as the chief buttresses of this assumption.

Of course, the covert cultural bias is obvious to us now.[4] The compelling argument from external evidence that the modern notion of 'literature for the masses', though long the basis of negative verdicts, is inapplicable, materially and sociologically, to antiquity, complements the recent reassessment of the novels' internal profile (see Stephens 1994). It follows that 'popular' and 'academic' readers were more or less the same people: the literate upper and middle classes of the Greek-speaking eastern Roman Empire.

We no longer think that entertainment as the purpose of fiction precludes a more complex, literary appreciation. It is widely accepted now that even the educated elite did (and does) read fiction, and during the 1980s aesthetic qualities characteristic of post-classical 'highbrow' texts were acknowledged in the sophistic novels of the second and third centuries. We can see now that *Callirhoe* has literary pretensions too. That the complexity beneath the surface of simplicity was discerned later in Chariton than in the other novels is due to his more straightforward narrative organization, lack of sophistic rhetoric and pre-Atticist language. The current academic reappraisal of the romances has turned scholars against the idea of an audience of 'women and children' (Bowie 1985: 688). The argument against a female readership is based on the same reasoning that was previously used in its favour, namely an association of the feminine with the disprivileged aspects of the text – but now in a reversed form. As the notions of popularity and sentimentality have been discarded so have women readers, who are now disqualified as lacking the high technical standard of education required to appreciate all the in-built complexity.[5]

It was indeed time to start reading the novels as skilfully constructed texts, but do we have to drop altogether the idea of a female audience, as a modern fancy no less anachronistic than their assumed mass appeal? The premises of the new debarment of women readers are nearly as unquestioned as was the supposed feminine character of the novels when they were still rated as trash. I wonder whether the current preference for technical merit really is the paramount reception implied. The concomitant disregard of 'romance' appeal resembles scholars' escape into studying the origins of the genre, which dominated research for almost a century. But the challenge of the affective and erotic interests of romance remains. To break out of the circle which equates the female with emotion, simplicity and triteness, and the male with literary and aesthetic refinement, we need to re-examine the notion of the ancient female reader of romance in the light of recent theory of romance reading, within an analysis of the genre's construction of gender.

We have learned from the heated debates in the audience-orientated branch of literary theory and from empirical reader-response research that a text does not prescribe the exact way it is received. But nor do I believe the absolute opposite, that it exerts no influence at all on the way individuals read it. The text offers guiding signals on several planes, but can be actualized in a variety of ways, depending on what readers bring to it and expect from it: their *Erwartungshorizont*.[6] Following the erudite leads and the interplay of allusions (which involves a measure of reflective distance from the plot) and tracing the vicissitudes of the love story or the upheavals and gratifications of passion (which imply a degree of empathy with the protagonists, or even – *horribile dictu!* – an emotionally or libidinally satisfying identificatory reading) are not mutually exclusive activities, even within an individual reader, much less across a varied audience group. Only scholars and critics set intellectual and emotional enjoyment of a text in opposition like this. In my search for a female text as one of the options for reception encoded in Greek romance, I shall focus on narrative patterns of identification and erotic vision operating alongside sophisticated intertextuality. I am not suggesting that ancient women read mainly for non-intellectual pleasure, but positing a female reader alerts us to the significance of sexual codes and so provides leverage for changing our apprehension of a text. Reading is a sexually divided practice today, as corroborated by cognitive research (cf. Crawford and Chaffin 1986). In a search for this gendered text inscribed in Greek romance, *Callirhoe* is the best test case, since the 'female feel' has always been sensed to be most compelling here.

I must clarify my concept of 'a female text' in the light of philosophical, psychological and sociological debate on the dilemma of female identity in a dominant patriarchal culture. When I use this term, I am not addressing the claims of an assertive, distinctive, non-male-identified female subjectivity – surely a legitimate goal for the present but hardly the practice of ancient texts produced, disseminated and transmitted within an unbroken history of androcentric institutions. Two recent studies of pornography and representation in the ancient novels look for this ideal, which would make a text 'useful reading' for women, but detect chiefly male-centred strategies rather than authentic female experience.[7] I shall argue that the female fantasies in *Callirhoe*, maybe predictably, resemble some of the more repressed constructs of femininity typically embraced by women in dominant patriarchal societies. But I shall also show that the text encompasses indeterminacies which leave room for subversive female thoughts, even if ultimately they may serve more as escape-routes and double messages of desire displaced and domesticated than as models of self-determination.

As I have said, internal textual structures delineating an implied external audience provide our main access to the elusive readership of Greek novels. Factual evidence for female literacy is unfortunately far from conclusive, but we know that some upper- and middle-class Greek women of the Hellenistic and early imperial periods could read and write, and so may be considered potential readers of fiction.[8] In approaching them, we must focus on internal patterns of imagination and rhetoric of gender. Authors design their work for specific groups, making assumptions, conscious or unconscious, about their beliefs, wishes and familiarity with conventions. Chariton presumes that his readers will appreciate allusions to the classical tradition, but that they will be fascinated by the love plot as well. He expects them to play along when he focuses on the heroine, who weds the man of her dreams, is battered into a coma by him, and is separated from him, but goes on loving him; who meets another attractive man and marries him to give a father to the child she is carrying; and who, after countless ordeals (mainly in escaping other men's designs on her amazing beauty) is reunited with her first lover, who has in the meantime redeemed himself and proved himself worthy of her. If this storyline sounds familiar, it only indicates how apparently immutable popular themes can be, and how little perhaps some female fantasies have changed.

Audience research has shown that reading can be influenced by generic expectations. Genres can serve as models not only for writing but also 'as different bundles of rules that readers apply in construing texts' (Rabinowitz 1984/5: 420). Some of these codes of ancient fiction have received more recognition than others. *Callirhoe* has been read as a latter-day epic, historical fiction, comedy, a failed religious *roman à clef*, juvenile literature, a document of social degeneration, most recently as a web of literary references. My aim here is to trace another textual level that has been scorned, at least by academic readers, both ancient and modern. I shall call this frame 'romantic'; its concerns are with emotion, sexuality, identification with the characters and the affective pleasures of reading, and it provides a striking construction of femininity.

Romance is a response centrally encoded in *Callirhoe*, through a prominent set of cues. 'I am going to tell a story of passionate love', declares the narrator at the beginning, an important announcement since the audience must consent to the topic if it wishes to proceed.[9] At 8.1.4 he makes a statement about the kind of readers he has in mind: interested in all the adventures and trials, but enjoying even more the ingredients of the happy ending: love and marriage, and re-established domestic order. He says nothing here of a taste for aesthetic sophistication: content and affective closure are meant to yield satisfaction.[10] There is no hint of irony in this description of a romantic target group which sets more store by the sentimental plot than by games of referentiality (as there is perhaps in Heliodorus' portrait of the naive and over-romantic 'reader', Cnemon). Chariton uses the masculine pronoun to denote this audience, but by the conventions of Greek grammar the masculine may subsume the feminine.

Internal audiences may serve as a first step in approaching female readers.[11] Throughout the Greek novels women are presented as literate. Callirhoe herself does not actually read but is intended to receive love letters (4.4.6). She does, however, write a secret letter of farewell and consolation to her second husband (8.4.4), and sets up an international correspondence with the queen of Persia (8.4.7). Of course, this is not the same as novel-reading,[12] but it does show that Chariton, like the other novelists, took literacy for granted among women of the leisured classes. However, in the novel, we find other women 'readers' of Callirhoe's story. The fate of the lovers is discussed and recounted at democratic assemblies at Syracuse, and the narrator stresses specifically that women are present at these story-telling occasions within the novel.[13] Similarly, the women of Babylon are gripped by Callirhoe's tale; as her case is debated all over the city, they comment, identify with her and offer advice as to which of her two husbands she should prefer (6.1.4–5). Such female interest and participation recur throughout the book. The fact that Chariton makes a point of including women among the internal audiences of *Callirhoe* suggests to me that he assumed they would also form part of the external audience. Why else should he emphasize their presence and engagement? But we must not overlook the fact that men are just as fascinated by the romantic plot. In the society depicted, the personal and the erotic are major political issues, and as such also a male concern. But where love as a public matter is at issue in Chariton's world, women join the audience.

My second angle is the centrality of the heroine in the story and the reaction of female characters to her. In many ways the novel is built more around Callirhoe than around Chaereas or the ideal of the couple.[14] However, we cannot simply assume that a narrative centred on the heroine, and a set of themes similar to those of modern romance, automatically imply a female audience. We must examine how the concentration on the female protagonist actually functions.

Callirhoe is the focus of the plot, which revolves around her and which, indirectly, she drives. Not only is she on-stage throughout long sections of the action, but even when she is absent, the thoughts, feelings and activity of all the other characters are directed towards her. Most strikingly the *gaze* of others is always on her: the gaze of men, women, the public, the narrator. Her incredible visual impact, on both individuals and crowds, is illustrated in episode after episode. The mere sight of her will make her famous (2.7.1). The frequency of words for looking, admiring, watching and so on is remarkable. One phrase among many sums it up: *tous hapantōn edēmagōgēsen ophthalmous* (4.1.10). Reardon's translation, 'She drew all eyes to her', makes good English of it, but there is more to it than that. Callirhoe is a *dēmagōgos*, a magnetic public figure, not by the force of words, but by her immense visual power.[15]

This constant gaze on the ravishing heroine is without question erotic. It lingers and dwells on her radiance, her stunning sensual beauty, which from the beginning is compared to that of Aphrodite, the goddess of sexual love. By being invited to concentrate on her appearance, the reader of course is also drawn into the role of gazer: this scopic tactic dominates the whole work. Feminist film criticism, working with concepts drawn from Freud and Lacan, terms such focusing 'the male gaze'.[16] It is the privilege of the male subject and an expression of patriarchal power, a means of reducing women to the status of object – the object of perception, of desire, of representation, of discourse.[17] The operation of this all-pervading male gaze may be briefly exemplified by two passages. The first is at 1.14, where Callirhoe, now a newly sold slave, is unveiled to her stunned buyer (and to the reader). Her role as object and victim is obvious here, as is a trace of a domination/submission fantasy. The second is at 6.4, when during a hunting-party arranged to take his mind off her, the Persian king finds himself unable to stop fantasizing about Callirhoe dressed as Artemis, in a revealing costume; his imaginary gaze lingers on her short skirt and heaving breasts. That she is not even present but constituted only by the projections of his desire confirms her appropriability.[18]

Yet this analysis does not exhaust the novel's visual strategies. If we go beyond the objectification of the female, which is virtually universal in patriarchal discourse, the question becomes: how do the women of romance, and their readers, react to it? We shall find female identification and collaboration with the male gaze, but also subtle traces of Callirhoe sabotaging a few gender norms.[19] The extraordinary fascination of the heroine affects women as an internal audience no less than men. Both these aspects are relevant to the issue of a female reader and her response to the text.

In analysing the complex functioning of the narrative gaze, I shall take as an example the bath scene at 2.2. Here Callirhoe is shown in the nude, while other slave women admire her overwhelming beauty. The terms of the description suggest the famous statue of Aphrodite of Cnidus (cf. Hunter 1994). On a purely technical level, this sculptural method of representation presumably facilitated the depiction of her body.[20] Making the heroine pose as Aphrodite (who as early as Homer is exposed caught in adultery and naked) was also a way to circumvent literary and social restrictions on the direct representation of femininity and the sexuality of a romance heroine. The parallel cases of Photis in Apuleius' *Golden Ass*, who is compared to the same Cnidian Aphrodite at the opening of a sex scene (2.17), and of Circe in Petronius' *Satyricon* (126), locate such depictions of women as statues in overtly libidinous contexts.[21] As characters in 'non-ideal' romance, Photis and Circe can possess explicit sexuality, but in Chariton too the assimilation of the heroine to the figure of the 'bathing Aphrodite' is more than just another chance for the narrator to portray Callirhoe's physical attractions: it has a more specific erotic meaning. This bath scene – a clear sexual marker – cleverly foreshadows her relationship with her second husband, Dionysius, and her more than merely passive role in it.[22] The servants compare her to Dionysius' dead wife and to the image of Aphrodite in the local temple. In setting the atmosphere for a new sexual encounter, this bath also prepares Callirhoe for her meeting with her new master in this very temple, and for a new wedding. The fact that it is women who gaze at Callirhoe's beauty here has partly to do with the need for modesty mentioned above. In the absence of a mirror, some third party has to act as focalizer; male onlookers (including the narrator, who would have to cast himself as a Peeping Tom) are impossible in this context. So the all-female cast is partly another device to show Callirhoe's seductive physique without violating the proprieties. But there is more to the presence of the peasant women.

This secret look into the bathhouse is surely male fantasy and voyeurism,[23] but the device of making the reader watch through the maids' admiring and appraising perspective also invites female interest. In androcentric discourse women share the male gaze, judging other women – and themselves – by its standards, thus reinforcing rather than reversing its circuit. This tactic of asking women to respond to the heroine on display as an object of desire has been described as 'co-opting women observers as both male-identified viewers and rival objects' (Elsom 1992: 221). But at the same time, they are clearly being encouraged to identify with

Callirhoe, as she gratifyingly outshines every other woman in the story, most memorably in her beauty contest with the glamorous Persian noblewoman Rhodogune, which all Babylon watches (5.3).

This perception that identification with the exposed heroine works differently for female and male observers connects with the ambiguous nature of the pleasure afforded by the heroine's visual centrality. On one hand it is passive, dependent on the gaze of others and requiring the woman reader to 'identify against herself' in her role as object (Fetterley 1978: xii). On the other, her optical allure endows the heroine with a special kind of power. Wherever she goes, people fall at her feet; four leading men of the Persian Empire have no concern but to plot her seduction; no one can withstand her beauty. Her irresistibility amounts to erotic omnipotence. Characteristically, she rejects or downplays her overabundant sex appeal, which is neither her fault nor her desire, the narrator stresses: she is fatally attractive despite herself. The same emotive patterns are still marketed in some types of popular romance today, when such protestations of innocence assuage guilt about active female eroticism raised in women readers who identify with the heroine.[24]

This ambiguity, however, opens the way to a more assertive reading of female identity. The gaze on a desired female object does not always confer mastery on the male observer: it can also unsettle him and threaten his subjectivity and authority. Callirhoe exerts an amazing impact on the men who see her. Extreme instances are the satrap Mithridates fainting when she appears (4.1.9), and her owner Dionysius preparing to kill himself because she seems unattainable (3.1). It is a recurrent scenario in the Greek novels for the heroine to be reduced to servitude but to force her captors into subjection by her sensual and emotional influence.[25] Once she has left home, she often finds herself without protection and compelled to rely for her safety on the one asset she has: her erotic appeal. Her attractiveness proves two-edged; first it lands her in danger of being raped, then it enables her to gain sway over her masters and so apparently reverse the real conditions of power. Typically, sexual denial keeps men at bay, or makes them more pliable. Thus, in a precarious balance of power, Callirhoe has a sort of schizophrenic control over the love-sick Dionysius and the Great King, because she can manipulate them by means of her sexy chastity – even, in Dionysius' case, by pretended virginity. It is not always clear who is the master and who the slave. The heroine's own identity is organized around the question of who has control over whom, in a dialectic of control typical of modern fantasties of erotic domination. In much western romance, ancient as well as modern, the male gaze that limits and defines women leads also to the taming or 'defeat' of the men who have the authority to look and command (cf. Newman 1990). The result is an apparent upgrading of the female object of desire, and a romantic (but fallacious) equipoise between the sexes.

But is there a more active role for Callirhoe beyond her disquieting effect as enthralling spectacle? Rarely is she explicitly said to experience desire, apart from her first encounter with Chaereas, when *she* gazes at *his* beauty, and unashamedly asks Aphrodite to give her the man she has shown her (1.1.7). Females who dare to gaze at men with sexual intent occur in the later novels: Lycaenion in Longus, and Melite in Achilles Tatius, for example. But such initiators who actively seek out the male protagonist are always cast as the antagonist, 'the other woman' of the story, who is permitted such sexuality but must never win. In Xenophon and Heliodorus, such female assertiveness is invariably presented negatively. Their anti-heroines (e.g. Manto or Arsace) are not only given to wild and illicit passion, but are also disqualified by being murderous barbarians who abuse their power to gratify their desires. Whereas in the other novels chastity and assertive sexuality are assigned to two contrasted female types, Callirhoe alone combines the two within herself.

The ambivalence of visual eroticism, with its combination of the passive and the operative, is reflected in the social construction of gender. On one hand, women are asked to empathize with overall female dependence and confinement: Callirhoe remains the object of constant male vision and supervision, the goal of men's desire and action, the victim of male legal and social authority, confined in enclosed spaces, a prize for the rivals vying to possess her (4.4.1, 6.2.7). She justly complains that she is being passed from one man's house and custody to another's like a piece of furniture, with no choice of her own (1.14, cf. Egger 1988). But there is a flip side to this picture of restraint, for the text offers its women readers vicarious gratification by dwelling on Callirhoe's stunning erotic effect, which amounts to an ersatz empowerment. In this narcissistic fantasy of female rule by eroticism, which tries to come to terms with patriarchal reality by romanticizing it, the idea of revenge lurks just beneath the surface of the narrative of seduction whenever the men are grovelling and the tables appear turned (cf. Modleski 1982). Though restricted socially, the heroine passively controls the central reality of romance, the erotic, in the dialectical manner I have analysed.

Finally, there is a textual indeterminacy to the highly ambiguous story of Callirhoe's second marriage which permits a reading of subjective female desire reaching beyond irresistible passivity. Every excuse is made to acquit Callirhoe of the charge of adultery, as pressing circumstances (her loss of freedom, pregnancy, a sly slave's manipulativeness) compel her to take Dionysius as a husband despite the fact that she is already married. The usual interpretation is that a 'virtuous bigamist' (Anderson 1984: 108) employs a cunning scheme reminiscent of New Comedy (a literary code suggesting a relaxation of moral standards) to safeguard her social rank, her child and her propriety. But at another level, the text suggests that her choice may be something more than merely a pragmatic reaction to her predicament, and that she may have more subjective, even subversive motives. The bath scene discussed above raises doubts as to the complete innocence of her stance. Thereafter her involvement with Dionysius can be read as one of unadmitted sexual interest (cf. Schmeling 1974: 103; Liviabella Furiani 1989: 47ff.). Among the gaps that the reader must interpret are her failure to mention her marriage to Chaereas, her blushingly alluring behaviour, her silent inability to choose between her two husbands at her trial. And she does, after all, end up actively courting Dionysius, through her intermediary, Plangon (3.1), and she does take a second lover – or husband, as she insists – something elsewhere permitted only to the female antagonist. Chariton leaves open the question of whether her seductiveness is really only a strategy to deal with an emergency,[26] or more self-motivated then usually conceded, and thus he eases the acceptance of her transgression of a major sexual taboo. Perhaps her second marriage is not, as critics since Heiserman have felt, a triumph of patriarchy, but, through a tangle of contradictions, a literary escape route from patriarchy for Callirhoe and her readers. She is, if not a widow of Ephesus, at least a widow of Miletus for a while, before she returns to domestic confinement in her home city. At the end of the story she reasserts her erotic visual power in her solution to the problem of having two husbands: asking Dionysius not to remarry, she fails to release him, leaving him with her child, but also with images of her on which he can gaze for the rest of his days (8.5.15).

In conclusion I want to look at how Chariton's evocation of traditional codes from other genres contributes to his treatment of issues of gender. The *Iliad* is an important intertext. Ancient readers would be sure to notice motifs from the epic in the plot fabric of the novel (the abduction of a beautiful wife, the trip to Asia Minor, the two husbands,[27] the war fought over the heroine, the role of Aphrodite), as well as various allusions and quotations, including two specific comparisons of Callirhoe's sexual fascination to the visual allure of Helen.[28] But whereas the epic focuses on the relations between the men in the two camps in the grip of the heroic honour code, their valiant combats and death, we hear little about Helen or men's feelings about her. Chariton introduces a parallel case of warfare in Book 7, where both Chaereas and Dionysius perform something like an Homeric *aristeia*. But martial endeavour is for him clearly secondary. The participation of the rivals in the campaigns serves mainly to demonstrate that Chaereas, suddenly a military hero and fabulously rich, is more eligible to be Callirhoe's mate after all. So a shift from the all-male perspective to an interest in the female eroticism has taken place in this frame also.

The use of other genres as intertexts brings into view a few expansions of the female role besides the amplification of her erotic power. When she offers her husband military advice, Callirhoe plays the part of Andromache from *Iliad* 6, except that she is not sent back to her weaving and her words are heeded (7.2.4). And if we switch to the frame of Hellenistic historiography, we see that not only Chaereas, as general, but also Callirhoe gets to play the part of Alexander, the noble conqueror who spares his Persian captives (8.3); a theme of friendship between women is sounded here that is new in Greek prose. However, these brief and intermittent cues remain subordinate to the general romantic configuration of the female ideal.

Gender is constructed through all these interlocking codes of reading, and the resulting image is more complex than I have been able to analyse here. My reading reveals a powerful double message, which on one hand triggers female fantasies of erotic omnipotence as a variety of narrative devices, notably visual focalization, concentrates the reader's attention on the heroine's indomitable passive eroticism, but at the same time evokes traditional restrictions on femininity. A more assertive aspect of Callirhoe's sexual identity, which emerges through textual indeterminacy, permits some release, but the focus on the seductive illusion of women's enhanced visual and sexual power channels reader interest to the ambivalent sphere of the erotic and contains female subjectivity there. Chariton, at the beginning of the Greek novel, experiments with several established literary genres, notably historiography and epic. Overlaying them with the erotic, he creates the dialectical message of romance highly accessible to female fantasy. Any inclusive reading of *Callirhoe* should integrate with its sophisticated literary texture this romance appeal inviting women readers' identification.[29]

NOTES

1 The name of the female protagonist alone seems to have been the original title since the narrator concludes (8.8.16) 'This is what I have written about Callirhoe'. This is corroborated by a second-century papyrus (P. Michael. 1) containing the subscript to Book 2. *Callirhoe* is also the title used by Persius, if we take 1.131 to be a reference to the novel (see below n. 3). The single manuscript of the novel uses the title *Chaereas and Callirhoe*, but this may be a later adaptation to the practice of other novelists. Cf. Plepelits 1976: 28f.; Lucke and Schäfer 1985: 181.

2 Chariton is probably predated by the *Ninus* romance. Hägg (1984: 79) suggests that he might be the author also of *Parthenope* and *Chione*, two other pre-Atticist novels preserved only in meagre papyrus fragments.

3 In our earliest piece of evidence, the first-century Latin satirist Persius mocks readers of a certain *Callirhoe*, quite possibly Chariton's novel rather than a popular mime of the same title; cf. Weinreich 1962: 13; Schmeling 1974: 18; Plepelits 1976: 29f. Philostratus, in the early third century, pours scorn on a certain Chariton, presumably the novelist, who is worth nothing in the present and will be forgotten in the future; cf. Perry 1967: 89ff.; Reardon 1991: 47f.

4 The female reader of romance was first postulated by Rohde in 1867, and has persisted into studies of the 1970s and 1980s, though the negative prejudice she aroused subsided. Cf. Egger 1988 and 1990.

5 Cf. Bowie 1985; Wesseling 1988; Treu 1989. In other recent studies such as MacQueen 1990, Reardon 1991 and Hunter forthcoming they are omitted from consideration. Elsom (1992) and Montague (1992), on new theoretical grounds, allow only for 'male-identified readers'.

6 Cf. Iser 1974, 1978; Jauss 1970; Radway 1984; Winkler 1985.

7 Elsom 1992; Montague 1992.

8 For the historical background of female novel readers and the evidence

from Graeco-Roman Egypt, see Egger 1988, 1990; also Cole 1981; Pomeroy 1977, 1981; Harris 1989; Kraemer 1991.

9 An allusion to Thucydides may be a signal to switch into historiographical gear (cf. Müller 1976; Hunter 1994), and readers may have focused on the tension between historical manner and private theme (although the gap between them was certainly narrowed by the practice of Hellenistic historiography). But the slight narratorial detachment revealed in the opening need not override the romantic interest of the promised subject.

10 'And I think that this last chapter will prove very agreeable to its readers; it cleanses away the grim events of the earlier ones. There will be no more pirates or slavery or lawsuits or fighting or suicide or wars or conquests; now there will be lawful love and sanctioned marriage' (8.1.4). (trans. B. P. Reardon, 1989: 110).

11 Cf. Doherty 1992 for a similar approach to the *Odyssey.*

12 The sole reader of books in the Greek novels is male, but even for him reading is not an activity with its own rewards, but is linked to an erotic motive: Clitophon, while courting Leucippe, pretends to be engrossed in a book only so as to be able to steal glances at her (Ach.Tat.1.6.6).

13 For instance when the pirate Theron gives an account of Callirhoe's fate (3.4.4), and at the final assembly when all (and Chariton writes this word in both its masculine and feminine forms, *pasai kai pantes*) demand to see her and learn everything (8.7.1). In general women may be assumed to form part of the public which takes an interest in her (e.g. 1.6.3, 3.5.3).

14 Chaereas becomes the centre of attention only in his rather unexpected role as martial hero in Book 7. But even here he is acting for Callirhoe's sake, in order to become worthy of her.

15 For other examples of the gaze fixed on the heroine, see 3.2, where the people of Miletus climb on roofs to catch a glimpse of her; 3.8, where she is compared to an admired painting; 5.5, where all of Babylon comes, ostensibly to hear the trial but in reality just to see her; 4.1, where people cannot bear the radiance of her beauty and turn away blinded and fall to the ground, even children.

16 Cf. Kaplan 1983; Newman 1990; de Lauretis 1987; Silverman 1988.

17 Hunter's interpretation of Callirhoe as a statue characterized by infinite projectibility illustrates this objectification (forthcoming). Elsom (1992) analyses it in Freudian terms: the 'phallic woman', always a sign and on sale, confirms the subjectivity of the men who compete for her.

18 Likewise, at 2.4, Dionysius, during one of many sleepless nights that her lovers suffer, relives in his imagination the time he has spent with her, again with emphasis on the visual.

19 Open female rebellion will not be found in novels until much later.

20 Apart from the bath scene, few physical details of her body are given. Elsewhere the narrator goes no further than baring her arms and describing her eyes and hair. Parallels at 4.1 and Ach.Tat.5.13.2 (cf.

5.11.5) suggest that this marble metaphor was a topos in representing the female body.

21 Hunter notes the comparison of Circe to the Diana of Praxiteles. The choice of Diana/Artemis, the goddess of chastity, foreshadows the negative outcome of Encolpius' sexual endeavours.

22 While a bath may seem a 'natural' frame for depicting the body, and thus the sexuality, of a romance heroine, it has a long tradition of erotic connotation in literature, going back to the *Odyssey* (6.85ff.). Nausicaa, who there bathes in the river, is, like Callirhoe, more beautiful than all other young women, but she is compared to Artemis, so that we can foresee that her encounter with Odysseus will not be sexual. Callirhoe is modelled partly on Nausicaa and her female companions, but also partly on the male Odysseus, the stranger who needs to wash after a long journey, to be anointed and given new clothes.

23 This voyeurism is even clearer in Heliodorus. The reader is encouraged to spy on Charicleia, through the eyes of a would-be rapist (5.31, where her bridal costume is an obvious sexual marker), or through a keyhole (7.15).

24 Erotic success actively sought by women is judged negatively; in both ancient and modern romances such behaviour is confined to the female antagonist. Sexual attractiveness has to be unintentional if it is to be a desirable female quality. This socio-erotic dilemma of modern women readers is analysed by Modleski 1982.

25 Such rape fantasies are less displaced in later novels. See Winkler 1990 and Montague 1992 (on *Daphnis and Chloe*). Some men in love with the heroine can be persuaded to spare her, with others brutality is avoided only in the act. For example, in Achilles Tatius Thersander has Leucippe locked up in a hideout, but when he comes to assert his rights of ownership 'he was totally her slave' (6.20.1). The idea is that rape can always be averted by a shrewd and truly pure woman. The menace is invoked, the imagination triggered, yet the stark reality of forced sex is never shown. The fantasy of a free woman temporarily enslaved and her chastity threatened has had an amazingly long life in western romance and pornography.

26 Other heroines in defenceless predicaments also use their sexual appeal to manipulate men, particularly Heliodorus' Charicleia (e.g. 1.21–3). Cf. Egger 1990.

27 Here Chariton has improved on his model. Not only is there a Greek husband (Menelaus/Chaereas) and a second, Asiatic one (Paris/Dionysius), but Dionysius also plays the role of Menelaus when he is opposed by further Asiatic rivals, 'many Parises' (5.2.7).

28 5.5.9 and 4.1.8; cf. Müller 1976: 130; Laplace 1980: 84.

29 My reading does not exclude a 'male aspect' to the text. For instance, through Chaereas' development, Chariton offers a story of empowerment that invites identification from men also; and, according to Elsom 1992, there is a quasi-pornographic satisfaction to be derived from the exhibition of the female.

BIBLIOGRAPHY

Anderson, G. (1982), *Eros Sophistes: Ancient Novelists at Play* (American Classical Studies 9), Chico, CA.

Anderson, G. (1984), *Ancient Fiction: The Novel in the Graeco-Roman World*, London and Sydney.

Bartsch, S. (1989), *Decoding the Ancient Novel: The Reader and the Role of Description in Heliodorus and Achilles Tatius*, Princeton.

Biraud, M. (1985), 'L'hypotexte homérique et les rôles amoureux de Callirhoé dans le roman de Chariton', in *Sémiologie de l'amour dans les civilisations méditerranéennes*, Paris, 21–7.

Bowie, E. L. (1985), 'The Greek novel', in P. Easterling and B. Knox (eds), *Cambridge History of Classical Literature* I, Cambridge, 683–99.

Cole, S. G. (1981), 'Could Greek women read and write?', in H. Foley (ed.), *Reflections of Women in Antiquity*, New York, 219–45.

Crawford, M. and Chaffin, R. (1986), 'The reader's construction of meaning: cognitive research on gender and comprehension', in P. Schweickart and E. Flynn (eds), *Gender and Reading*, Baltimore and London, 3–30.

de Lauretis, T. (1987), *Technologies of Gender*, Bloomington.

Doherty, L. (1992), 'Gender and internal audiences in the *Odyssey*', *AJP* 113, 161–77.

Egger, B. (1988), 'Zu den Frauenrollen im griechischen Roman: Die Frau als Heldin und Leserin', *GCN* 1, 33–66.

Egger, B. (1990), 'Constructing the feminine: women in the Greek novels', dissertation, University of California.

Egger, B. (1994), 'Women and marriage in the Greek novels: the containment of romance', in J. Tatum (ed.), *The Search for the Ancient Novel*, Baltimore, 260–80.

Elsom, H. (1992), 'Callirhoe: displaying the phallic woman', in A. Richlin (ed.), *Pornography and Representation in Greece and Rome*, New York and Oxford, 212–30.

Fetterley, J. (1978), *The Resisting Reader: A Feminist Approach to American Literature*, Bloomington.

Hägg, T. (1983), *The Novel in Antiquity*, Berkeley and Los Angeles.

Hägg, T. (1984), 'The Parthenope romance decapitated?', *Symbolae Osloenses* 59, 61–91.

Harris, W. (1989), *Ancient Literacy*, Cambridge, MA.

Heiserman, A. R. (1977), *The Novel before the Novel*, Chicago.

Hunter, R. L. (1983), *A Study of Daphnis and Chloe*, Cambridge.

Hunter, R. L. (1994), 'History and historicity in the romance of Chariton', *ANRW* II, 34.2.

Iser, W. (1974), *The Implied Reader*, Baltimore.

Iser, W. (1978), *The Act of Reading*, Baltimore.

Jauss, H. R. (1970), *Literaturgeschichte als Provokation der Literaturwissenschaft*, Frankfurt (Engl. translation 'Literary history as a challenge to literary theory') (*New Literary History* 2, 7–37).

Jensen, M.A. (1984), *Love's $weet Return: The Harlequin Story*, Toronto.

Johne, R. (1989), 'Übersicht über die antiken Romanautoren bzw. -werke mit Datierung und weitergeführter Bibliographie', in H. Kuch *et al.* (eds), *Der antike Roman: Untersuchungen zur literarischen Kommunikation und Gattungsgeschichte*, Berlin, 198–230.

Kaplan, E. A. (1983), 'Is the gaze male?', in A. Snitow *et al.* (eds), *Powers of Desire: The Politics of Sexuality*, New York, 309–27.

Kraemer, R. (1991), 'Women's authorship of Jewish and Christian literature in the Greco-Roman period', in A. Levine (ed.), *'Women Like This': New Perspectives on Jewish Women in the Greco-Roman World*, Atlanta, 221–42.

Kuch, H. *et al.* (eds) (1989), *Der antike Roman: Untersuchungen zur literarischen Kommunikation und Gattungsgeschichte*, Berlin.

Kussl, R. (1991), *Papyrusfragmente griechischer romane* (Classica Monacensia 2), Tübingen.

Laplace, M. (1980), 'Les légendes troyennes dans le "roman" de Chariton, *Chairéas et Callirhoé*', *REG* 93, 83–125.

Liviabella Furiani, P. (1989), 'Di donna in donna: Elementi "femministi" nel romanzo greco d'amore', in P. Liviabella Furiani and A. Scarcella (eds), *Piccolo mondo antico: Le donne, gli amori, i costumi, il mondo reale nel romanzo antico*, Naples, 43–106.

Liviabella Furiani, P. and Scarcella, A. (eds.) (1989), *Piccolo mondo antico: Le donne, gli amori, i costumi, il mondo reale nel romanzo antico*, Naples.

Lucke, C. and Schaefer, K. (1985), *Kallirhoe: Übersetzung und Anmerkungen*, Leipzig.

MacQueen, B. (1990), *Myth, Rhetoric and Fiction. A Reading of Longus'* Daphnis and Chloe, Lincoln and London.

Maehler, H. (1990), 'Symptome der Liebe im Roman und in der griechischen Anthologie, in *GCN*, 4, 1–12.

Merkelbach, R. (1962), *Roman und Mysterium in der Antike*, Munich and Berlin.

Modleski, T. (1982), *Loving with a Vengeance: Mass-produced Fantasies for Women*, New York.

Montague, H. (1992), 'Sweet and pleasant passion: female and male fantasy in ancient romance novels', in A. Richlin (ed.), *Pornography and Representation in Greece and Rome*, New York and Oxford, 231–49.

Morgan, J. (1982), 'History, romance and realism in the Aithiopika of Heliodoros', *Classical Antiquity* 1, 221–65.

Morgan, J. (1991), 'Reader and audiences in the "Aithiopika" of Heliodoros', in *GCN* 4, 69–83.

Müller, C. W. (1976), 'Chariton von Aphrodisias und die Theorie des Romans in der Antike', *A&A* 23, 115–36.

Newman, Beth (1990), 'The situation of the looker-on: gender, narration, and gaze in *Wuthering Heights*', *PMLA* 105, 1029–41.

Papanikolaou, A. D. (1973), *Chariton-Studien*, Göttingen.

Perry, B. E. (1967), *The Ancient Romances: A Literary-historical Account of Their Origins*, Berkeley and Los Angeles.

Pervo, R. I. (1987), *Profit with Delight: The Literary Genre of the Acts of the Apostles*, Philadelphia.

Plepelits, K. (1976), *Chariton: Deutsche Übersetzung, Einleitung, Erläuterungen*, Stuttgart.

Pomeroy, S. (1977), 'Technikai kai Mousikai: The education of women in the fourth century and in the Hellenistic period', *AJAH* 2, 51–68.
Pomeroy, S. (1981), 'Women in Roman Egypt: a preliminary study based on papyri', in H. Foley (ed.), *Reflections of Women in Antiquity*, New York, 303–22.
Rabinowitz, P. (1984/5), 'The turn of the glass key: Popular fiction as reading strategy', *Critical Inquiry* 11, 418–31.
Radway, J. A. (1984), *Reading the Romance: Women, Patriarchy, and Popular Literature*, Chapel Hill and London.
Reardon, B. P. (1982), 'Theme, structure and narrative in Chariton', *YCS* 27, 1–27.
Reardon, B. P. (1991), *The Form of Greek Romance*, Princeton.
Reardon, B. P. (ed.) (1989), *Collected Ancient Greek Novels*, Berkeley, CA.
Richlin, A. (ed.) (1992), *Pornography and Representation in Greece and Rome*, New York and Oxford.
Rohde, E. (1914), *Der griechische Roman und seine Vorläufer*, 3rd edn, Leipzig.
Sandy, G. N. (1982), *Heliodorus*, Boston.
Schmeling, G. L. (1974), *Chariton*, New York.
Silverman, K. (1988), *The Acoustic Mirror*, Bloomington.
Stephens, S. (1994), 'Who read ancient novels?', in J. Tatum (ed.) *The Search for the Ancient Novel*, Baltimore, 405–18.
Treu, K. (1989), 'Der antike Roman und sein Publikum', in H. Kuch *et al.* (eds), *Der antike Roman: Untersuchungen zur literartischen Kommunikation und Gattungsgeschichte*, Berlin, 178–97.
Weinreich, O. (1962), *Der griechische Liebesroman*, Zürich.
Wesseling, B. (1988), 'The audience of the ancient novel', *GCN*, 1, 67–79.
Wiersma, S. (1990), 'The Ancient Greek novel and its heroines: a female paradox', *Mnemosyne* 63, 109–23.
Winkler, J. (1982), 'The mendacity of Kalasiris and the narrative strategy of Heliodoros' *Aithiopika*', *YCS* 27, 93–158.
Winkler, J. (1985), *Auctor and Actor: A Narratological Reading of Apuleius's The Golden Ass*, Berkeley, CA.
Winkler, J. (1990), 'The education of Chloe: hidden injuries of sex', in *The Constraints of Desire: The Anthropology of Sex and Gender in Ancient Greece*, New York and London, 101–26.
Zeitlin, F. (1990), 'The poetics of Eros: nature, art and imitation in Longus' *Daphnis and Chloe*', in D. Halperin (ed.), *Before Sexuality*, Princeton, 417–64.

3

XENOPHON OF EPHESUS[1]

Eros and narrative in the novel

David Konstan

The Greek romantic novels exploit a formula involving young love, hair-raising adventures and close escapes culminating in a happy conclusion, like the romances published by Harlequin or Mills and Boon, and this has worked to discredit them as literature. Critics today, however, have come to appreciate the individuality and sophistication of these ancient prose fictions – with one exception: the *Ephesiaka* or *Ephesian Tale* by Xenophon of Ephesus, which is universally regarded as the worst of the lot. This is a mistake. The novel is not only good fun, it is also very cleverly constructed, and subtly examines the erotic conventions that underpin the genre as a whole.

While nothing is known of its author, the simple, idiomatic style of the *Ephesian Tale*, and its resemblance to the novel of Chariton which is no later than the second century CE, suggest that this may be the earliest of the surviving Greek novels. The Byzantine lexicon known as the *Suda* identifies Xenophon of Ephesus as the author of an *Ephesiaka* in ten books, and this has been taken as evidence that the existing text, in five books, is abridged. It is true that some passages in the *Ephesian Tale* as we have it seem condensed or obscure, but the case for abridgement is inconclusive.[2] The work survives in a single manuscript, and the first edition was published in 1726.

We may begin by considering a scene early in the second of the five books or chapters into which the novel is divided. In Book 1, Habrocomes and Anthia, the hero and heroine, had fallen in love, and were married with their parents' consent. On their honeymoon voyage, however, they were captured by pirates, who at this point are holding them under guard in a hut in Tyre. Corymbus, the leader of the pirate squad, has fallen violently in love with Habrocomes. He confesses his passion to his shipmate, Euxinus, who reveals in turn that he is enamoured of Anthia.

In pleading their love, each of the pirates undertakes to represent the other. After they have heard the pirates' arguments, Habrocomes and Anthia each request a brief interval in which to deliberate about their offers. When they are together again,

> flinging themselves down they wept and wailed. 'O Father!' they said, 'O Mother! Dear country! relatives! family!' Finally Habrocomes recovered and said, 'Wretches that we are, what then shall we suffer in this land of barbarians, delivered to the insolence of pirates? What was prophesied is beginning. Now the god is exacting vengeance on me for my arrogance. Corymbus is in love with me, Euxinus with you. O for my beauty, unseasonable for us both![3] For this, then, have I kept myself chaste until now, that I might subject myself to a robber who loves me with a foul passion? What kind of life remains for me when I have become a whore instead of a man, and have been deprived of my Anthia? No, by the chastity that has been my companion from childhood until now, I cannot subject myself to Corymbus. Sooner shall I die and prove chaste as a corpse.'

Anthia gives vent to a similar desperation, and concludes:

> But may I never be so in love with life, nor survive, having been violated, to look upon the sun. Let this be our decision: let us die, Habrocomes. We shall have one another after death, troubled by no one.
>
> (2.1.1–6)

The speeches of Habrocomes and Anthia seem virtually identical in tone and content, on the basis of which one could scarcely determine which is the woman's and which the man's. Each is committed to preserving faith with the other, each fears being overpowered and violated, each turns to death as a means of escaping the sexual violence of the pirates. The similarity between the protagonists is quite different from the Mills and Boon formula, with its virile heroes and wilting heroines.

We may compare the scene, shortly before, in which the pirates board the ship on which Habrocomes and Anthia are passengers:

> Thereupon some in panic flung themselves into the sea and

> perished; others were slain attempting to defend themselves. But Habrocomes and Anthia ran to the pirate Corymbus, clasped his knees, and said, 'Take the money and ourselves as slaves, master, but spare our lives and cease murdering those who have become your willing subjects'.
>
> (1.13.5–6)

The hero conspicuously declines to fight against his assailants. One critic has remarked: 'The reactions of Habrocomes and Anthia are noteworthy for that pair's unmitigated pusillanimity.'[4] But this submissiveness cannot be taken simply as a sign of cowardice or unmanliness. Later, Habrocomes will himself be a valued member of a band of robbers under the leadership of Hippothous, who will remain his loyal friend to the end of the story. This is not, I think, inconsistency of characterization; rather, it reveals a convention observed by the Greek novels generally. As lovers, Habrocomes and Anthia plead with one voice before their captors. Xenophon eschews any differentiation between the roles of hero and heroine when their bond to one another is challenged. She reacts as resolutely as he in her willingness to die, while he is as resigned as she to their helplessness, and as concerned for his chastity as she is for hers.

Xenophon also knows other representations of masculine desire. In Book 3, the pirate Hippothous, with whom Habrocomes has fallen in, tells his new associate how he, as a young man in Perinthus, had fallen in love with a youth named Hyperanthes. The two were able to enjoy each other because, Hippothous explains, 'the fact of our equal age was unsuspicious' (3.2.4). However, a wealthy rival from Byzantium induces Hyperanthes' father to commit the boy to his keeping. Hippothous follows the pair to Byzantium, where he steals into the house of his rival and slays him in his bed with a dagger. Hippothous thus rescues Hyperanthes, and they sail off together to Asia. During the voyage, however, the ship capsizes in a storm, and despite Hippothous' efforts to save him, Hyperanthes drowns as they swim for the shore. Hippothous buries the body, and enters upon a life of brigandage.

Hippothous' narrative can be read in counterpoint to that of Habrocomes.[5] Where Habrocomes is passive and pleading in the face of rivals, Hippothous is active and resourceful. Even though Hippothous and Hyperanthes are of the same age and gender, their relationship is clearly an unequal one. Hippothous is cast in the role of the rescuer, who must pursue his beloved, snatch him from the side of his rival, plan and direct the escape, and assist the weaker man in time of danger. But Hippothous' action leads to the death of his beloved, whereas Anthia will, like her lover, survive this and other trials through her own steadfastness. Her willingness to die rather than endure the embraces of someone other than Habrocomes is worlds apart from the submissiveness of Hyperanthes.

In Book 4, when Anthia, unrecognized, falls into the hands of Hippothous' own gang of bandits, the brigand who is assigned to guard her falls in love with her, and when persuasion fails, he tries violence while Hippothous and the rest of his men are out on a foray. As he hovers over her, Anthia seizes a sword and slays him (4.5.5). The vengeance that Hippothous contrives upon his return is gruesome, but Anthia, despite the extreme risk, actively protects her chastity by the very means that Hippothous had employed against the man who was sleeping with Hyperanthes, while Hyperanthes himself evidently found no way to repel his unwelcome attentions. Though her name derives from the Greek word for flower (*anthos*), Anthia is not delicate about defending her fidelity to Habrocomes. Hyperanthes, however, whose name suggests flowers in excess and marks him as a foil to Anthia, is wholly dependent upon Hippothous.[6]

The erotic relationship between Hippothous and Hyperanthes, then, is in contrast to that of the main characters. The formula of heroic rescue is predicated on an opposition in the roles of the lovers, according to which one partner is active and dominant, the other passive and dependent. It is not entirely arbitrary that Xenophon should have chosen a homoerotic attachment to illustrate this type of relationship. The reason is not that Xenophon means to denigrate love between men. Nothing suggests that Hippothous has anything but a noble temperament, and as for his career as a bandit, we may recall that Habrocomes becomes his associate in this. But the practice of pederasty, in which an older man is the lover of a younger, provides the model of a bond that is asymmetrical with respect to power or authority, and Xenophon invokes the pattern even though he specifies that, contrary to custom, the ages of the two men are equal in this case. While this latter circumstance facilitates their secret amour, it also renders the relationship between Hippothous and Hyperanthes parallel to that between the hero and heroine of the novel

(Habrocomes is 16, Anthia 14). But the differences highlight the equality and reciprocity of the passion that unites Habrocomes and Anthia.

Uniquely in classical love literature, the Greek novels as a genre portray *erōs* or amatory passion as a mutual bond between equals eventuating in marriage. The primary couple, invariably heterosexual, are either fellow citizens or members of the same social class, and of more or less the same age – very young. They fall in love at the beginning of the story, and the larger part of the narrative relates their subsequent adventures, in which they endure shipwrecks and separations, and fall captive to brigands, pirates, princesses and satraps, who are susceptible to the beauty of the hero or heroine and are in a position to force compliance. Both partners bear up under these trials with a certain fortitude, though they may yield to thoughts of suicide.

Especially surprising to the reader of the modern romantic novel is the extent to which the actions and reactions of the hero and heroine are alike. Both tend to be represented as victims, both give way to tears, lamentations and despair, sometimes in language that is all but identical. Correspondingly, the novels avoid episodes in which the hero intervenes actively to save the heroine. There are no scenes in which the valiant lover comes to the rescue of his lady. Indeed, the apparent passivity of the male protagonist has exposed him, as we have seen, to charges of cowardice on the part of critics who have not appreciated the conventions of the Greek novel. Where resolute action, however, is required in defence of chastity or safety, the heroine, no less than the hero, will show spirit and determination.

The erotic reciprocity that characterizes the protagonists in the Greek novels distinguishes them from cases in which the couple are differentiated into a lover and beloved, in Greek *erastēs* (an agent noun) and the passive participles *erōmenos* (masculine) or *erōmenē* (feminine). The latter pattern informs the structure of homoerotic, or more accurately, pederastic relations as they were predominantly imagined in classical antiquity,[7] as well as the structure of traditional heteroerotic relations. As in the English language of a generation ago, the active term 'lover' in Greek (*erastēs*) specifically designated a male rather than a female.

Let us return to the scene in which Habrocomes and Anthia are captured by brigands and transferred to their vessel, in order to illustrate a third paradigm of erotic interaction. The pirates, under the command of Corymbus, have set sail for their base in the Phoenician city of Tyre, where their leader, Apsyrtus, has his headquarters. Xenophon continues:

> In the course of the voyage, as a result of seeing him frequently each day, Corymbus had fallen mightily in love with Habrocomes, and his intimacy with the lad kindled him the more. During the voyage itself he did not think it possible to persuade Habrocomes, for he saw that he was in a dreadful state of discouragement, and he saw too that he was in love with Anthia. It was apparent to him as well that it would be difficult to use force, for he feared that he might do something terrible to himself.
>
> (1.14.7–15.1)

Corymbus, as we have seen, confides in his chief mate, Euxinus, who is himself 'in a dreadful state on account of Anthia, and had fallen fearfully in love with the girl' (1.15.4). Euxinus recommends that they prosecute their case energetically with the young couple.

> 'For in fact', he said, 'it would be mightily ignoble if we who run the risks and expose ourselves to danger cannot enjoy in peace of mind what we have earned with our labour. We shall be able', he added, 'to obtain them specially as a gift from Apsyrtus.'
>
> (1.15.5)

In their pleas to the young couple, Corymbus and Euxinus urge (on one another's behalf) the helplessness of their position as captives, and promise to restore their fortunes should they yield, as indeed they must, to their new masters. They declare as well the intensity of their passion, and profess a sincere and honourable commitment, extending, in the case of Euxinus, to the promise of lawful marriage with Anthia (1.16.7). Habrocomes and Anthia resolve, as we know, to die rather than submit to the advances of their enamoured captors; they survive only because Apsyrtus, recognizing their exceptional value on the slave market, decides to keep the two in his own custody.

The episode just recounted presents a homoerotic and a heteroerotic passion in strictly parallel terms, emphasized by the fact that each lover pleads the case of the other. The asymmetry of power in the situation is apparent: Habrocomes and Anthia are entirely at the mercy of Corymbus and Euxinus. As opposed to the reciprocal affection between the hero and heroine, the relationship between the pirates and the protagonists is conceived on the model of pursuer and pursued, hunter and prey.

We might be tempted to construe the desire of the pirates as a matter of sexual domination, bringing home to the captive couple their new status as slaves. Their protestations of love, made from a position of power, are coercive. Euxinus, as we have seen, views the captive pair as fair reward for services rendered in the trade of piracy, and he assumes that Apsyrtus will freely make a gift of them. In principle, they are a part of the booty. Habrocomes, for his part, understands that he and Anthia are vulnerable to sexual violence (see 2.1.1–6, quoted above).

Nevertheless, Corymbus and Euxinus do not set about to compel the two young people with the immediate application of force. They are constrained by their feelings for Habrocomes and Anthia, and are loath to do them harm or cause them to harm themselves. Corymbus and Euxinus are not motivated by a desire that is indifferent to the consequences for the beloved – by the urge, for example, to have sex willy-nilly with the attractive young people in their possession. Aggressive and lawless as they are, the pirates are represented as moved not so much by lust (in Greek, *epithumia*) as by love, or rather *erōs*, a passion something like being in love.

Love in the Greek novels normally inspires a desire for sex, and in this respect, the pirates' passion is not different from the desire that draws Habrocomes and Anthia together, a desire that is assuaged only by sexual congress. 'Each was overcome by the same passion', writes Xenophon of the wedding night (1.9.1).

> Clinging to each other, they prepared to retire and enjoy their first taste of the passions of Aphrodite. They rivalled one another in love throughout the entire night, contending which should appear more loving. When daylight broke, they arose much gladder and much cheerier, because they had enjoyed what they had long desired of one another.
>
> (1.9.9–10.1)

Love finds its expression and its balm in sexual intercourse. The sexual ardour of the protagonists is mutual and equal, in conformity with the symmetry that characterizes their relationship, but it is no less physical than the passion that seizes the pirates Corymbus and Euxinus.

While Euxinus perceives Anthia as a kind of war prize, he also tenders (via Corymbus) an offer of lawful marriage. There is no suggestion in the text that Euxinus is being cunning or hypocritical in his promise to wed Anthia. What is more, the congruence between the passions of the two pirates suggests that Corymbus too intends to maintain an enduring relationship with Habrocomes, rather than the kind of affair that terminates when the beloved boy or *paidika* reaches maturity.

In Book 5, at the conclusion of the novel, the hero and heroine are reunited, and they return to Ephesus in the company of Habrocomes' dear friend, Hippothous, and the handsome young Clisthenes, whom Hippothous had brought with him from Sicily (5.9.3, 5.13.6). Hippothous decides to remain permanently in Ephesus with Habrocomes and Anthia, and he adopts Clisthenes as his son (5.15.4). The parallel between the two couples at the end of the novel seems to echo in a positive key the twin desires of Corymbus and Euxinus, and to offer a model for an enduring association, comparable to marriage, arising out of an original pederastic relationship.[8]

While the pirates' desire, then, is not reciprocated, it aspires to a lasting relationship with a willing partner. In this regard it does not differ qualitatively from the love that first drew Habrocomes and Anthia together. If anything, the pirates' sentiments are more considered than those of the hero and heroine. Xenophon emphasizes that the feelings of Corymbus and Euxinus matured gradually, and were fostered by continual association with their charges: their passion seems to have been stimulated as much by the character or *ēthos* of the pair as by their physical beauty. This is in the nature of what the Greeks called *philia*, conventionally translated as 'friendship' (the verb *phileō* has much the same range of meanings as the English word 'love').[9]

Habrocomes and Anthia, on the contrary, were overcome by a sudden and arbitrary infatuation for one another, which is more in accord with the general conception of *erōs*.[10] Because of his pride in his handsome looks, Habrocomes was, at the beginning of the novel, humbled by the god Eros (Cupid), and made to fall violently in love with Anthia. He was excited first by reports of her beauty. The moment they beheld one another, each was stricken with desire – Anthia to the point of openly defying the modesty required of a Greek maiden so that she might gain Habrocomes' attention. Thereupon, they began to waste away, in the passive fashion of protagonists in the Greek novel, and took to their beds.

In Xenophon's story, everyone who conceives a passion for Habrocomes or Anthia is moved by *erōs*. Thus, when the protagonists find themselves in the custody of the pirate leader Apsyrtus, Apsyrtus' daughter, Manto, falls desperately in love with Habrocomes. She makes trial of his affections through a messenger, and when Habrocomes proves steadfast in his attachment to Anthia, she sends him a peremptory letter which reads, in part:

> I beg you, do not disregard me, and do not outrage one who has taken your side. For if you obey me, I shall persuade my father Apsyrtus to marry me to you, and we shall get rid of your present wife, and you will be rich and blessed.
> (2.5.1–2)

She indicates also the tortures that await Habrocomes and Anthia, should he refuse to submit to her.

Manto's emotion is exactly comparable to that of Corymbus and Euxinus, and so too is her strategy of blandishments, promises and threats. Nothing in the text suggests that her offer of marriage is a ploy rather than a pledge in good faith. In so far as Manto is enamoured of Habrocomes, she is assumed to desire a permanent or conjugal union with him. Her passion, like that of Corymbus or Euxinus, is not distinguished in this respect from that of Habrocomes and Anthia: everyone who is under the spell of *erōs* wants it to last forever.

Later, Anthia comes into the possession of Manto, who orders her death, but she is sold instead to traders; the ship on which she is carried sinks, and she is subsequently captured by brigands who are on the point of sacrificing her, when they are routed by the forces of the local governor Perilaus.

> Perilaus got possession of Anthia, and when he learned of her impending misfortune he took pity on her. But that pity for Anthia in turn contained the seeds of a great misfortune. . . . The habitual sight of the girl drew him to love, and little by little Perilaus was conquered by Anthia.
> (2.13.5–6)

Perilaus presses marriage upon her, which she evades only by swallowing poison, as she thinks; in fact, it proves to be a sleeping potion that induces a death-like trance. Anthia is buried, awakens, and is carried off by tomb-robbers.

An Indian prince named Psammis purchases Anthia for her beauty and, 'being a barbarian', tries to force her sexually. She puts him off by explaining that she has been consecrated to Isis by her father 'until the season of her marriage, and she said that the appointed time was still in a year' (3.11.4). Psammis is subsequently slain by bandits, into whose hands Anthia falls. Perhaps his respect for Anthia's condition, which Xenophon imputes to a barbarian weakness for superstition, implies an intention of making her his wife (the text we possess of the *Ephesian Tale* may have been slightly abridged here and at some other places).

Among the bandits, Anthia is placed in a pit with savage dogs as punishment for slaying one of them (in the episode mentioned earlier), but she is saved when Amphinomus, who is assigned to guard her, turns out to be in love with her, and swears to 'keep her holy and undefiled by marriage until she herself should be persuaded and willingly agree' (5.2.5). As luck would have it, she and Amphinomus are taken prisoner by a patrol under the leadership of Polyidus, a relative of the ruler of Egypt. Polyidus – need one say it? – falls in love with Anthia, and tries flattery and force, but when she takes refuge in a temple of Isis, he promises that he will 'never force Anthia or commit any outrage against her' (5.4.7). Polyidus, however, has a wife, and she in jealousy sells Anthia to a brothel-keeper, where she escapes violation by feigning epilepsy. The brothel-keeper finally puts her up for sale, and she is bought by Hippothous, the leader of the brigand gang into whose power she has twice fallen already. He too becomes enamoured of her, but ceases to press his love upon her when he learns that she is the wife of Habrocomes, who is his dearest friend.

The element common to all the rivals is the one-sided unreciprocated character of their passion, and their power over the lives of the hero or heroine. The mutual love between Habrocomes and Anthia is associated with their powerlessness in the face of intrusive competitors as well as with their passive submission to the force of *erōs* itself. It would appear that Xenophon has denatured the aggressive and asymmetrical character of passionate desire by rendering both the protagonists of his novel young and helpless.

Let us return to the love at first sight that unites the protagonists themselves. On their wedding night, Anthia kisses Habrocomes' eyes and apostrophizes them:

> You, who have often hurt me, who first planted the goad in my heart (*psukhē*), arrogant then, passionate now, you have ministered to me well, and well have you guided love for me into the heart of Habrocomes. Therefore do I kiss you again and again and match with you my own eyes as ministers of Habrocomes. May you always see the same, and do not show another woman beautiful to Habrocomes, nor may another man seem handsome to me. Preserve the hearts, which you yourselves have ignited; keep them as they are.
>
> (1.9.7–8)

This pretty piece of rhetoric fixes the eyes as the conduit of love. But the eyes do not simply register beauty; they are active in seeing things as beautiful or not, and render the heart faithful by their constancy.

At the end of the *Ephesian Tale*, Habrocomes and Anthia arrive by coincidence simultaneously upon the island of Rhodes. Their faithful slaves, Leuco and Rhode, who chance to be residing there, meet first Habrocomes and then Anthia, but recognize neither of them (5.10.9, 5.12.3). Each is then told of the proximity of the other. 'As they saw one another, they immediately recognized each other, for this is what their hearts desired' (5.13.3). Xenophon spares the reader the poignancy of a reunion marred by misrecognition, but makes it plain that Habrocomes and Anthia know each other on sight only because each has been informed in advance of the presence of the other. And yet, moments afterward, the Rhodians cry out before the goddess Isis, 'Once more we behold the beautiful Habrocomes and Anthia' (5.13.3). Beauty is the beginning of *erōs*, and remains its emblem, even when the hero and heroine are so transformed in looks that they are unrecognizable. At the beginning of Book 5, an aged man who is Habrocomes' host in Sicily explains that he keeps in his house the embalmed body of his wife, who died a few years earlier; what he sees, however, is not her shrivelled body, but the young girl she was when they first eloped from Sparta (5.1.11). The vision that originally induced love is imprinted on the memory.

When they are reunited, Habrocomes and Anthia reassure each other of their steadfastness (5.14.2–4). To have engaged willingly in sex would, as Anthia says, be a sign that Habrocomes had found another woman more beautiful than her, and this Habrocomes sincerely denies. Submission under constraint, however, does not in and of itself mark a lapse in faith. In certain situations, the protagonists of the Greek novels, male or female, may accept a sexual association with another partner, but this is not registered as a failure of fidelity.

When Habrocomes is purchased as a slave by a retired soldier named Araxus, his wife Cyno, or 'Bitch', falls immediately in love with him.

> Cyno proposed sex and begged him to accede and promised to take him as her husband and kill Araxus. This seemed terrible to Habrocomes, and he thought of various things simultaneously: Anthia, his vows, the restraint that had harmed him many times ere now. Finally, when Cyno became insistent, he agreed. At nightfall, she killed Araxus, since she was going to take Habrocomes as her husband, and told Habrocomes what she had done. He, however, could not endure the woman's wantonness, and fled the house, abandoning her, in the conviction that he could never sleep with a murderess.
>
> (3.12.4–5)

Under duress, and especially in view of Cyno's intention to slay her lawful husband, Habrocomes consents to Cyno's proposition. His self-control or chastity (*sōphrosunē*) in cases such as this has already done him damage, or, to render the Greek term more literally, has victimized him, done him an injustice (*tēn pollakis auton sōphrosunēn adikēsasan ēdē*). The danger that, in submitting to Cyno, he is forsaking his commitment to Anthia, is registered in Habrocomes' recollection of the oaths he swore to her, but his decision to sleep with Cyno is not taken as evidence of an unforgivable betrayal. He flees, indeed, because she is defiled by murder, and not for reasons of conjugal fidelity. His original motive for agreeing to her demands may well have been to forestall her plan of doing away with Araxus, for it is specifically this that strikes him as terrible or awful (*deinon*).[11] For a modern writer of romances, the tension here between sexual fidelity and the moral requirement to prevent a murder might have been the focus of the narrative, the more so in that Xenophon tells us that Araxus was exceptionally fond of Habrocomes and treated him as his son. If Xenophon shifts attention to the danger of pollution, it is because Habrocomes' chastity is not of unique interest as the touchstone of his fidelity. Habrocomes has certainly not found Cyno more beautiful than Anthia, and that is the essence of the matter.

When Perilaus, the principal authority in Cilicia, presses marriage upon Anthia, she evades his solicitations, as we have seen, by choosing to imbibe poison, which produces not the intended suicide but a death-like coma. She thus appears more steadfast in her vows than Habrocomes. But she too has a moment of indecision. 'At first', Xenophon writes,

> she resisted, but because there was nothing she could do if he used force or was very insistent, and she was afraid that he would attempt something more violent, she agreed to the marriage, but implored him to wait a short while, some thirty days, and to keep her unsullied.
>
> (2.13.8)

Like Cyno, Perilaus is importunate (*enkeimai*), and Anthia, like Habrocomes, gives her assent (*sunkatatithēmai*). Later, Anthia will reconsider; revolving in her mind 'various things simultaneously: her love, her vows, her city, forefathers, compulsion, marriage' (3.5.2), she chooses to die on the day of her wedding, rather than marry, and hear the wedding song and enter the bed of Perilaus. She will, she says, remain Habrocomes' bride until death (3.5.4). The means of doing away with herself is provided by the opportune arrival of a doctor from her home city of Ephesus, who, as we have seen, substitutes a sleeping potion for the poison she requests. Anthia's ability to resist Perilaus' entreaties is thus represented as contingent rather than wholly within her power. The preservation of her sexual fidelity is not something that rests entirely with her.

Xenophon's *Ephesian Tale* exhibits a structure of amatory relations substantially different from that which is represented in modern popular romances. Love between the hero and heroine is symmetrical rather than differentiated into an active and a passive role. Rivals are aggressive, though they too are motivated by love, while both the protagonists are cast as victims. The love of the hero and heroine is distinguished by its steadfastness against violence and the changes wrought by time, for it transcends the original allure of beauty, and survives a radical alteration of appearance. Chastity, which is not always in one's power, is not so much an issue in itself as a sign that the lover remains committed to the original vision of the beloved, which is the source of desire.

The classical image of *erōs* was that of a one-sided, aggressive and transient passion. The lover was likened to a hunter, and the prey was a young man or woman whose charms inspired the ardour of the pursuer. The Greek novel inaugurates an ideal of *erōs* as the basis of a mutual and lasting union which achieves its ultimate expression in marriage. Xenophon's *Ephesian Tale* is elegantly contrived to dramatize this new conception of passionate love.

NOTES

1 This chapter is based in part on the first chapter of my book, *Sexual Symmetry: Love in the Ancient Novel and Related Genres*, Princeton: Princeton University Press, 1994; I am grateful to the Princeton University Press for permission to republish portions of that chapter. An earlier version appeared in *Classicum* 17 (1991), 26–33, published in Sydney, Australia.

2 See Tomas Hägg, 'Die Ephesiaka des Xenophon Ephesios – Original oder Epitome?', *C&M* 27 (1966), 118–61.

3 The meaning must, I think, be 'my beauty', rather than 'our beauty', which the translators prefer; all translations are my own.

4 Gareth Schmeling, *Xenophon of Ephesus*, Boston: Twayne, 1980, 34.

5 Schmeling, *Xenophon*, 54–5 notes some of the analogies.

6 On the names, cf. Tomas Hägg, 'The naming of the characters in the romance of Xenophon Ephesius', *Eranos* 69 (1971), 36.

7 Plato, in *Phaedrus* 255d8–e1, allows the beloved to feel a reflected kind of love (*anterōs*) in return.

8 For the idea that pederastic love can survive the maturation of the beloved, see Aristotle, *Nicomachean Ethics* 8.4.1157a3–12, and cf. A. W. Price, *Love and Friendship in Plato and Aristotle*, Oxford: Clarendon, 1989, 247–9; Hippothous' adoption of Clisthenes marks the termination of the pederastic relationship.

9 On *philia* in the Greek philosophical tradition, see Martha Nussbaum, *The Fragility of Goodness*, Cambridge: Cambridge University Press, 1986, 354–72.

10 On the contrast between the instantaneous passion of the protagonists in the novel and the more protracted enamourment characteristic of rivals, especially in Xenophon of Ephesus, see Massimo Fusillo, *Il romanzo greco: polifonia ed eros*, Venice: Marsilio, 1989, 203.

11 John Moschus, *Pratum spirituale*, 76 (in Migne *Patrologia Graeca* 87. iii) tells a story of a woman in love with a man who puts her off on the grounds that she has children; when she kills her children in order to remove the obstacle, he rejects her as a murderess.

BIBLIOGRAPHY

Fusillo, Massimo (1989), *Il romanzo greco: polifonia ed eros*, Venice: Marsilio.

Hägg, Tomas (1966), 'Die Ephesiaka des Xenophon Ephesios – Original oder Epitome?', *C&M* 27, 118–61.

Hägg, Tomas (1971), 'The naming of the characters in the romance of Xenophon Ephesius', *Eranos* 69, 25–59.

Konstan, David (1994), *Sexual Symmetry: Love in the Ancient Novel and Related Genres*, Princeton: Princeton University Press.

Nussbaum, Martha (1986), *The Fragility of Goodness*, Cambridge: Cambridge University Press.

Price, A. W. (1989), *Love and Friendship in Plato and Aristotle*, Oxford: Clarendon.

Schmeling, Gareth (1980), *Xenophon of Ephesus*, Boston: Twayne.

4

DAPHNIS AND CHLOE

Love's own sweet story

J. R. Morgan

If the Greek romance seems to be a stereotyped genre, the single surviving specimen which most stretches the possibilities of the form is Longus' *Daphnis and Chloe*.[1] The outlines of the conventional plot remain easily discernible in its storyline: Daphnis and Chloe are lovers, young and beautiful, who endure a series of setbacks, including separation, shipwreck and a brush with pirates, before finally achieving static wedded bliss. But the deviations from the norm are so striking that they must form the basis of any integrative reading of the work.

Instead of being members of the social élite, for instance, Daphnis and Chloe grow up in the countryside as goat-herd and shepherdess. The social proprieties of the genre are salvaged to the extent that they finally turn out to be the offspring of the urban aristocracy, and from the very first pages the reader is aware that they are not what they seem, having been exposed as babies by parents wealthy enough to leave valuable tokens of recognition beside them (1.2, 1.6). On its way to revealing their true identities the story unfolds in a new and humbler ambience; its episodes revolve around the routines of the agricultural year and its properties are milking pails, fresh cheeses and cottage gardens.

Longus has not given us a novel of social realism, however. The countryside in which his story is set is ostentatiously derived from the tradition of pastoral poetry, known to us chiefly from the *Idylls* of Theokritos.[2] The hero's very name recalls Theokritos' most famous shepherd. Elements of Longus' description allude verbally to Theokritos, and motifs of Theokritos' poetry are redeployed to become episodes within a developing narrative. Just in case these hints are missed, Longus slips in a reference to a Sicilian goat-herd as source for a story told by one of his rustics (2.33;

Theokritos was Sicilian). An important secondary character, the retired herdsman Philetas, shares his name with another Hellenistic poet, Philetas of Kos, whom Theokritos seems to acknowledge as a master in the same field (7.39ff.). Philetas' poetry does not survive, but I should be very surprised indeed if the lyrical description of an epiphany of Eros which Longus allots to his Philetas (2.3ff.) were not replete with allusions to it.

By thus stressing the literary pedigree of his bucolic milieu, Longus is deviating in another way from the normal practice of the novels, which, despite the inherent improbability of their plots, devote considerable energy to locating themselves in the real world. Longus, on the other hand, parades his unreality. Pastoral is not about photographic depiction of the countryside, but about the indulgence of urban nostalgia for a world of bucolic simplicity, sunshine and leisure, where a man's only problems are those of the heart, and even they find relief in an outpouring of spontaneous song beneath a shady tree. It is a literary holiday, whose whole point is that the world it depicts does not, and never could exist. Longus even seems to poke fun at the fantasy of his countryside by exposing the distance between the muck and toil of real agricultural life and the hygienically packaged artefact which pastoral purveys to its fastidious urban clientele. So, for instance, when the wealthy absentee landlord Dionysophanes proposes to visit his estates and play the tourist at the festival of the grape harvest, the wells have to be cleared of refuse and the farmyard dunghills carted away out of sight (4.1). Most importantly, Longus uses a prologue to stake out the relationship between his creation and reality. He tells us that while hunting in Lesbos he came across a beautiful painting of erotic scenes, the elucidation of which by a local exegete provided the basis for his novel. This is as much a fiction as the story itself, of course, but it serves, among other things, to make the point that Longus' immediate inspiration lies in art rather than in experience.

The story which plays out against this background is also profoundly mutated. The staples of the canonical novels are love and adventure, but Daphnis and Chloe experience very little in the way of adventure. In contrast to the other heroes, whose wanderings take them all over the Mediterranean, Daphnis and Chloe never leave Lesbos. Within this narrow geographical compass, their experiences are also decidedly small-scale. Daphnis is abducted by some local pirates, but is not taken beyond swimming distance from the shore, and is soon rescued when Chloe plays a special tune which induces some trained cows to jump overboard and capsize the ship (1.28–30). An unpleasantness arises when the pleasure-trippers from the city of Methymna find their boat set adrift by a comic accident: their mooring cable is 'borrowed' by a man who needs a rope for grape-crushing, and a stray goat eats through the green willow shoot they use as a replacement (2.12–13). Matters escalate to fisticuffs, and then to a punitive military expedition from Methymna, which succeeds in capturing Chloe and her sheep. However, she is taken only ten stades from home before being rescued by divine intervention (2.20–7). Although for a moment it looks as if full-scale war is about to break out between Methymna and Mytilene, this storm in a tea-cup dies down as soon as the authorities take stock of the situation (3.1–2).

It is difficult to resist the feeling that these atrophied incidents are intended as dead-pan caricatures of conventional romantic adventures. Although they are integrated into *Daphnis and Chloe* in the sense that they give rise to events which form part of Longus' real agenda, in themselves these 'adventures' are narrative dead ends, whose function in the development of the plot does not justify the length with which they are treated. Here too Longus seems to be looking to an acquaintance with earlier literature, more typical romances, to control his reader's response.

In the area of love Longus is clearly reacting critically against the generic stereotype. The normal schema is that the hero and heroine fall in love at first sight. Their love is born fully formed and undergoes no alteration during the story. Indeed the ethics of conventional romance presuppose that true love is the one stable point in a universe of shifting and hostile contingencies. The convention, however, tends to shift the focus of the narrative away from the experience of love itself, which becomes merely a static datum around which other kinds of intrigue can be built. Longus, on the other hand, has made the growth of the love between Daphnis and Chloe the central theme of his novel. Travel in space has been internalized to become psychological and emotional development, and the protagonists' real adventures are the stages through which they pass on their journey to maturity.

Daphnis and Chloe begin as innocent children, at one with nature, imitating the songs and frolics of the natural world (1.9–10). One spring day when Daphnis is 15 and Chloe 13, he falls into a wolf-trap, and has to take a bath. Chloe is entranced by the sight and touch of his naked body, and suffers an anguish which she cannot understand, but which the reader recognizes as love-sickness (1.13). This is not romantic love but the awakening of sexual instinct, and as befits a child of nature Chloe knows no reason to feel ashamed or inhibited; in fact at this stage she tends to take the initiative, innocently engineering situations in which she can see Daphnis naked again.

When wooed by the cow-herd Dorkon, Chloe does not understand the purpose of his gifts, 'having no experience of a lover's wiles' (1.15). This is an index of the distance between her (and Daphnis) and someone like Dorkon who 'knows the name and acts of love'. The acquisition of these two items of knowledge forms the agenda for the rest of the narrative. Daphnis' sexual awakening occurs when he wins a kiss from Chloe, and like her he has no comprehension of the feeling it arouses (1.18). Even when Dorkon attempts to rape Chloe disguised as a wolf, she takes it for no more than a merry prank (1.21).

As spring passes into summer (1.23), the heat of their feelings increases, and their childish games become more physical, culminating in a pleasurable occasion when Daphnis retrieves a cicada from Chloe's dress. But still a shared bath arouses in Daphnis feelings more painful in their inexplicable intensity than any injury inflicted by the pirates, for 'he was still ignorant of the piracy of love' (1.32).

With autumn comes the time for their relationship to move forward, and Philetas duly comes to tell them about an epiphany of the child Eros in his garden (2.3–6). He explains the power of love, and, having now heard the word for the first time, Daphnis and Chloe are at last able to put a name to their feelings (2.8), so completing the first stage of their education. But with knowledge comes inhibition. Philetas has told them the remedies of love: 'a kiss, an embrace and lying down together with naked bodies', but somehow they cannot bring themselves to try more than the first two of these, except in their dreams. The balance of their relationship is also subtly altered: instead of innocent reciprocity, Daphnis emerges increasingly as the more active partner, beginning with a passionate clinch beneath a tree (2.11), and there are new elements of competition as they swear oaths of fidelity, and of gender differentiation in that they swear by different gods, Chloe by the Nymphs, Daphnis by Pan (2.39). While Daphnis is perfectly satisfied with her oath, Chloe 'in her girlish simplicity' suspects that the promiscuous Pan would fail to punish any infidelity on Daphnis' part (2.39). There is a clear gap opening up between the programmes of male and female sexuality.

After a winter of separation, the sight of the animals mating in spring inflames Daphnis. He presses Chloe to try Philetas' third remedy (3.14), but she coyly deflects his overtures, pointing out that the animals do not have to lie down or take off their fur to do what they do. They end up trying to imitate the goats copulating, but without success. This second impasse is resolved by the intervention of Lykainion, a woman from the city, who has witnessed Daphnis' futile attempts at love-making and teaches him the 'acts of love' at first hand (3.18). Again knowledge brings inhibition: Daphnis is alarmed by Lykainion's warning of pain and blood should he try out his new skills on Chloe, and Chloe is suddenly too ashamed to ask the reason for his apparent loss of ardour (3.24). Daphnis' knowledge, which he does not share with his beloved, has given him, as a man, the power to control Chloe's progress to fulfilment, and she, as a woman, surrenders the initiative to him.

Daphnis has grown into a conventional role. His aim is no longer the satisfaction of shared natural appetite, but institutionalized marriage (3.25ff.), and with the formal declaration of his suit Chloe's virginity, which she would happily have lost in ignorance of its significance, becomes an issue for the first time. Marriage, however, is a serious responsibility. Simple love is overlaid by considerations of finance, parental ambition and social propriety. The decision is taken out of the lovers' hands entirely and adjourned until their urban lord and master Dionysophanes visits his estates. The third book ends with another symbolic episode when Daphnis climbs to a dangerous height, disregarding Chloe's pleas, to fetch her the last remaining apple in a tree (3.34). This looks very like an assertion of his dominance and manhood, and the importance he attaches to this lover's gift is in marked contrast to Chloe's misconstrual of Dorkon's purposes in the first book.

The fourth and final book concerns the progression of Daphnis and Chloe to ultimate self-knowledge: the discovery of their true identities. Daphnis is the first to be recognized, when his foster-father has to produce his recognition tokens to save him from the homosexual advances of the parasite Gnathon, a member of Dionysophanes' retinue. Daphnis is the son of Dionysophanes himself, but the immediate effect of his new-found status is to divorce him from what he loves most, from Chloe, and from his precious rustic tools, which he tearfully dedicates to Pan and the Nymphs, like a young adult making his last farewells to his childhood toys (4.26). Selfhood has brought pains that almost outweigh the gains. Eventually, however, when Chloe's tokens prove that she too is a person of quality, Dionysophanes gives his consent to their marriage. Chloe is dressed in city finery, 'and then you could learn what beauty is like when it is properly presented' (4.32). In the city, predictably enough, Chloe is reunited with her true parents, and now that the couple have both truly found themselves, their wedding can take place. The formalities completed, Daphnis can share his sexual knowledge with Chloe, and she finally understands that 'All they had done in the woods had been nothing but shepherds' games' (4.40).

By the end of the novel Daphnis and Chloe have both travelled far, from natural childhood to social adulthood, and although they return to the countryside to celebrate their marriage and spend much of their lives there, they will never be able to recapture that natural innocence, will forever be nostalgic day-trippers in a world which is no longer really theirs. Their love has been brought to the only satisfactory consummation, but Longus has shown clearly that there are losses to be faced as well.

For instance, the main story is counterpointed by a series of inset narratives or myths told by characters within it. First Daphnis tells Chloe the story of a young cow-girl, who sang the story of Pan and Pitys, but was defeated in a singing contest by a young man, who also lured away her animals (1.27). Her distress was such that the gods in their pity metamorphosed her into a wood-dove. This double myth has a hidden agenda. The story of Pitys is not fully narrated, but the reader may remember her as a victim of Pan's aggressive sexuality. The anonymous cow-girl is also a victim of male superiority. In the second inset these themes emerge more clearly. After Chloe's delivery from the Methymnaians, Lamon, Daphnis' foster-father, tells the story of the invention of the Pan-pipes or syrinx (2.34). Syrinx was originally a maiden, who attracted Pan's amatory attentions. She tried to escape, but could do so only by metamorphosis into reeds, from which Pan made the pipes. Again, the female is shown as the victim of the male, and this time the relevance of the myth to what is happening to Daphnis and Chloe is underlined when they take it upon themselves to assume the roles of Pan and Syrinx in a mime. In the third book, Daphnis tells Chloe the story of Echo, another victim of Pan's violence, this time in an extreme form: she was torn limb from limb, but her dismembered remains were hidden in the earth and preserved their power of beautiful song (3.23). These stories convey the violence of male sexuality, and offer a paradigm of the gender roles, which is of clear relevance to Longus' protagonists as they move from natural innocence to socially acceptable matrimony.

However, Longus is not preaching a feminist sermon here. All three of the inset myths issue in musical beauty: the song of the wood-dove, the music of the pipes of Pan, the never-dying echo. Longus is intimating that violence and loss are necessary preconditions for the creation of true harmony, that the old and good has to pass away before the new and better can come into being. Chloe has to be acculturated into the passive role because that is the only way that she can escape the sterility of innocence.[3] Although she has to be cast, in a physical sense, as the victim of the male, I think Longus is at some pains to show that both parties have an emotional cost to bear. The knowledge that Daphnis acquires from Lykainion carries fear and responsibility, and he is not immediately the happier for having acquired it. He has to part with the symbols of his pastoral happiness before he can become his real self. Longus even suggests that Daphnis, like Chloe, has to become the victim of a sexual predator as an inevitable stage in his maturation. This is accomplished through the recurrent symbol of the wolf.[4] Chloe's first sexual awakening is the result of Daphnis' tumble into a wolf-trap; Dorkon, somewhat unnecessarily, dresses in a wolf-skin when he goes out a-raping; but interestingly, Daphnis' sexual initiation is by Lykainion, whose name means 'little she-wolf', and Longus has taken care to demonstrate that she is acting for her own gratification as well as from sympathy for the frustrated young lovers.

Another important aspect of Longus' conception of love is its relation to nature. The pastoral scenario allows love to come into being in its most natural form, isolated from all cultural influences. At several points Daphnis and Chloe imitate nature: in their songs, in their first attempt at sex, in Daphnis' rejection of Gnathon's homosexuality. Not only does their sexuality emerge naturally, in natural surroundings, but it keeps time with the rhythms of the natural year. Love is awakened in the spring, becomes more heated through the summer, and takes its first step towards fruition with the intervention of Philetas at the autumn vintage. Winter is a dead time for both nature and love, but spring brings rebirth, the second summer provokes crisis, resolved by marriage in the season of nature's fruiting. Longus wrote his novel in four books, and although it is not the case that each book covers a single season, the total is hardly fortuitous.

Longus, however, wants to say more than this. He uses the mouthpiece of Philetas to identify the power growing in his hero and heroine with the motive principle of the whole natural world:

> Zeus has not so much power as Love: he rules the elements; he rules the stars, he rules his fellow gods – more completely than you rule your goats and sheep. All the flowers are the work of Love; all the plants are his creation; thanks to him the rivers flow, the winds blow.
>
> (2.7)

This concept of love as nature joins with the antithesis of town and country which underlies all pastoral. The essential point of the bucolic world, from Theokritos onwards, is not what it is but what it is not: it is not the city. The values which it enshrines are not those of the real countryside, but the reverse of those of the real town. The two environments, by definition, form the terminals of an ethical polarity: the peace, beauty and purity of rural nature are set against the greed, corruption and ugliness of urban culture. So in Longus' novel, not only is the rural landscape described in terms of almost incantatory beauty, but the town constitutes a threat to its peace. The city-slickers from Methymna blunder in and cause havoc and disruption; the city-dwelling landowner brings parasitism, sexual deviance and the threat of separation in his train; the city-bred Lykainion is casually promiscuous. The material wealth of the city-folk has no place in the jolly poverty of the land, and on the one occasion when Daphnis needs money, he finds it, symbolically, in a dead and decomposing carcase (3.28). At the very end, the protagonists' choice to return to the country is nothing less than the espousal of the positive moral values associated with it.

This facile antithesis is implicit in the pastoral form, but Longus, to his credit, evokes it only to deconstruct it. If the city brings violence, violence was already present in the country, in the shape of wolves and lycanthropic rapists. The materialistic values of the town are mirrored in the shrewdness of Chloe's foster-father over her bride-price, and even in the barely resisted temptation Lamon feels on first discovering the baby Daphnis to help himself to the recognition tokens and leave the child to die. Similarly, the negatives of the town are only equivocally so. Lykainion acts to satisfy her selfish desires, but her tuition of Daphnis is also partly motivated by altruism and beneficially forms one of the two crucial stages in the education of the protagonists, as staked out in the programmatic phrase 'name and acts of love'. It comes when the natural way, imitation of the beasts, has proved ineffective. Unlike Dorkon, who is eliminated from the story as punishment for his attack on Chloe, Lykainion is a guest of honour at the wedding, alongside Philetas, who shares her status as structural pivot. Chloe is beautiful throughout, but her beauty reaches its true perfection only when the cosmetic skills of the city are applied to it. Even after their marriage Daphnis and Chloe apparently pass some of their time in the city.

Longus in fact has gone out of his way to show that nature alone is insufficient. Just as the violence of adult sexuality is the necessary price for escaping the happy sterility of childhood innocence, so human skill, *technē*, is complementary rather than antithetic to nature. Again he uses a symbol to convey this idea in his story: the symbol of a garden, the unique space where the beauty and fecundity of nature are shaped and improved by the work of human hands. There are two gardens in the novel, and both occupy crucial positions. The first is that of Philetas, where he witnesses the epiphany of Eros (2.3ff.). The interplay of ideas and images here is profound. Love, as a natural principle, is the source of the fertility of Philetas' garden, but Love, like the garden he inhabits, requires human help to attain his potential. Thus Philetas is able to present Eros simultaneously as a primal power and an object of instruction. The second garden is described with even greater elaboration (4.2–3).[5] This is the walled garden which Daphnis' foster-father Lamon works for Dionysophanes. Here art seems nature and nature seems art; the fusion of the two is more beautiful than either by itself. But if the garden is an image for Love, at its centre stands a temple of Dionysos, decorated with paintings depicting scenes of the utmost violence, the deaths of Semele, Lykourgos (another wolfman!) and Pentheus, together with the sleeping Ariadne, an image found on Dionysiac sarcophagi, where her union with Dionysos represents the union of the believer's soul with his god.[6] This garden thus seems to unite the themes of violence and harmony which I have been tracing in this essay. It is itself subjected to violence when Lampis, a rejected suitor of Chloe, vandalizes it in order to antagonize Dionysophanes towards Daphnis. Here the aggression of the inset myths spills over into the main story, but in terms of the plot the desecration of Lamon's garden is curiously inconsequential, and simply initiates the series of events leading up to the recognition of Daphnis. Lampis, despite a further act of anti-social behaviour when he tries to kidnap Chloe after Daphnis has been found by his parents, is even, like Lykainion, rewarded by being included among the wedding guests on the novel's last page. It is as if the destruction of the beautiful garden – like Daphnis the object of Lamon's care – is, while lamentable in itself, a part of a larger process by which that which is beautiful and beloved must suffer violation so that a profounder joy can arise, in a never-ending and deeply religious cycle of loss and gain, in which human pain and loss, like the natural sequence of the seasons, represent points of transition rather than finality, and every passing away implies a transfiguration.

Longus' thought-world seems to revolve around the sequential harmonization of opposites, regardless of conventional evaluations: country and town, innocence and experience, peace and violence, sheep and wolves, nature and culture. But I think there is one layer of meaning further to be explored: the opposition between truth or reality and fiction. This is an issue from the first page of the novel to the last. Longus tells us in his prologue that his story is the verbal counterpart of a work of visual art. In fact the painting which supposedly gave rise to his narrative turns out to be an autobiographical document of the novel's protagonists, dedicated by them at the end of their story. *Daphnis and Chloe* is thus our first self-begetting novel and it is hardly surprising that it is preoccupied with its own status and function as a fiction, and the relation between fiction and experience in general.

That same prologue makes some sweeping claims. The novel is described as 'a pleasurable possession (*ktēma terpnon*) for all mankind', which 'will cure the sick, comfort the distressed, stir the memory of those who have loved, and educate (*propaideusei*) those who haven't'.

These claims both echo and subvert those of the historian Thucydides in his famous programmatic statement (1.22):

> it may be that my work will seem less pleasurable (*aterpesteron*) because of its unmythlike quality (*to mē muthōdes*); but it will be enough for me if my work is judged useful by those who want to understand clearly the events which happened in the past and which (human nature being what it is) will be repeated in the future. My work is not a piece of writing designed to meet the taste of an immediate public, but is a possession (*ktēma*) for all time.

Just as Thucydides' history serves a propaedeutic function by embodying universal truths of human nature which readers in the future will find helpful in making sense of their own experience, so Longus' novel will act as preparatory education for the inescapable experience of love. His readers will be able to draw from the fiction knowledge of universals which can be applied in reality. But where Thucydides contrasted the utility of his history with the pleasures of myth (or could we say fiction?), Longus sees pleasure and utility as yet another pair of harmonizing opposites: as a garden combines art and nature, so a novel fuses myth and history, fiction and truth. Thus, in his prologue, Longus can describe his story as a history of love, *historia erōtos*.

In Thucydides' history the central theme which narrative specifics served to exemplify was human nature, *to anthrōpinon*. In Longus its place is taken by Love. We have seen too that, in contrast to other romances, love is not just a static precondition to Longus' plot: love, in a new dynamic conception, *is* the plot.

But love is not just the subject of the plot; in its personification as Eros it also controls it, both directly and through Pan and the Nymphs, who represent its masculine and feminine aspects. So, for example, Eros initiates the first contact between Daphnis and Chloe by appearing, unrecognized, to their foster-fathers in a dream and telling them to send the children out to pasture (1.7). In a symmetrical dream at the end of the story, Eros appears again, this time to Daphnis' real father, to tell him to prepare a wedding feast for Daphnis and Chloe, thus resolving the intrigue of recognition (4.34). The whole plot unfolds under Eros' supervision, so that the Nymphs can tell Daphnis that Love will take care of all the couple's affairs (2.23). He intervenes at crucial junctures in the story to act as the motor of plot development, contriving, for example, Daphnis' fall into the wolf-pit (1.11), and engineering a chance meeting with Chloe's foster-father in the winter snow

(3.6–7). Editors and translators of *Daphnis and Chloe* are in some perplexity as to when they should use upper or lower case letters for the words *erōs* and love. Longus did not have that problem, and so was able to preserve the continuity between personification and abstract. What the controller of the plot, personified Eros, brings Daphnis and Chloe to full awareness of is himself, as abstract Love, and its power to shape and inform their experience.

However, Longus seems to want to go further even than this. The presentation of experience as story recasts the controller of experience as the author of the story. At one level, this emerges, for example, when the word used of Love's contrivance is one which can also be used of fictional literary composition (1.11, *aneplase*), but most important is a startling instance of self-reference. When Chloe is abducted by the invaders from Methymna, Pan appears to their leader Bryaxis in a nightmare vision to lambast him for taking away 'a maiden from whom Love wishes to make a story' (2.27). The story that Love will make out of Chloe is nothing other than the text of *Daphnis and Chloe*, the novel we are reading, and, just as Eros shapes the experiences of Daphnis and Chloe to bring them to a full comprehension of himself and themselves, so he has *ipso facto* shaped the vicarious narrative by means of which all humanity also can attain to similar instruction in and by Love. A second-time reader will realize that the description in the prologue of the seminal painting as a 'history of love' (*historia erōtos*) can mean both a 'history *about* love' and a 'history *by* love', an ambiguity which clearly extends to the novel.

The interplay of levels is complex. In effect the work has three separate but intertwined authors. First Eros, who devises and scripts the story of Daphnis and Chloe. Second the protagonists themselves, who transmute their lived experience into the artistic representation of the painting they dedicate to the Nymphs. And finally, of course, there is Longus, who poses as an essentially uncreative promulgator of someone else's truths but nevertheless, as we have seen, by the very literariness of his writing, draws attention to the unreality of his pastoral romance and his own status as its author. Eros' control of the story can thus be read as a cypher for Longus' control over his own invention. The conceit we have been examining emphasizes the factual unreality of the story, but at the same time suggests that the fiction is a channel for a non-factual truth of general applicability.

The story that Love makes of Chloe is a *muthos*, precisely the kind of narrative that Thucydides equated with pleasure, in opposition to the utility of truthful history. Indeed, the word *muthos* was commonly used by rhetorical theoreticians to denote a narrative both untrue and unlike the truth.[7] However, by marking crucial stages in the protagonists' growing awareness of themselves and Love, the inset *muthoi* (this is the word Longus himself uses of them) act as demonstration that untrue stories can embody lessons relevant to real life. But Love himself, the force that governs and gives meaning to their lives, is to Daphnis and Chloe also a *muthos*. When Philetas tells them of the epiphany of Eros in his garden, they react with joy, 'as if they had heard a *muthos* not a *logos*' (2.7). Longus here picks up the terminology of Plato's distinction between fictional and true narrative,[8] and in so doing raises serious issues about what truth really is. Even within the frame of the novel, the status of Philetas' story is problematic: Longus never makes clear whether he really has seen the winged child trampling his herbaceous border or whether he is instructing through parable. In a way it does not matter. From the perspective of the real audience, the reader, the whole text is a fiction and Philetas' narrative perhaps doubly so, while as far as Daphnis and Chloe are concerned, they derive instruction about the deepest truths in their life from something in which they do not believe factually, which they perceive, rightly or wrongly, as a fiction.

This seems to be what Longus is saying – and the ideas he implies run directly counter to those of Thucydides, making the intertextual dialectic of the prologue rather more subversive than decorative. To understand our experience and ourselves fully, we must become aware of the forces which shape our lives. But to do this necessarily involves interpretative processes of selection, generalization, simplification, organization, categorization, all distortions of the myriad diversity of daily existence. It means imposing structure on life, turning it into narrative; experience understood, in short, becomes fiction. Fiction in its turn is the vehicle of truth, about ourselves and about the world. Through fiction we can pool our experiences and learn imaginatively what we cannot or choose not to learn experientially. Fiction is at the heart of Daphnis and Chloe's progress to adulthood and to be without it is to be locked into the charming sterility from which they begin, to be a child forever. In that sense, fiction and the understanding it brings are beneficially destructive, as is Love itself. We can feel nostalgia for the loss of innocence, and even use pastoral fiction to indulge that nostalgia, but every human being must sooner or later abandon the countryside of childish ignorance for the city of adult awareness, and Longus' fiction is the vehicle that plies that road.

Obviously we should be cautious in attributing to Longus articulated theories of fiction too like our own, but it seems to me beyond doubt that he had a clear perception that fiction reveals deep-level truths, and intended *Daphnis and Chloe* both as an ironic commentary on its own generic strategies and as a self-referential defence of fiction.

NOTES

1 This is the title usually given to the work in translation, but the manuscripts suggest it was originally called *Poimenika* or *Pastoral Story*. Of the author nothing is known. His name suggests that he was a Roman citizen, and it is tempting to link him with the family of Pompeii Longi attested by inscriptions from Lesbos, especially as he seems, for all the deliberate artificiality of his setting, to show some knowledge of Lesbian topography and agriculture; on this see H. J. Mason, 'Longus and the topography of Lesbos', *TAPhA* 109 (1979), 149–63; P. Green, 'Longus, Antiphon and the topography of Lesbos', *JHS* 102 (1982), 210–14; and H. Kloft, 'Imagination und Realität: Überlegungen zur Wirtschaftstruktur des Romans Daphnis und Chloe', *GCN* 2 (1989), 45–61. His dating is equally a matter for speculation; the consensus is to place him in the second century and connect him with the cultural movement known as the Second Sophistic.

2 This aspect of Longus' novel has been much studied; for more detail on his relation to Theokritean pastoral see: G. Rohde, 'Longus und dic Bukolik', *RhM* 86 (1937), 23–49; M. C. Mittelstadt, 'Bucolic-lyric motifs and dramatic narrative in Longus' *Daphnis and Chloe*', *RhM* 113 (1970), 211–27; L. R. Cresci, 'Il romanzo di Longo Sofista e la tradizione bucolica', *Atene e Roma* 26 (1981), 1–25.

3 It is tempting to identify the three females of the inset myths, Pitys, Syrinx and Echo, with the three Nymphs who act as Chloe's guardians; for the number see 2.23. If we make this equation, my point becomes clearer than ever. First, the stories of the Nymphs and Pan become even more explicitly analogues of the story of Chloe and Daphnis. And second, the Nymphs are now acting in harmony with their erstwhile aggressor in order to bring about a repetition (albeit in a metaphorical sense) of their own destruction. Although these figures were traditionally identified as nymphs, Longus seems to equivocate as to their status, and even specifies that Echo was mortal (3.23), as if to emphasize the irrevocability of their necessary destruction.

4 On the symbolism of the wolf, see especially P. Turner, '*Daphnis and Chloe*: an interpretation', *Greece and Rome* 7 (1960), 117–23.

5 Lamon's garden seems to be recognizably of the formal Persian kind; see P. Grimal, 'Le jardin de Lamon à Lesbos', *RA* 49 (1957), 211–14; but Longus' description also echoes that of the garden of Alkinoos in *Odyssey* 7.112ff.

6 On the relation of *Daphnis and Chloe* to Dionysiac religion, see E. Simon, 'Dionysischer Sarkophag in Princeton', *Mitteilungen des deutschen Archäologischen Instituts (Röm. Abt.)* 69 (1962), 136–58; H. H. O. Chalk, 'Eros and the Lesbian pastorals of Longos', *JHS* 80 (1960), 32–51; R. Merkelbach, *Die Hirten des Dionysos*, Stuttgart: Teubner, 1988.

7 On this division of narrative by truth-relation and its relevance to the novel, see K. Barwick, 'Die Gliederung der Narratio in der rhetorischen Theorie und ihre Bedeutung für die Geschichte des antiken Romans', *Hermes* 63 (1928), 261–87.

8 See Plato, *Gorgias* 523a, *Phaidon* 61b. This distinction became common currency in the Second Sophistic. The story of Herakles and the peaks in Dio's first oration is introduced as a *logos* in the guise of a *muthos*, i.e. as a fiction purveying truth. Conversely Achilleus Tatius has one of his characters refer to a *logos* which is like a *muthos* (1.17), i.e., something which is true but incredible.

BIBLIOGRAPHY

Chalk, H. H. O., 'Eros and the Lesbian pastorals of Longos', *Journal of Hellenic Studies* 80 (1960), 32–51.

Effe, B., 'Longos: Zur Funktionsgeschichte der Bukolik in der römischen Kaiserzeit', *Hermes* 110 (1982), 65–84.

Forehand, W. E., 'Symbolic gardens in Longus' *Daphnis and Chloe*', *Eranos* 74 (1976), 103–12.

Hunter, R. L., *A Study of Daphnis and Chloe*, Cambridge: Cambridge University Press, 1983.

McCulloh, W. E., *Longus*, New York: Twayne, 1970.

MacQueen, B. D., *Myth, Rhetoric and Fiction: A Reading of Longus's 'Daphnis and Chloe'*, Lincoln: University of Nebraska Press, 1990.

Merkelbach, R., *Die Hirten des Dionysos*, Stuttgart: Teubner, 1988.

Mittelstadt, M. C., 'Longus: *Daphnis and Chloe* and Roman narrative painting', *Latomus* 26 (1967), 752–61.

Mittelstadt, M. C., 'Bucolic-lyric motifs and dramatic narrative in Longus' *Daphnis and Chloe*', *Rheinisches Museum* 113 (1970), 211–27.

Mittelstadt, M. C., 'Love, Eros and poetic art in Longus', in id., *Fons Perennis: Saggi critici di filologia classica raccolti in onore di Vittorio d'Agostino*, Turin: RSC, 1971, 305–32.

Montague, H., 'Sweet and pleasant passion: female and male fantasy in ancient romance novels', in A. Richlin (ed.), *Pornography and Representation in Greece and Rome*, Oxford: Oxford University Press, 1992, 231–49.

Pandiri, T. A., '*Daphnis and Chloe*: the art of pastoral play', *Ramus* 14 (1985), 116–41.

Philippides, M., 'The "digressive" aitia in Longus', *Classical World* 74 (1980/1), 193–9.

Philippides, M., 'The prooemium in Longus's *Lesbiaka*', *Classical Bulletin* 59 (1983), 32–5.

Rohde, G., 'Longus und die Bukolik', *Rheinisches Museum* 86 (1937), 23–49.

Teske, D., *Der Roman des Longos als Werk der Kunst*, Munster: Aschendorff, 1991.

Turner, P., '*Daphnis and Chloe*: an interpretation,' *Greece and Rome* 7 (1960), 117–23.

Winkler, J. J., *The Constraints of Desire*, London: Routledge, 1990 (especially Ch. 4 'The education of Chloe: hidden injuries of sex').

Zeitlin, F. I., 'The poetics of Eros: nature, art and imitation in Longus' *Daphnis and Chloe*', in D. M. Halperin, J. J. Winkler and F. I. Zeitlin (eds), *Before Sexuality*, Princeton: Princeton University Press, 1990, 417–64.

5

ACHILLES TATIUS AND EGO-NARRATIVE

B. P. Reardon

Of the three so-called 'sophistic' Greek novels, that of Achilles Tatius has probably been the least generally read and admired.[1] Whereas Longus and Heliodorus have seemed more immediately accessible, Achilles has often puzzled and troubled readers and scholars by the mixture that *Leucippe and Clitophon* offers: sensational melodrama side by side with sophisticated psychology and complex intrigue, simplistic novelistic convention along with a difficult narrative technique and elaborate rhetoric. Reactions have been varied. On the one hand, various degrees of dislike, from the moral disapproval of Photius in the ninth century to the contempt of Rohde in the nineteenth and the critical strictures of the early twentieth; later, a gleam of understanding, mixed with puzzlement and irritation; most recently, re-evaluation as some form of comic narrative, though hard to situate – parody, comedy, sick humour?[2] None of these judgements is altogether without foundation. No doubt because of this uncertainty about how to approach the story, it has not often been the object of sustained analysis, compared to its fellows.[3] The present paper will try to find a standpoint that will allow the various ingredients of *Leucippe and Clitophon* to come into proper perspective, and allow us to align our reactions with Achilles' intentions. Although no unchallenged interpretation exists, there is a degree of common ground in our own day; to the taste of the late twentieth century, the story is some form of comedy. What is offered here, then, is a reconsideration of some ideas by now familiar enough in themselves, in the hope that it may be useful to reshuffle them.

The features of the story that merit attention here have been touched on; they are:

1 the technique of ego-narrative;
2 psychological realism;
3 sensational adventures and melodrama;
4 the use of standard novel conventions;
5 sophistication of manner and style;
6 variety of content.

The most profitable approach will be to consider how these features are interrelated. The general questions that need to be answered are, how serious is Achilles? Is this melodrama or comedy – or, if it is both, what is the relation between them? What is the place of this novel in its genre? One preliminary comment should be made. It is virtually certain that Achilles wrote in the latter part of the second century, and therefore is a near-contemporary of several other writers of fiction whose dates are fixed firmly enough for present purposes: certainly Apuleius (*Metamorphoses*), Lucian (*True Story, Philopseudes, Toxaris*, perhaps a version of the *Asinus*-story), Iamblichus (*Babyloniaca*), and very probably others including Longus (*Daphnis and Chloe*) and the authors of several stories of which we possess fragments of varying tone. Working in this creative age, Achilles assuredly had every incentive to experiment, as did his contemporaries, with the form of this fashionable genre, and in fact several of the qualities of his writing can be found in the above works. A priori, therefore, we may reasonably expect to find in him originality and ingenuity in the treatment of familiar themes.

The most notable formal feature of *Leucippe and Clitophon* is that it is cast as ego-narrative.[4] Why has Achilles chosen this form? What does he gain by abandoning the more obvious and easier omniscient authorial narrative method of earlier fiction of this kind, such as *Ninus* and *Chaereas and Callirhoe*? What difficulties does it entail, and how does he deal with them? This complex of questions will be seen to lead to a number of important aspects of the structure and content of the story.

One thing that ego-narrative notoriously can do is to make it impossible, if the writer so wishes, for narrator (and hence reader) to 'see' some of the action. The reader, in this convention, can learn only what the narrator learns as events unfold, without benefit of any knowledge acquired subsequently by the narrator. Alternatively, the narrator can be represented as learning part of the story subsequently to his own participation in the events it contains, and as being therefore in a position, at the time of his narration, to tell the listener (= reader) not only what he knows from his own participation, but also what he found out later. That is to say, the writer can have it both ways. He can let the reader learn the whole story of a given incident the first time that incident occurs in the ego-narrator's account of events; in that case the ego-narrative is being used not to keep the reader ignorant but for some other purpose. Or he can deliberately hide some of the story from the reader; in which case the ego-narrative form is being used *in order to* mystify, or produce some comparable effect on, the reader.

If we examine what Achilles does in this respect, we find that his practice varies.[5] In the first part of the story he conscientiously represents Clitophon as narrating only what he himself knew at the time of the action in question, namely the arrival of Leucippe in Tyre, the death of Charicles, the flirtation with Leucippe and its immediate sequel in the lovers' journey to Egypt – all of which we see through his eyes, as it happened at the time to his own knowledge. But at 2.13–18 comes the story of how Callisthenes abducted Calligone, mistaking her for Leucippe, and at this point in his story Clitophon could not know about some of this – for instance, about Callisthenes' desire to marry Leucippe, and his request to Sostratus in Byzantium for her hand. He got to know about all of this later (8.17.2); so he is here, at 2.13, introducing subsequent knowledge into his account of events. That is to say that Achilles has moved from one mode of ego-narration to another, in order to put the reader in possession of the necessary knowledge and relevant explanations.

All very well so far; this can be considered a legitimate version of ego-narrative. It certainly simplifies matters for the author, since it can add greatly to the coherence of the action, from the reader's point of view – although it can, of course, tend to turn the narrator into an 'omniscient author', and thus spoil the specific ego-narrative effect. Achilles, at any rate, seems after this point to prefer to stay consistently on this less uncompromising level. At two major points, however, he reverts to the stricter technique, and they are significant points indeed. First, at 3.15 Clitophon tells us about the 'sacrifice' of Leucippe, and once more describes events as he saw them *at the time they happened*, including the gruesome details about how Leucippe's belly was slit open and her entrails spilled out, only to be seized, cooked and eaten. That is to say that we, the readers, are deliberately prevented from knowing what has really happened, as we should have known with omniscient narrative or with ego-narrative with hindsight. Obviously this is for the sake of sensational effect. And that is the point of making this observation: having tacitly dispensed himself from respecting his own original narrative practice, Achilles chooses to return to it here – for what purpose? In order to give himself the opportunity to invent a singularly lurid incident of human sacrifice and cannibalism. There was, after all, no need whatever to concoct so grotesque an episode. But Achilles has stacked the cards ruthlessly: he invents the rhapsode's theatrical equipment, conjured up handily by a pirate attack on a ship, and he invents also the requirement that Menelaus and Satyrus perform human sacrifice as an initiation rite for entry into the robber band. This point should be stressed: he is not simply taking advantage of a situation that the story has thrown up of its own accord, so to speak, he has deliberately fixed the whole scene, gone out of his way to set it up, expecting his audience to enjoy the kitsch,[6] to relish the *frisson* such an incident would induce. It is one of the vicissitudes of the *tyche* attaching to the survival of the Greek novel that in our day a papyrus has come to our knowledge describing in even more revolting detail an episode of startling similarity from another novel of the period, the *Phoenicica* of Lollianus.[7] Together with the Grand Guignol of Iamblichus' *Babyloniaca*, with its ghosts, suicides, mutilation, poison, murder, magic practices and other entertaining features, these episodes demonstrate that there was undoubtedly a taste for fiction as sensational in its methods as any modern ghost or science fiction story.

The reader, duly mystified, naturally wants to know what happened. But before his curiosity is satisfied a few pages later (3.20–2), Achilles takes advantage of the situation he has set up to attribute to Clitophon a soliloquy that revels in the nauseating details of the incident, in the fact that Leucippe's entrails have been eaten by human beings. Winkler's translation nicely catches the tone and a crucial antithesis: 'Your body is laid out here, but where will I find your vitals? Oh, far less devastating had the fire devoured them, but no – your insides are inside the outlaws, victuals in the vitals of bandits'[8] (3.16.4). Gaselee's version of 1917 just as nicely catches the tone not of Achilles Tatius but of so much scholarship on him; translating the passage lamely – 'now has the burial of them been at the same time the robbers' sustenance' –

he comments that 'the appalling ill taste of this rhetorical outburst prevents the English translation from being anything but ludicrous'.[9] It is of course exactly that – a question of taste – and one may of course deplore it; kitsch is not to everyone's liking. But the point is that the episode is very evidently constructed precisely in order to set up this appalling ill taste. It is deliberate, and it is the point of the whole episode. Far from being crude sensationalism, this is, for better or for worse, highly sophisticated sensationalism.

Having milked his resuscitated device of strict ego-narrative, Achilles repeats the trick once, at 5.7, where apparently Leucippe is decapitated. This time, however, no doubt aware that he cannot expect to deceive his reader a second time in the same way, Achilles varies the recipe. Instead of being enlightened almost at once, the reader is explicitly fended off at 5.20, where Satyrus tells Clitophon 'you will hear in due course', and has to wait almost beyond patience for the explanation, until virtually the end of the whole novel (8.15–16); at which point Achilles himself archly says 'this is the only episode left incomplete in the whole story'. But again we have had an aria from Clitophon, though a short one (5.7). The central antithesis this time is between the useless bulk of the surviving trunk and the smallness of the dominant but lost head; a perfect specimen of the contorted rhetoric of the Second Sophistic – and again, the last thing we should do is take it seriously.[10] Had these two episodes occurred in Xenophon's *Ephesiaca* or Iamblichus' *Babyloniaca* they would indeed have been 'serious', in the sense of being part of the real fabric of the story. In Achilles they are isolated and special episodes, staged for their effect in their own right, for which the author has chosen to revert to an uncomfortably severe form of ego-narrative that he has in principle already abandoned.[11]

More commonly Achilles allows his narrator to tell us not only what he saw happening at the time it happened, but also what he came to know subsequently; this is in fact his normal procedure after the watershed of 2.13. Occasionally there is a passage where the stricter form interplays with the looser, and this can lead to irony. At 7.1.3, for example, we hear the story of Leucippe's third 'apparent death' (her alleged murder by the agents of Melite), which Clitophon recounts as he heard it at the time; but by then we as readers know what Clitophon at the time of the incident did not know, namely that Leucippe is alive; the narrative has by now become complex. In some cases, where we might wonder how Clitophon learned what had really happened, Achilles will throw in a brief justificatory remark.[12] As the story proceeds, however, the conventions are observed more and more loosely, until in the final two books the ego-narrator in effect turns into an omniscient narrator, for all the world like an omniscient author. For even given the fullest information after the event, Clitophon could never have come to know some of the things Achilles represents him as telling us on his own authority. From the point at which Thersander enters the plot (5.23) to the end of the story we are repeatedly told not only what Thersander did but also what went on in his mind. For instance, at 6.11 (an interview between Thersander and Melite), and again at 6.18 (Thersander and Leucippe), feelings are attributed by Clitophon to Thersander that Clitophon could not possibly learn about subsequently from the only conceivable source, namely Thersander himself; Thersander was his bitterest enemy, and cannot be imagined as communicating such intimate matters to Clitophon, and in any case Thersander disappears abruptly from Ephesus and from the novel at 8.14. Sometimes Achilles tries to explain away this apparent omniscience – notably at 8.15, where we are told that Sosthenes (Melite's steward, who abets Thersander), when threatened with torture, described Thersander's machinations in detail; Sosthenes cannot however be credibly represented as reporting Thersander's unspoken thoughts. There are other instances of such justification, sometimes encapsulated in a single phrase.[13] But Achilles is fighting a losing battle. The root of the matter is that he has set himself a task that is difficult enough from the very beginning, and by the final movement of his story he cannot credibly maintain the fiction of watertight ego-narrative – particularly if he wants to get inside Thersander's mind at this point as he has earlier got inside Clitophon's, Leucippe's and Melite's, all of them via his only channel, namely his narrator Clitophon. The longer his story goes on, the more complex it becomes, and the less strictly can he observe his own narratorial convention. It is the story that wins; the convention suffers. Wolff was not exaggerating very much when he said long ago that Clitophon 'assumes omniscience wherever Achilles finds it convenient'.[14] It is not that he is without conscience in the matter; on the contrary, he tries very hard to clear up loose ends where he can, notably the story of Callisthenes and Calligone. But there are limits to what he can do. In practice, Clitophon is used increasingly as the voice of the omniscient author.[15]

All of which brings us to the question of why Achilles embarked on ego-narrative in the first place. How does this structure serve his aim, and what does it tell us about it? What kind of story did he want to write?

Fundamentally *Leucippe and Clitophon* is a 'standard' Greek novel. It contains all the ingredients one would expect: lovers, travel and adventures, separation and tribulations, rivals and fidelity, divine intervention and *tyche*. We have already seen some of the adventures, and have seen that they are distorted; and we shall see distortion or at least modification of other elements as well. This does not necessarily mean that the whole story flouts the generic conventions; it is, however, the distortions that give it its special flavour, and we should examine them. In doing so we shall find the feature of ego-narrative recurring frequently as a major factor contributing to that distortion and that flavour.

First, the lovers, and the element of love. In the less sophisticated specimens of the genre, *Chaereas and Callirhoe* and the *Ephesiaca*, love is simply a given, born in a moment, totally simplistic and unexamined throughout the story. In Achilles' story the picture is different; neither Clitophon nor Leucippe is naive or sentimental. Clitophon, it is true, falls in love at first sight, but what he aims at in the first place is not ideal marriage but simply sexual satisfaction; his approach to it is highly sophisticated, based as it is on realistic psychology rather than romantic convention, and Chariton's or Xenophon's few lines of bare assertion of love become two books of quite unideal courtship. Leucippe does not fall in love at first sight; she has clearly read her Ovid and knows the rules, and she unideally yields to seduction – that it does not come to completion is not her fault. This is the first instance of another of Achilles' devices, which one may call brinkmanship: he very nearly abandons the convention, in order to produce a thrill in the reader. But thereafter Leucippe turns into a conventionally virtuous virgin heroine; when, at 4.1, at the first opportunity since the couple's flight from home, Clitophon again seeks satisfaction, Leucippe refuses it. The real reason for this refusal is that Achilles wants to change tack. He has used the modified love-motif to get his story off to a convincing start: the departure of the lovers is motivated not by some melodramatic intervention of the gods (as in Xenophon) or of *tyche* (the apparent death of Callirhoe in

Chariton), but by the realistic indignation of Leucippe at being unjustly disbelieved by her mother when she protests that she has not lost her honour – a very Achillean irony. Having thus put this particular departure from convention to effective use, he needs now to get back again to the main structural beam of such a story, namely the impregnable virtue of the heroine; and in order to do so he is quite ready to resort to another convention, divine intervention, in the shape of a dream sent to Leucippe by Artemis, enjoining her to remain a virgin until she is married to Clitophon. Having begun his story by standing conventional love on its head, Achilles now retreats into conventional love.

During this first stage the strict ego-narrative technique has been put to use in the realistic representation of Clitophon's – that is, the narrator's – psychology, which sets the tone for the whole novel; and we have already seen that in the subsequent stage of the action, the adventures of the couple in Egypt, the technique is used to produce sensational effects. In the third stage – Clitophon's entanglement with Melite – it is used quite simply to get Leucippe out of the way. Since Clitophon thinks Leucippe is dead, his narrative will naturally leave her out of account; it will concentrate, and therefore we shall concentrate, on Melite. We may here turn to the standard ingredient of rivals and fidelity; and here too Achilles has stood novel-convention on its head. As the heroine's rival, Melite could be expected to be cast as a female villain, anything from the black-and-white caricatures Manto and Cyno of Xenophon to the impressive predatory *femme fatale* Arsace of Heliodorus. In fact she becomes something close to a secondary, or even simply a second, heroine. The female interest is now transferred to Melite, and once more Achilles embarks on an impressively realistic piece of psychology in presenting this substitute lover; if there is one character in the story who has regularly attracted readers' sympathy, it is Melite.[16]

And once more Achilles indulges in a piece of brinkmanship, comparable to the episode of Leucippe's near-capitulation in Book 2. This time, of course, it is Clitophon whom we half-expect to give in; Leucippe's mother appeared just in time to save her daughter from the wrong kind of love, we remember, but will Leucippe herself appear (or reappear) in time to save Clitophon from another version of it? As Ephesus comes closer and closer we wonder how long Clitophon can hold out. How is this crisis to be dealt with? Of course Leucippe does reappear in time – just; and because she does, Melite can unconsciously assure her of Clitophon's fidelity precisely by enlisting her, ironically, in a final attempt to subvert it by employing Leucippe's alleged magical abilities as a 'Thessalian' to conjure Clitophon's affections. Brinkmanship . . . but this time, having only just pulled his hero back from the brink, Achilles trumps his own ace by suddenly throwing him over the brink after all, as after all Clitophon suddenly does give way to Melite – when, and precisely because, the situation has been saved and he is no longer in danger. Yet a further piece of realism: 'I felt as any man would', says Clitophon (5.27). Yet again Achilles had disconcerted us with the unexpected, and made of it his masterstroke. Here we revert to the situation in Books 1–2, in that we are made to see the operation of love through Clitophon's eyes; in the degree in which this is (after all) a love-story, the verisimilitude accruing from the use of ego-narrative in both cases in itself adds to the realism of the emotions thus treated, and makes of the story something more than a generic exercise.

Yet structurally the function of even this realistic episode is not to make Melite central to the story, but on the contrary to get rid of her so as to bring the story to its expected conclusion. Clitophon pays his dues to passion and passion bows out. We return to novel-convention; this time, to reunion. Yet again, however, it is convention distorted. For this double reunion – Leucippe and Clitophon, Melite and Thersander – is precisely what prevents the standard reunion of lovers, through the agency of Thersander, who becomes the other rival and the obstacle to that reunion. And once more the story changes key; we have seen that variety of episode is one of its main features. Parallel adventures now become intrigue, a veritable amatory fugue – or perhaps a better analogy would be musical chairs: who will be left out when the music stops – Clitophon, Leucippe, Melite, Thersander? Of course we know who will *not* be left out; but the process has to be visible, credible, 'natural' – if the word can be applied to such a product of artifice. And we should recall now that all this is too much for Achilles' ego-narrative framework, which will not sustain the complications of action and motive that characterize this final movement. *Leucippe and Clitophon* becomes simply a different kind of story, much closer to New Comedy than is, say, the *Ephesiaca*.

Thus, one thing the device of ego-narrative has been used for is to create suspense in the reader in regard to the unexpected and sometimes grotesque turns of the plot; and another is the pursuit of psychological realism. One of the principal effects of ego-narrative, in fact, is to induce credibility: the actor in events is telling you himself what happened, and he ought to know. But with Achilles it is primarily psychological realism that is achieved, and that is one of his most marked features. Careful attention to the nature and sources of human behaviour is, we have seen, built into the structure of the story; the actions of the characters, at any rate the principal characters, arise from their personalities, in a way that is not true of Chariton or Xenophon. This is true of Clitophon's pursuit of Leucippe, of Leucippe's own reactions in the early part of the story,[17] and certainly true of the passionate Melite. Admittedly, other elements of the action are motivated by *tyche* (which is sometimes guyed), and some characters are drawn largely in black-and-white (Thersander) or are purely functional (Menelaus, Satyrus) in a plot whose main lines are determined by other causes.

Other elements on our initial list of Achillean features have already been touched on in the perspective of ego-narrative, but may warrant some further comment. The adventures of Books 1–2 are grotesque, certainly, but not more so than those of the *Ephesiaca* or *Babyloniaca* or *Phoenicica*, or even Apuleius' *Metamorphoses;* there is no need to take them more seriously in themselves. The point about their appearance in Achilles is not the fact that they appear, but the purpose for which they are used – suspense – and the mixture of so lurid an element with realism and with a developed love-interest, neither of which figures in Xenophon or Iamblichus. Clearly such episodes constituted 'popular entertainment'; but this entertainment is sophisticated.

To continue with the catalogue of novel-conventions as used by Achilles Tatius, one notorious problem for a writer of such stories is how to handle the separation of the lovers and the parallel story-lines it entails. Xenophon and Chariton find it difficult; their solution is to pass alternately from one to the other, which involves either a not very satisfactory ping-pong effect or losing sight of one lover for a long time for no very positive reason. Heliodorus and Longus separate their lovers only marginally, so do not really have to solve the problem. Achilles has contrived a very good reason for losing sight of one lover: he makes his ego-narrator lose sight of Leucippe himself, to the point of thinking her dead. It is of course true that by the time of her 'deaths' Clitophon has broken the strictest ego-narrative rule, as we have also seen, by reporting that what he had come subsequently to learn, in the case of Callisthenes and Calligone; but as he tells his dramatic story we as readers hardly expect him to know what was really happening to Leucippe, so caught up are we in the melodrama. As far as the narrative is concerned, Leucippe can credibly disappear from it, and be brought back into play when convenient to the author; not only that, but her adventures during her absence from the narrative can all be apparent deaths, and the *frissons* multiplied. Here too, then, Achilles uses standard conventions with a wry twist.

It may also be noted that whereas the 'primitive' Chariton and Xenophon use the separation of their lovers to underline the isolation of each of them, Achilles uses it rather for the purpose of mounting a complex intrigue: each of the two is beset by an importunate rival. The topic of parallel action is in fact inseparable from that of another novel-convention, the theme of the rival, the 'other man' or 'other woman'. All of the novels make play with this kind of danger to ideal love; if in Xenophon the theme is represented by brief and crude passing incidents (Manto, Cyno), in Chariton it is the basis of the whole plot, which is built not on the simple opposition of good guy (or girl)/bad guy (or girl), but on the very nobility of Chaereas' rival Dionysius. The eternal triangle is of course a – perhaps *the*– fundamental romantic narrative situation. Achilles plays all his cards here: psychological realism (Melite and Clitophon), melodrama fit for the Victorian stage as Leucippe cries to Thersander, in effect, 'Unhand me, villain!', and above all complication. Not only does the plot produce rich possibilities of misunderstanding and reproach between the two basic couples, but there are cross-currents: Melite/Clitophon and Leucippe/Thersander, obviously, but also jealousy between the males Clitophon and Thersander and ironic misprision between Leucippe and Melite. The eternal triangle becomes a quadrilateral, and an irregular one at that. Achilles, that is, develops intrigue more fully, and in so doing comes closer to New Comedy, than any of the other novelists. It is another of his major characteristics, and another aspect, along with realism and melodrama, of his mixture of fictional styles, of the disparate ingredients that constitute his story. But we have seen that he does so at the cost of effectively abandoning ego-narrative. It breaks under the strain – but at this point he has no further real use for it.

To close the account of Achilles' treatment of novel-conventions, we may glance at the reverse side of the theme of rivalry, namely the theme of fidelity, and its concomitant chastity. Again, what we find is an Achillean grimace at a romantic cliché; for in one way or another all of the principal characters offend against the rules. Clitophon and Melite offend by commission, however excusably; if Leucippe does not, it is not her fault. This is an unromantic view of sexual purity. But ultimately Achilles does just stay within the convention, in that his heroine does recover her virginal stability; as for Clitophon, he is at any rate no more blameworthy, or not much, than Longus' Daphnis – and is there not a margin accorded to men? By another irony, the striking example of observance of the romantic code comes not from a major actor, but from one of the extras – Callisthenes, who, initially moved by romantic passion for a Leucippe he has never seen, ends up romantically falling in love with her understudy Calligone and respecting her honour with the utmost rigour. Callisthenes and Calligone, we may note, are in no way necessary to the plot; they simply serve as a backdrop of normality in a story which throughout distorts the romantic norms.

The present analysis started from Achilles' technique of ego-narrative, and may at this concluding stage return to it as a point of entry into the central question posed at the beginning, namely how 'serious' is Achilles, and what is the nature of his story? Ego-narrative is a common device of comedy (Petronius, Apuleius' *Metamorphoses, Moll Flanders*), for a reason already adduced: it authenticates the narrative, and in particular the realistic detail that is the stuff of comedy. There is a strong link, furthermore, with psychological realism, in that we are inside the narrating character. Now, the tendency of realism is to abandon the moral high ground, the level of tragedy and of ideal behaviour. People 'as they really are' are not ideal, and representation of their behaviour turns readily to comedy. This moral migration is what characterizes this version of the ideal romance. Realism is the distinguishing feature of *Leucippe and Clitophon*. The most scathing assessment of it came from Rohde, who asserts that Achilles' realistic psychology consists in debasing his characters, all of whom are worthless – as if novels should be manuals of high-minded behaviour (which is assuredly what Rohde did think).[18] A more temperate and just view was expressed by Perry, for whom in Achilles

> the comic or picaresque tradition of epic narrative has been grafted onto the ideal, thereby greatly widening the scope of

the genre romance and its capacity as an artistic medium for the criticism or interpretation of life in all its aspects.[19]

But this point had already been made by Rattenbury; 'Achilles Tatius seems to have been to Greek Romance what Euripides was to Greek Tragedy. He broke down the conventions.'[20] This judgement has been taken farther. Some years after Rattenbury's formulation of Achilles' place in the history of the genre, Durham went so far as to suggest that *Leucippe and Clitophon* was in effect a parody of the form.[21] More recently Heiserman saw it as quite simply a comic novel, and Anderson as 'carefully calculated sick humour'.[22] This battery of comments highlights the relation between the novel and the New Comedy tradition which is one of its principal ancestors, and illustrates the problems that this example of the form has created for scholars.

The shape of the answer, already adumbrated in the 1930s, is easier to discern today. In recent decades it has become more apparent (partly as a result of papyrological discoveries and partly through the serious attention increasingly accorded to the genre) that these texts are not the simplistic things they were once thought to be, all formed on the same simple pattern and written by solemn, unsophisticated writers. We are now armed with enough knowledge of the chronology and cultural context of these stories to be able to see them in better perspective than was possible in the nineteenth century, or even in the early twentieth. We are also, thanks to shifts in our own attitudes, more free than were earlier scholars to see late Greece as by no means simply a tired leftover from classical Hellenism, but on the contrary a highly sophisticated society. It is this note of sophistication that is important for the immediate purpose of placing Achilles Tatius. We can allow ourselves, as earlier periods had difficulty in doing, to see various qualities and merits in the novel. In particular, we can accept the possibility of humour in the ideal romance,[23] and can see Achilles' story as essentially an amused comment on its own genre. It is above all a sophisticated work, whose sophistication lies partly in its narrative structure, partly in its realism and partly also in the way it juxtaposes romantic elements: it plays the lurid off against the refined, melodrama against realism.[24] The mixture of ingredients, far from being a problem for scholars, should be seen as the point of the work. It is not yet exactly parody; a parody would be concerned exclusively with making fun of its genre, whereas

Achilles does have a story to tell of the conventional kind, and carries it through to its end conscientiously. That story is a version of the familiar pattern, not a sustained send-up of it; it is written for its value as a story, not for its value as parody. Nor is it yet altogether a 'comic novel'. The romantic conventions ultimately hold; they are strained, but they hold. Achilles takes too much trouble over the story for us not to take it seriously as a genuine if offbeat specimen of its genre.

But serious is not solemn. Achilles is markedly unsolemn, irreverent. He deflates the very romantic conventions he uses, pushes them to the limit: decapitation, forsooth! One may perhaps think of it as a 'comedized' version of the standard novel plot – if one can properly talk of that hypothetical creation. It is at once inventive, self-conscious and critical; it employs alike ego-narrative and falsetto voice. But it does have a serious side to it. It explores, convincingly, real human psychology, and in particular, like most of the novels, feminine psychology; the pathos of Callirhoe, the melodrama of Anthia, give way to the more recognizable, more accessible behaviour of Leucippe and Melite. Rattenbury's comment is as close to the mark as any.

NOTES

1 Modern editions: Garnaud 1991; Vilborg 1955/1962; Gaselee 1917 (2nd edn, 1969). Translations: English, Winkler 1989, Gaselee 1917; French, Garnaud 1991, Grimal 1958; German, Plepelits 1980; Italian, Cataudella 1958.

2 Photius, *Bibliotheca* 87 and 94; for the other reactions, see later.

3 Besides the works mentioned in later notes, there are useful sections in Fusillo 1991: esp. 97–108, and Plepelits 1980: introduction.

4 Technically, as reported ego-narrative, since the main story is told in the first person by Clitophon to the ostensible narrator, who himself is represented as now recounting it to the reader. That is to say that initially the story is in double ego-narrative – initially, because this 'reporting frame' is not closed at the end. On the ego-narrative mechanism in this novel, see Fusillo 1991: 166–78. The modern distinction between an ego-narrator who himself participates in the action (like Clitophon) and one who does not (like Clitophon's interlocutor in the opening chapter) may be noted, since it is Clitophon's personal participation that is the basis of Achilles' narrative strategy.

5 Hägg 1971: 124–36, 'Points of view: Achilles Tatius'; this meticulous examination is fundamental to the present study.

6 *Webster's Dictionary* defines kitsch as 'gaudy trash . . . writing of a

pretentious but shallow kind, calculated to have popular appeal'. The element of self-consciousness is strong in this specimen.

7 Henrichs 1972; preliminary publication Henrichs 1969.

8 Winkler 1989: 217.

9 Gaselee 1917: 168–9.

10 'No translation can make this laboured rhetoric anything but ridiculous' – Gaselee 1917: 253.

11 A third scene picked out by Hägg 1971: 133, is 5.17.3ff., where Clitophon describes meeting 'Lacaena' without saying that she was actually Leucippe (as he obviously knew at the time of narration); here, however, the effect of surprise is spoiled by Clitophon's comment that she reminded him of Leucippe. Here Achilles is doing his best to get out of a patently absurd situation in which his hero would not in any way recognize his heroine; that is, Achilles is not in this case exploiting the situation (he is in fact trying to disentangle himself from his own plot).

12 To take one case of a number listed by Hägg 1971: 132ff., already at 2.30 Clitophon, reporting Leucippe's reaction to her mother's irruption into her room (which had caused Clitophon to escape unseen, so that he could not himself have witnessed Leucippe's reaction), retails what she said to his servant Satyrus with the phrase 'When I heard about this'.

13 See Hägg 1971: 132.

14 Wolff 1912: 199f., quoted with approval by Hägg 1971: 134 n.2.

15 We may note here in passing that the frame of Clitophon's story is never closed. This has worried scholars, who have sometimes accused Achilles of forgetfulness or incompetence. Neither is a very likely explanation, given so much evidence of care in construction in general. More probably he thought that a logically satisfactory closure would be pedantic and would detract from the ending of the real story, thus creating worse problems than it solved; and as has been pointed out before now, he had the precedent of Plato's *Republic* and other dialogues to justify him – the best possible precedent for so literary an author. See Hägg 1971: 125: the opening frame launches the whole story – and that is all Achilles wants it to do. Most 1989 attributes this 'weakness' to a 'taboo against excessive self-disclosure' and a convention whereby autobiography in Greek literature has to be a tale of woe, which does not suit a Greek romance with its happy ending; this, it is claimed, explains both Clitophon's otherwise inexplicable sadness at the beginning of the story and the omission, at its end, of reference to the autobiographical nature of this ultimately happy story. This seems specious; it is hardly likely that Achilles would go to so much trouble in order to end up painting himself into a corner. In setting out his position Most defends the complete integrity of the ego-narrative, but he does not meet adequately the evidence adduced by Hägg.

16 Rojas Alvarez 1989.

17 One might well think it is true of the later, obstinately virginal Leucippe too; now that the stage of flirtation and capture is over, and she

and Clitophon are committed (as English says, 'engaged') to each other, *Leucippe* – not Achilles – retreats, at 4.1, into convention; perhaps Artemis' injunction that she remain virgin until marriage is merely a cover (conscious or unconscious) on her part for what she intends to do anyway? Compare the (understandably) proprietorial tone of her letter to Clitophon at 5.18. Leucippe cannot be accused of lacking personality.

18 Rohde 1876: 511. For Rohde's attitudes see Cancik 1986.

19 Perry 1967: 115.

20 Rattenbury 1933: 256–7. It is true that Rattenbury was making the point to argue that Achilles was later than Heliodorus, which was disproved by the later publication of papyri; but although this complicated the literary history of the form, it does not affect the essential point made by Rattenbury.

21 Durham 1938; specifically, of Heliodorus' *Ethiopica*. His article was another contribution to the debate about chronology; ironically, it was in the same year that the first of the more recently published papyri appeared. As with Rattenbury's article, the point at issue here is not fundamentally invalidated.

22 Heiserman 1977; Anderson 1982: 32.

23 Anderson 1982 devotes a whole book to this theme, though with unequal results.

24 There is also another feature that is 'sophisticated' in the very strict sense of reflecting the literary culture of the Second Sophistic. It is to be found in the elaborate stylistic and rhetorical devices used throughout by Achilles: the digressions and ecphrases, couched invariably in very complex language (unlike the narrative, which employs a quite straightforward style), the carefully mounted and polished monologues and debates, the numerous references both overt and covert to Greek cultural tradition. Some of this can be studied with profit in Bartsch 1989, a most perceptive study. Bartsch perhaps overstates her case, namely that the descriptions in Heliodorus and Achilles Tatius are integral in the conception of these novels and should be integral in their interpretation; but her basic contention is not unjust, in that the rhetorical elaboration of the story is very much of a piece with the approach visible in its structure, as considered in the present study. It would be somewhat difficult, however, to develop this theme in the present context, that is to say without reference to the original Greek.

BIBLIOGRAPHY

Anderson, G. (1982), *Eros Sophistes: Ancient Novelists at Play*, (American Philological Association), Chico, CA.

Cancik, H. (1986), 'Erwin Rohde, ein Philologe der Bismarckzeit', in W. Doerr (ed.), *Semper Apertus: Sechshundert Jahre Ruprecht-Karls-Universität Heidelberg 1386–1986*, Berlin and Heidelberg, 436–506.

Cataudella, Q. (1958), *Il romanzo classico*, Rome (2nd edn 1973), 353–523.

Durham, D. B. (1938) 'Parody in Achilles Tatius', *Classical Philology* 33, 1–19.

Fusillo, M. (1991), *Naissance du roman*, tr. Marielle Abrioux, Paris (Italian original: *Il Romanzo greco: Polifonia ed Eros*, Venice, 1989).

Garnaud, J-Ph. (ed. and tr.) (1991), *Achille Tatius: le roman de Leucippé et Clitophon* (Collection Budé), Paris.

Gaselee, S. (ed. and tr.) (1917), *Achilles Tatius* (Loeb Classical Library), Cambridge, MA and London (2nd edn 1969).

Grimal, P. (1958), *Romans grecs et latins*, Paris, 871–1023.

Hägg, T. (1971), *Narrative Technique in Ancient Greek Romances: Studies of Chariton, Xenophon Ephesius, and Achilles Tatius*, Stockholm.

Heiserman, A. (1977), *The Novel before the Novel*, Chicago.

Henrichs, A. (1969), 'Lollianos, Phoinikika. Fragmente eines neuen griechischen Romans', *Zeitschrift für Papyrologie und Epigraphik* 4, 205–15.

Henrichs, A. (ed.) (1972), *Die Phoinikika des Lollianos*, Bonn.

Most, G. W. (1989), 'The stranger's stratagem: self-disclosure and self-sufficiency in Greek culture', *Journal of Hellenic Studies* 109, 114–33.

Perry, B. E. (1967), *The Ancient Romances: A Literary-Historical Account of their Origins*, Berkeley and Los Angeles.

Plepelits, K. (tr., intro., comm.) (1980), *Achilleus Tatios: Leukippe und Kleitophon*, Stuttgart.

Rattenbury, R. M. (1933), 'Romance: traces of lost Greek novels', in J. U. Powell (ed.), *New Chapters in Greek Literature*, Oxford, 211–57.

Rohde, E. (1876), *Der griechische Roman und seine Vorläufer*, Leipzig (3rd edn, 1914, ed. W. Schmid, repr. Hildesheim 1960, 1974).

Rojas Alvarez, L. (1989), 'Realismo erótico in Aquiles Tacio', *Nova Tellus* 7, 81–90.

Sedelmeier, A. (1959), 'Studien zu Achilleus Tatios', *Wiener Studien* 72, 113–43.

Vilborg, E. (1955/1962), *Achilles Tatius: Leucippe and Clitophon*, Stockholm (1955 ed. Vilborg/1962 comm. by Vilborg).

Winkler, J. J. (1989), translation of Achilles Tatius in B. P. Reardon (ed.), *Collected Ancient Greek Novels*, Berkeley and Los Angeles, 170–284.

Wolff, S. L. (1912), *The Greek Romances in Elizabethan Prose Fiction*, New York.

6

THE *AITHIOPIKA* OF HELIODOROS

Narrative as riddle

J. R. Morgan

In the last book of Heliodoros' *Aithiopika* (*Ethiopian Story*), Hydaspes, king of Ethiopia, returns in triumph, after a spectacular victory over the forces of Persia. During the celebrations he is presented with commemorative gifts by his subject nations, including:

> a specimen of an unusual and bizarre kind of animal: in size it stood as tall as a camel, but its hide was marked with garish leopard spots. Its hindquarters and rear parts were squat and leonine, but its withers, forelegs, and chest were disproportionately taller than the rest of its anatomy. Notwithstanding the bulk of the rest of its body, its neck was as slender and elongated as the crop of a swan. In appearance its head was like a camel's, in size not quite twice that of a Libyan ostrich. Its eyes were rimmed with a black line like mascara and darted hither and thither with an expression of pompous disdain. Even its method of locomotion was unique, since it rolled from side to side like a ship at sea, in a manner quite unlike any other creature, terrestrial or aquatic: it did not advance each of its legs individually, in rotation, but its two right legs moved forward in unison, separately from the two left legs, which also functioned as a distinct pair, thus leaving each side of its body in turn without support. It was so halting in its gait and so docile in its temperament that its keeper could lead it on a slender cord wound around its neck, and it obeyed the directions of his will as if it were a chain that brooked no disobedience. The arrival of this beast produced universal amazement. The people

> spontaneously invented a name for the creature derived from the most prominent features of its anatomy: *kamēlopardalis* [the normal Greek word for 'giraffe'].
>
> (10.27.1–4)

It is worth spending a little time analysing what is going on in this passage. The first point to note is that an essential piece of information, the creature's name, is not divulged until the last possible moment, after the description is completed.

The information contained in the description itself is not imparted directly by the narrator to the reader. Instead it is channelled through the perceptions of the onlooking crowd. They have never seen a giraffe before, and the withholding of its name from the reader re-enacts their inability to put a word to what they see. From their point of view the creature is novel and alien: this is conveyed partly by the naive wonderment of the description, and partly by their attempts to control the new phenomenon by fitting it into familiar categories. Hence the comparisons with leopards, camels, lions, swans, ostriches, eyeliner and ships. Eventually they assert conceptual mastery over visual experience by coining a new word to name the animal, derived from the naively observed features of its anatomy. However, their neologism is given in Greek (*kamēlopardalis*), although elsewhere Heliodoros is scrupulously naturalistic in observing that Ethiopians speak Ethiopian.

The reader is thus made to watch the giraffe from, as it were, inside the skull of a member of the Ethiopian crowd. The narration does not objectively describe what they saw but subjectively re-enacts their ignorance, their perceptions and processes of thought. This mode of presentation, involving the suppression of an omniscient narrator in direct communication with the reader, has the effect that the reader is made to engage with the material with the same immediacy as the fictional audience within the frame of the story: it becomes, in imagination, as real for him as it is for them.

But there is a double game going on, since the reader, as a real person in the real world, differs from the fictional audience inside the novel precisely in that he does know what a giraffe is. This assumption is implicit in the way the description is structured. If Heliodoros' primary aim had been to describe a giraffe for the benefit of an ignorant reader, he would surely have begun with the animal's name, not withheld it. So for the reader the encounter with the giraffe is not a matter of coming to terms with a new experience, so much as an exercise in matching Heliodoros' deliberately eccentric formulations with what is already known about giraffes.[1] Knowledge about giraffes in late antiquity will have derived from autopsy in only a very few cases, although exotic animals were regularly exhibited in the arena. However, there exist a number of descriptions in classical authors which confirm that a literate reading public could be counted upon to have at least second-hand information about the animal.[2]

What all this means is that the description of the giraffe functions on a second level as a riddle aimed at the reader. The information it releases at such a measured pace serves as a series of clues from which the animal can be identified, although Heliodoros does not observe the modern protocol in such games of making the clues progressively easier.[3] The answer to the riddle of course is the name of the creature: the rules of riddling entail both that the answer should be postponed until all the clues have been supplied and that it must be properly given, even when it has become perfectly obvious. So although the Greek word *kamēlopardalis* is introduced in a way formally consistent with the dramatic frame of the narrative (i.e., it is supplied by people within the story rather than by authorial statement), it functions to confirm to the reader that this passage truly was a riddle, and that the riddle is now over.

Heliodoros has taken some pains to observe the proprieties of realism here. The use of an ignorant audience within the fiction allows the riddle to be accommodated without damage to dramatic illusion. Nevertheless, once the riddle is recognized as such it becomes a game played directly between author and reader, bypassing the dramatic situation and even the narrative structure. Perhaps we can think of two Heliodoroi, first the author, a real man sitting in a room somewhere writing this text, and second the narrating voice in the text, which is just as much part of the fiction as the events it narrates. The narrator maintains the dramatic realism, but the author grimaces over his shoulder at the reader, playing with the etymology of the word *kamēlopardalis* in a way which is not meaningful for the Ethiopian-speaking spectators. Similarly the reader operates on two planes: one addressed by the narrator, responding to events with the immediacy of real experience, the other bookishly responding to the author's textual game, which challenges him into interpretative activity, into being a solver and realizer of the text rather than just a passive consumer of it.

I have subjected the giraffe to such prolonged analysis because it is an emblematic beast. The point I want to stress in this paper is that Heliodoros' whole novel demands an active interpretative response from his reader. The *Aithiopika* is a much more challenging read than any of the other Greek novels, precisely because it is pervaded at every level by the kind of self-conscious game-playing typified by the riddle of the giraffe.

Here, for instance, is the Egyptian priest, Kalasiris, who acts as narrator for about a third of the whole novel, describing a dream he had on the island of Zakynthos:

> as I slept, a vision of an old man appeared to me. Age had withered him almost to a skeleton, except that his cloak was hitched up to reveal a thigh that retained some vestige of the strength of his youth. He wore a leather helmet on his head, and his expression was one of cunning and many wiles; he was lame in one leg, as if from a wound of some kind.
> (5.22.1)

The vision reproaches Kalasiris for failing even to pay him a visit while in the vicinity, prophesies punishment for the omission, but conveys greetings from his wife to Kalasiris' charge, the heroine Charikleia, 'since she esteems chastity above all things' (5.22.3).

Again a riddle is set up by not immediately identifying the old man, and again the description is presented from the point of view of a character within the story. Here, however, the situation is rather more complicated, since Kalasiris himself has two aspects, as narrator and character within his own narration. As narrator he knows the identity of the dream figure, but in his presentation of his own experience he omits any explanatory gloss, and re-enacts the perplexity of his initial reaction. He describes the dream as he saw it, rather than as he subsequently understood it. Again the reader is challenged to disambiguate the riddle by matching the points of the description with knowledge acquired elsewhere. Every detail corresponds to something in the Homeric poems.[4] This time Heliodoros has succeeded in keeping the easiest clues to the end, particularly the formulaic epithet *polytropos* ('of many wiles'), proverbially associated with one epic individual, and the reference to a wound in the leg which also clinches its owner's recognition in the original. Further clues are offered by the fact that the old man has a home not far from Zakynthos and a wife associated with chastity.

From all this any half-educated reader would have little difficulty in identifying the figure as Odysseus. Again, by the rules of the game, a formal answer must be supplied, and again it is supplied realistically without breaching the narrative frame. A few sentences later Kalasiris makes this final request of his host on Zakynthos:

> Take your boat over to Ithake and make an offering to Odysseus on our behalf. Ask him to temper his wrath against us, for he has appeared to me this very night and told me that he is angry at having been slighted.
>
> (5.22.5)

In these cases, the game is played gently. Heliodoros wants to stimulate his reader, not defeat him. Ample help is given so that the identification can be made correctly; the game is collaborative rather than competitive. However, it concerns material from outside the novel, and is perhaps not so very far above the level of a general-knowledge quiz. When Heliodoros starts playing comparable games with his own invented story, where all readers start equal, he is apt to make greater demands.

Let's start with an easy example. At the very end of the novel, Charikleia has returned to her native Ethiopia after eloping with her beloved Theagenes from Delphi, where she was brought up as the daughter of the priest of Apollo, Charikles. She has been recognized by her real parents, Hydaspes and Persinna, king and queen of Ethiopia, but Theagenes stands in mortal peril, since he has been designated a sacrificial victim in celebration of the Ethiopians' victory over the Persians. At this juncture a message arrives from Oroondates, the defeated satrap of Egypt, asking Hydaspes to restore to her father a girl captured by the Ethiopians while on her way to Memphis; Oroondates adds that he is himself attracted to her, and knows that she has been brought to Ethiopia on Hydaspes' orders (10.34.3–4). Hydaspes allows the father, an old man in pitifully shabby clothing, to look around for his daughter. Unable to find her among Hydaspes' captives, the old man weeps, but suddenly rushes at Theagenes, drags him from the sacrificial altar, calling him villain and scoundrel, and informs the king, 'This is the man who kidnapped my daughter' (10.35.1–2).

Again a vital piece of information is withheld: the identity of the old man. And again we are presented with a series of clues provided dramatically from inside the narrative frame: partly through the satrap's letter, which the reader of the novel reads through the eyes of a character in the novel (Hydaspes), and partly through the subsequent action, description of which is limited to what could have been seen and heard by those present, thus enabling the narrator to conceal his omniscience about the old man's identity and motives.

The contents of the letter, however, cohere so closely with events already narrated that it is plain that the daughter the old man is seeking is Charikleia. This is confirmed when he fails to find her among Hydaspes' captives, since she has been removed after her recognition by her natural parents. But even when the reader has become sure that the object of the old man's quest is the heroine of the novel, he may still be reluctant to identify the old man himself as Charikles, because of the sheer improbability of the priest of Delphic Apollo suddenly turning up in rags beyond the southern frontiers of Egypt – until, that is, he recognizes Theagenes and refers to the elopement from Delphi which took place six books previously. These clues are quite sufficient to enable the reader to work out who the old man is before Heliodoros gives us the answer: 'Pressed by Hydaspes to explain more clearly what he meant, the old man (who was none other than Charikles) . . .' (10.36.1).

What must be noted here is that the reader can entertain and confirm the identification of Charikles only because he has a surplus of knowledge over the Ethiopians which is the result of his having read the novel so far and their having not. The riddle this time does not involve material from outside the text and is more than just an incidental piece of fun. The game which the reader is being invited to join is a riddle which not only tests his memory of earlier sections of the plot, but also has a crucial bearing on its future. For if the identity of Charikles is enigmatic, even more so is how he might affect the prospects of Theagenes; the hero is condemned to die as a human sacrifice, but the reader's expectations are geared up to a reprieve, partly by the knowledge that romantic heroes do not get killed on the last page,[5] but also, more specifically, by Theagenes' exhibition of prowess in wrestling a runaway steer and an Ethiopian giant, and by suggestions that, despite her maidenly inhibitions, Charikleia is on the verge of coming clean about him to her parents. The sudden intervention of her wronged foster-father confounds all expectations, and his well-founded accusations make Theagenes' future look decidedly bleak. The solution of the riddle, then, moves the plot forward into a new and more unpredictable (and hence exciting) phase.[6]

This characteristic pattern of withholding information (riddle), releasing it obliquely and gradually (clues), and then explaining it in retrospect (answer) also informs larger spans of narrative. In Book 8, for example, the hero and heroine have fallen into the clutches of the nymphomaniac Persian princess, Arsake. Charikleia is sentenced in a rigged trial to be burned at the stake for a murder she did not commit, a sentence she welcomes as a release from the miseries of her life. The fire is lit, and with a fearsome denunciation of Arsake and assertion of her own innocence, Charikleia leaps into the heart of the flames:

> There she stood for some time without taking any hurt. The flames flowed around her rather than licking against her; they caused her no harm but drew back whenever she moved towards them, serving merely to encircle her in splendour and present a vision of her standing in radiant beauty within a frame of light, like a bride in a chamber of flame. Charikleia was astounded by this turn of events but was nonetheless eager for death. She leapt from one part of the blaze to another, but it was in vain, for the fire always drew back and seemed to retreat before her onset.
>
> (8.9.13–14)

A miracle! At least it seems so because a vital piece of information is omitted: *how* does a romantic heroine escape being fried to a crisp when she jumps into a bonfire? The passage exhibits all the by now familiar features. Events are presented from partial viewpoints, first Charikleia's in her dramatic speech; then the moment of her mounting the pyre and her unexpected survival are seen through the crowd's eyes (note how *visual appearance* is stressed); and finally the heroine's again in her astonishment. The absence of any authorial explanation for such an inexplicable and unexpected development constitutes a riddle, and invites speculative interpretation. Knowledge from outside Heliodoros' novel is of marginal utility, and consists mainly of an awareness that romantic novels simply do not incinerate their heroines with two books still to go, so that the reader was in some sense expecting Charikleia to survive.[7] The actual course of the plot was never really what was at issue, so much as the means by which the inevitable outcome would be accomplished, and it is precisely those means which are problematized by the riddle structure.

As usual, the answer is provided retrospectively and within the dramatic frame, but in this case the solution involves the introduction of new 'facts' of which the reader has hitherto been quite unaware. That night, in their prison cell, Theagenes and Charikleia talk over the day's remarkable events. Charikleia suddenly remembers a dream vision of her now dead mentor Kalasiris that had visited her the previous night and delivered this prophecy:

> If you wear *pantarbe* fear-all, fear not the power of flame
> Miracles may come to pass; for Fate 'tis easy game.
> (8.11.2)

The solution to the riddle is itself a riddle, which Charikleia elucidates for her sceptical beloved: thinking she was about to die, she had secreted about herself the recognition tokens left her by her mother, including a ring set with the jewel called *pantarbe* and engraved with mystic characters. This, she surmises, protected her from the fire (8.11.7–8).

Heliodoros' manipulation of his narrative is obvious. Any 'honest' writer would have narrated this self-evidently important dream in its proper chronological place. The postponement is half-heartedly explained within the dramatic frame by the suggestion that Charikleia simply forgot about it, but this is only for form's sake.[8] Heliodoros is deliberately withholding information, to induce puzzlement and speculation, to encourage the reader to take, in Umberto Eco's notorious phrase, 'inferential walks'.

In comparison with the other riddles we have discussed, this one may seem adversarial rather than collaborative. Rather than slowly releasing material which will guide the reader safely to the correct solution, Heliodoros' aim appears to be to keep us in the dark until such time as it suits him to tell us something we could not have otherwise known. But, although the author is playing more roughly here, he is still observing the rules: the clues *are* there, though probably their significance is realized only in retrospect. As Charikleia goes to face trial, intending to denounce herself and find release from the torment of her existence, Heliodoros duly records that she wore her recognition tokens 'as a kind of burial shroud, fastened around her waist beneath her clothes' (8.9.8). And this reference to the tokens takes us back, across half the novel, to the embroidered message in Ethiopian hieroglyphs which Persinna exposed with her daughter and which remained unread until Kalasiris tracked her down in Delphi and deciphered it:

> Above all, be sure to find among the treasures that I laid beside you a certain ring. Keep it by you always. It was a gift that your father gave me during our courtship, engraved all around with the royal crest and set with a *pantarbe* jewel that endows it with holy, mystic powers.
>
> (4.8.7)

These holy, mystic powers are unspecified.[9] Nevertheless, the mere mention of them would lead a competent reader to surmise that the plot would exploit them sooner or later, and an exceptionally alert reader might beat the author to the connection in Book 8.

It is not difficult to find other sections within the narrative of the *Aithiopika* which are constructed as riddles, a vital piece of information being kept back and then released as an answer. Two more examples can be mentioned briefly, both from the ninth book, whose military subject matter could easily lead to the false assumption that its narrative technique is simple.

Oroondates is besieged by the Ethiopians in Syene. He parleys with them, and secures their permission to send two envoys to his troops at Elephantine, *ostensibly* to negotiate their surrender at the same time as his. His real motives are not divulged, nor are they when he makes an apparently impossible break-out and stealthily enters Elephantine by night (9.7ff.). The riddle set is: what is his plan?, and, as is by now familiar, the reader's ignorance is produced by the exploitation of partial in-text viewpoints. In this case all Oroondates' actions are described as seen by the Ethiopians without authorial explanation. Some additional clues are given later in the narrative, but the full answer is withheld until the moment when the Persian army from Elephantine suddenly turns up with Oroondates at its head (9.13), at which point the omniscient narrator intervenes to fill in the gaps he had left in his own narrative.

There ensues a battle, in which the Persians have a seemingly decisive weapon, their armoured cavalry. A lengthy description stresses the totality of the protection of both rider and horse and the awesome power of their arms (9.15). Against them Hydaspes stations troops of the Blemmyes and Seres, two subject nations, with special instructions which are not communicated to the reader. This is the riddle. The answer emerges in the battle, when the Blemmyes rush forward like madmen (all this is seen from the Persian point of view, without explanation), throw themselves to the ground and stab upwards with their swords into the horses' unprotected bellies as they thunder over their heads (9.17–18), and then butcher the dismounted knights through the one vulnerable point in their armour, between the legs, as they lie helpless, too heavy to move. Meanwhile the Seres part ranks to reveal Hydaspes' corps of elephants, the sight of which throws the cavalry into panic. Ethiopian archers pick off the survivors by shooting arrows through the eye-slits in their helmets. Unobtrusive clues to the stratagem were furnished in the description of the armour, where all the details which become important in the battle were unostentatiously included.

These examples present the riddle format over a medium-term narrative span. The pattern recurs with sufficient frequency for us to identify it as a characteristic feature of Heliodoros' narrative technique. To reiterate, release of information is deliberately controlled so as to entice the reader into identifying and answering, with varying degrees of certainty, questions posed by the narrative. The implied reader of the *Aithiopika* is compelled to be constantly engaged in interpretation and speculation, and must respond to the author's games in order to actuate the text fully. Formalist critics earlier this century made a distinction between what they called *histoire*, that is the story as it 'actually' happened, complete and in chronological order, and *récit*, that is, the way that the story is presented, the textual surface. To use their terms, Heliodoros' *récit* consistently omits or postpones important aspects of the *histoire*, and the author communicates directly with the reader about the *histoire* through riddles, over the head of the narrator and his *récit*.

By this stage, it has probably become clear to anyone who knows the *Aithiopika* and the recent secondary literature on it that what I have been discussing is an exact counterpart in microcosm to the macrotextual structure of the whole work. This is where Heliodoros marks a spectacular advance over his predecessors in the romance form. At the end of the tradition, when Heliodoros was writing,[10] two weaknesses of conventional romantic narrative must have become obvious. The first was its predictability: curiosity to know what happens next is the motor of reading any fiction, but with a stereotyped basic plot there can never be any real doubt about the ending. Heliodoros redirected curiosity from outcome to explanation. The second problem is lack of direction and unity: romance was prone to fall apart into a series of exciting but only loosely connected adventures, at the end of which the protagonists recovered their lost happiness and simply lived out the rest of their lives as if nothing had happened. By leaving central questions unanswered Heliodoros is able to hold large spans of text together, and the most important answers, when they do arrive, involve decisive change for the protagonists. Both these strategies imply an interpretatively active reader.

The opening of the novel is deservedly famous.[11] A gang of bandits come across a beached ship, surrounded by twitching corpses and the wreckage of a banquet. Through their eyes, and with their ignorance of what has taken place, the reader is made to assimilate the scene in obsessive but unexplained visual detail. In the midst of the carnage sits a fabulously beautiful young woman, nursing a fabulously handsome young man. It does not take long to identify them as the hero and heroine of the novel, and learn that their names are Theagenes and Charikleia, but Heliodoros tantalizes us over further details. Thus at the very beginning of the novel two riddles are established: what has happened on the beach? and who exactly are the hero and heroine? Heliodoros prolongs the reader's ignorance by his characteristic use of partial viewpoint. Sometimes, as with the bandits, there is a fictional audience whose specific perceptions act as a channel of partial information to the reader, but elsewhere Heliodoros as narrator simply relates what an uninformed witness of the events would have seen or heard. For example, we are only allowed to find out about the hero and heroine as they speak to others or are spoken about: Heliodoros as author knows all about them but keeps quiet in favour of his recording but not explaining narrative voice.

The opening scene is eventually disambiguated by Kalasiris, an Egyptian priest. He regales Knemon, a surrogate reader within the text who shares the real reader's curiosity about the protagonists, with a long story, beginning in Book 2, of how he met Charikleia at Delphi, witnessed the birth of her love for Theagenes and helped the lovers to elope. He chronicles their subsequent experiences, until at the end of Book 5, half-way through the novel, the story circles back to its own beginning and at last resolves the mystery of the scene on the beach.

Kalasiris, however, is no more a straightforward narrator than is Heliodoros.[12] In fact, he comments himself (2.24.5) on the apparently tricksy quality of his story-telling. By the time he tells Charikleia's story to Knemon, Kalasiris has long known her to be the natural daughter of the King and Queen of Ethiopia, exposed by her mother at birth because of her white skin, but he suppresses this knowledge so that Knemon (and through him the reader) can actively participate in the discovery. First he learns (through a reported narrative, 2.30ff.) that she is only the adopted daughter of her ostensible father, Charikles, the priest of Apollo, and how she came to be adopted. Then (2.35) he is granted an enigmatic prophecy by the Delphic oracle, and visited in his sleep (3.11) by Apollo and Artemis who tell him to take the young lovers with him to Egypt and onwards. Assisting their love against Charikles' wishes through a complex and duplicitous intrigue, he eventually tricks Charikles into allowing him to see the embroidered band exposed with her, a message from the Ethiopian queen to her abandoned child.[13] The performance of Kalasiris is in many ways emblematic of the whole novel, intensely self-aware, theatrical, manipulative, enigmatic. He is the focus where the roles of author and reader intersect. Like the reader he has to make speculative sense out of cryptic fragments of information, and like the author he employs less than complete release of information to puzzle and please his audience; he is both a solver and setter of riddles.

But his narrative does not resolve all the ambiguities it poses. The obscure oracle is in fact a predictive armature around which the whole future course of the plot is built.[14] Some elements of it are obvious and others are resolved by Kalasiris, but it also looks beyond his death to the very end of the novel. It is another large-scale riddle, whose answers are supplied by the course of the story itself. Its last couplet, which predicts that the lovers will:

> ... reap the reward of those whose lives are passed in virtue:
> A crown of white on brows of black

only receives full explication in the last sentence of the work, when Theagenes and Charikleia, now formally to be married and honorary Ethiopians (hence the brows of black), don the white mitres of the High Priest of the Sun and High Priestess of the Moon in Ethiopia. In the interim, it has served to elicit deliberately misguided guesses about the ending of the novel, for example as the terms of its prophecy appear to be fulfilled in the human sacrifice which threatens Theagenes and Charikleia when they reach Ethiopia.

To conclude: it is characteristic of Heliodoros at every level of narration to withhold information, not simply to produce effects of shock and surprise, but to enlist the reader into an actively interpretative role. If this essay has dwelt on specific examples from the second half of the work, that is because there has been a tendency in scholarly work on the novel to dwell on its overall structure and particularly the figure of Kalasiris and to regard the sections narrated by Heliodoros himself as technically simpler and less interesting. This is untrue; the technique is all-pervasive. The plot itself contains frequent examples of characters compelled to speculate interpretatively, notably in response to dreams, not surprisingly since the narrator so conspicuously fails to provide an authoritative centre of final meaning. Heliodoros was clearly very interested in these issues of cognition and comprehension, but I do not think his interest was a post-modernist one in hermeneutic theory, nor that these recurrent situations are intended to focus the reader's attention on the reading process *per se*.[15] For all the self-conscious artificiality of individual examples, I would prefer to see the enigmatic narrative mode of the *Aithiopika* as an attempt to move fiction closer to life.

Real life, after all, tends to be confused and senseless. We are not always immediately aware of the causes or meanings of what we see and suffer. These things more often become clear only in retrospect, as we learn more or impose patterns on raw experience. Whereas other Greek novelists, in predigesting the story for us, reduce us to the role of audience, Heliodoros has contrived to make his reader an imaginative participant in the story of Theagenes and Charikleia.[16]

NOTES

1 An illuminating modern parallel is provided by Craig Raine's poem 'A Martian Sends a Postcard Home', in which an alien from outer space describes familiar Earth objects with disorienting unfamiliarity:

> In homes a haunted apparatus sleeps
> that snores when you pick it up.
>
> If the ghost cries, they carry it
> to their lips and soothe it to sleep
>
> with sounds. And yet, they wake it up

deliberately, by tickling with a finger.

2 In fact, our passage itself probably derives from literary sources rather than first-hand experience, and may well share a source with an account of the beast by the fifth-century grammarian Timotheos of Gaza, preserved in the second book of the so called *Sylloge Constantini*, printed in the *Supplementum Aristotelicum*, vol. 1, Berlin, 1885, 94, §270. Compare my note 'Two giraffes emended', *CQ* 38 (1988), 267–9. For other descriptions of giraffes see Diod.2.51 (preserving Poseidonios); Strab.16.4.7 (preserving Artemidoros); Plin. *Nat. Hist.*8.69; Oppian, *Kyn.*3.462ff.; Philostorgios, *Hist.Eccl.*3.11.

3 In fact he gives the game away rather early by mentioning camels and leopards in the first sentence; but perhaps this heavy hint should be read as a signal that the animal is not going to be named any more directly – in other words that there is a riddle being set at all.

4 The withering of age refers to the disguise given to Odysseus by Athene at *Od.*13.398ff.; the strong thigh revealed by a hitched-up cloak recalls the preparations for the wrestling bout at *Od.*18.66ff.; the leather helmet comes from the nocturnal raid of *Iliad* 10.

5 I am oversimplifying the dynamics of fiction here. Even when readers know (from their acquaintance with the conventions of the genre) what is going to happen next, they are often quite happy to pretend that they do not and respond accordingly. This is one term of the contract we make in reading a work of fiction, and is an aspect of Coleridge's famous 'suspension of disbelief'. Nevertheless, many novelists – and Heliodoros is one – exploit the tension between what generic rules say ought to happen and what looks likely to happen. For the manipulation of expectations in this scene see my article 'A sense of the ending', in *TAPhA* 119 (1989), esp. 315–18.

6 In this case, the answer to the riddle is given by the author himself, not one of the characters inside the narrative frame. Such explanatory interventions are rare in Heliodoros (but not unique: compare those at 2.12.2ff., 5.4.3ff., 9.13.2ff., all incidentally good examples of medium-scale narrative riddles). The present instance can be explained partly by the fact that none of the characters in the narrative knows as much about Charikles as the reader does, and partly by the consideration that Hydaspes must not be allowed to hear Charikles' name since its similarity to that of Charikleia would make it very implausible for him not to realize that the old man's 'daughter' is actually his own recently recovered child.

7 In fact Heliodoros himself signals as much a few sentences previously, when Charikleia embraces her beloved 'for what she thought would be the last time' (8.9.8).

8 It is not even that considerations of mimetic realism have led Heliodoros to postpone mention of the dream until it can be spoken of by his characters. Elsewhere dreams, which are invariably significant, are narrated in due sequence by the omniscient narrator; for example, those at 1.18.4 and 2.16.1, although a similar example of a duplicitously

postponed dream occurs at 9.25.1. We are dealing here with a deliberate device to produce a specific effect in its context.

9 The *pantarbe* is an unidentified red gem; various powers were ascribed to it, such as that of attracting other jewels; cf. FGH 688 F 45 (Ktesias), Philostr. *Vit.Apoll.* 3.46, but no writer apart from Heliodoros, so far as we know, linked it with fireproofing.

10 Heliodoros' dates are a matter of dispute. There is clearly some connection between the spectacular siege of Syene in the ninth book of the novel, and the references to an exactly similar stratagem used at Nisibis by the Parthians in CE 350 in two orations by the Emperor Julian. This would indicate a date for Heliodoros after 350, except that other sources for the siege of Nisibis describe significantly different tactics, which leaves open the possibility that Julian was copying from Heliodoros rather than vice versa, and that Heliodoros could have written his novel up to a hundred years earlier. However, no one disagrees that the *Aithiopika* is the latest romance that we know of, and papyrus fragments suggest that although novels continued to be read into the sixth and seventh centuries, the composition of such texts had ceased by the fourth.

11 For more detailed analysis of this scene, see my paper 'Reader and audiences in the *Aithiopika* of Heliodoros', in *GCN* 4 (1992), 86–90.

12 Kalasiris has been the focus of much important work on this novel; see esp. J. J. Winkler, 'The mendacity of Kalasiris and the narrative strategy of Heliodoros' *Aithiopika*', *YCS* 27 (1982), 93–158; G. N. Sandy, 'Characterization and philosophical décor in Heliodorus' *Aethiopica*', *TAPhA* 112 (1982), 141–67; M. Futre Pinheiro, 'Calasiris' story and its narrative significance in Heliodorus' *Aethiopica*', *GCN* 4 (1992), 69–83.

13 At which point his narrative takes another twist into its infinite regress, because he tells Charikleia (if he is to be believed) that he had been commissioned by her mother to find her, so that what he reads in the embroidery is not a discovery so much as a confirmation of what he already knew (4.12.2ff.). The answer seems to be that, although enlisted to look for Persinna's daughter, the search was not the reason for his coming to Delphi; only gradually did he come to realize who she was and to recognize the subtlety of the divine governance which had united the two strands of his experience (4.9.1). However we read Kalasiris' motivation (see Winkler, 'The mendacity of Kalasiris' and Futre Pinheiro, 'Calasiris' story'), this is clearly a spectacular, and hyper-enigmatic example of the postponement of explanatory material.

14 On this oracle and its structural function, see my paper 'A sense of the ending' in *TAPhA* 119 (1989), 299–320.

15 Against, for example, Winkler and Bartsch.

16 In life an external centre of authoritative meaning can be provided by religion; in a text of literature that centre is represented by the author himself, which is why the elusive omniscient Heliodoros tends to allow us a fleeting glimpse of himself in riddling situations, which thus become simultaneously the most lifelike and the most artificial aspect of his fiction. Perhaps we can accept his intrusions as a kind of

divine epiphany. At the very deepest level of understanding, when all the patterns finally cohere, god and author are indistinguishable. Certainly epiphanies of coherence within the novel are ascribed to realization of the divine economy; I think particularly of Kalasiris' realization that his personal pursuit of wisdom at Delphi and his care for the love of Theagenes and Charikleia are one and the same as his mission to find the Ethiopian princess (4.9.1), and of the supreme moment at the end of the novel when Charikles, of all people, who has been an uncomprehending victim of seemingly malign events, is granted a realization that everything has happened as the oracle predicted and nothing has been random (10.41.3). Disguised as God, Heliodoros takes his final bow.

BIBLIOGRAPHY

Altheim, F., *Literatur und Gesellschaft im ausgehenden Altertum*, vol. 1, Halle: Niemayer, 1948, 93–124.

Bartsch, S., *Decoding the Ancient Novel*, Princeton: Princeton University Press, 1989, esp. 109–43.

Feuillâtre, E., *Etudes sur les Ethiopiques d'Héliodore*, Paris: Presses Universitaires de la France, 1966.

Futre Pinheiro, M., *Estruturas técnico-narrativas nas Etiópicas de Heliodoro*, Lisbon, 1987.

Futre Pinheiro, M., 'Fonctions du surnaturel dans les *Éthiopiques* d'Héliodore', *Bulletin de l'Association Guillaume Budé* (1991), 359–81.

Futre Pinheiro, M., 'Calasiris' story and its narrative significance in Heliodorus' *Aethiopica*', *GCN* 4 (1992), 69–83.

Hefti, V., *Zur Erzählungstechnik in Heliodors Aethiopica*, Vienna: Holzhausen, 1950.

Keyes, C. W., 'The structure of Heliodorus' *Aethiopica*', *Studies in Philology* 19 (1922), 42–51.

Kövendi, D., 'Heliodors *Aithiopika*: eine literarische Würdigung', in F. Altheim and R. Stiehl (eds), *Die Araber in der alten Welt*, vol. 3, Berlin: de Gruyter, 1966, 136–97.

Morgan, J. R., 'History, romance and realism in the *Aithiopika* of Heliodoros', *Classical Antiquity* 1 (1982), 221–65.

Morgan, J. R., 'A sense of the ending: the conclusion of Heliodoros' *Aithiopika*', *TAPhA* 119 (1989), 299–320.

Morgan, J. R., 'The story of Knemon in Heliodoros' *Aithiopika*', *JHS* 109 (1989), 99–113.

Morgan, J. R., 'Reader and audiences in the *Aithiopika* of Heliodoros', *GCN* 4 (1992), 85–103.

Paulsen, T., *Inszenierung des Schicksals: Tragödie und Komödie im roman des Heliodor*, Trier: Wissenschaftlicher Verlag, 1992.

Sandy, G. N., 'Characterization and philosophical décor in Heliodorus' *Aethiopica*', *TAPhA* 112 (1982), 141–67.

Sandy, G. N., *Heliodorus*, Boston: Twayne, 1982.

Szepessy, T., 'Die *Aithiopika* des Heliodoros und der griechische sophistische Liebesroman', *Acta Antiqua Academiae Scientiarum Hungaricae* 5 (1957), 241–59; reprinted in H. Gärtner (ed.), *Beiträge zum griechischen Liebesroman*, Hildesheim: Olms, 1984, 432–50.

Winkler, J. J., 'The mendacity of Kalasiris and the narrative strategy of Heliodoros' *Aithiopika*', *YCS* 27 (1982), 93–158.

Wolff, S.K., *The Greek Romance in Elizabethan Prose Fiction*, New York: Columbia University Press, 1912.

Part III

THE GREEK CONTEXT

7

THE *ALEXANDER ROMANCE*

From history to fiction

Richard Stoneman

The inclusion of the *Alexander Romance* in a volume concerned with Greek fiction may need a word of defence. The Romance is almost unique among the Greek novels in having a historical character as its protagonist: the only analogous cases are two fragmentary works, the *Ninus Romance* and the *Sesonchosis Romance*, and Xenophon's *Education of Cyrus* (itself something of a taxonomic problem). Because it concerns a historical character there may be a temptation to regard it as a kind of history (bad history, or perhaps an extreme version of 'tragic history') and to treat it differently from other Greek romances. This temptation might be enhanced by the attribution in some of the MSS of the ß-recension (composed between 300 and 500 CE) to Callisthenes, Alexander's court historian: the attribution is impossible because Callisthenes died before Alexander, whereas the Romance describes Alexander's death. In fact the Romance shows more similarities with other narrative texts about individuals, including the novels, which need to be explored in order to characterize the work properly.

The term 'romance' is a will-o'-the-wisp which is better ignored in discussion of this text. The Greek romances have been so called mainly because of a reluctance by critics to refer to them as novels, implying a nineteenth-century model of character development and psychological analysis. In fact the Greek romances have rather little in common with the medieval romances from which the term has been borrowed. French and German scholars are spared this problem by having only the single word *roman/Roman* for both novel and romance. The Greeks had no word corresponding to either term, and if a name were to be given to any of the romances it would probably be *diegema*, narrative.[1] A narratologist might insist that it is unrealistic even to distinguish between fictional and historical narratives;[2] but we do not need to go so far as this to reach an acceptable view of the *Alexander Romance* as a kind of historical novel. The *Alexander Romance* is a text which uses the freedom of fiction to explore more fully, through philosophical and psychological means, the quality of a particular historical epoch. Like *War and Peace* or *Waverley* it adds to history in order to explain history. It is an exploration of a career which like few others in history genuinely was epochal: the Greek world was quite different after Alexander's reign from what it had been before it.

The *Alexander Romance* concerns the historical Alexander and gives an account, albeit a garbled one, of his campaigns in Greece and his conquest of the Persian Empire. But it also contains much material that does not appear in the surviving historians. Some of this may be broadly historical: the chronology of the foundation of Alexandria, the detail of Alexander's will which, while it was not written by Alexander, does preserve a propaganda document of the period soon after his death. Rhetorical elaboration has produced the long debate in Athens about how to respond to Alexander's demands, in which the participants include Demosthenes, Aeschines and Demades as well as figures from previous centuries like Lysias and Heraclitus. Much more is derived from folk-tale and other non-historical narrative genres. These elements include the long description of Alexander's conception, as a result of the Pharaoh and wizard Nectanebo cohabiting with Alexander's mother Olympias in the guise of the god Ammon, and the extensive adventures in India and Central Asia which follow the death of Darius and include the search for the land of the blessed and Alexander's interviews with the god Sesonchosis in which he seeks in vain to learn the hour of his death. Yet other historical elements are fictionalized, notably the elaborate and important encounter with the Brahmans.

The date of composition of the *Alexander Romance* is quite uncertain, though we have a *terminus ante quem* in the translation into Latin by Julius Valerius, consul in 338 CE. Scholars differ as to the date at which the Romance took the form known to us in its earliest recension (A), some putting it as late as the third century CE. It is probable that the Romance had assumed something much like that form already in the third or second century BCE, when a good deal of nationalistic material was being composed in Egypt.[3]

The Romance is an amalgam of several different kinds of material: a poetic history of Hellenistic type,[4] a series of letters between Alexander and Darius, a series of letters about marvels and a rhetorical set-piece in the Debate in Athens (only in recension A). The later recensions β and γ add increasing detail to the wonder-tales while reducing the material belonging to the Greek historical context.

I HISTORY AND SAGA

Alexander ensured that his deeds would be the subject of history by taking several writers with him on his travels to write up what they saw: these included Callisthenes and Aristobulus, as well as the bematists (recorders of the route) Baeton, Diognetus and Philonides of Crete. Accounts were also written by members of his military staff, the general Ptolemy and the admiral Nearchus. Another of Alexander's companions, Nicanor, may be the same Nicanor who wrote a 'Life' of Alexander in which he stated that Alexander's career had been foretold by the Persian Sibyl (FGrH146). In the period immediately following his death the story of his life was recomposed by many other historians, including Cleitarchus (date uncertain, but probably early third century BCE), whose work, now lost, became the source of the Vulgate tradition known to us in Quintus Curtius Rufus, Diodorus Siculus and others. Jacoby's *Fragmente der griechischen Historiker*[5] contains fragments from thirty-seven different Alexander historians. Though Ptolemy and Aristobulus were regarded by Arrian as the most reliable of all the sources, many of the other writers did not hesitate to include strange and wonderful tales in their narratives: Onesicritus' account of India is a case in point, while Cleitarchus was renowned for unreliable and exciting stories.

In addition to these written accounts, we can scarcely doubt that tales began to circulate orally about the great conqueror throughout the area of his conquests. The phenomenon is almost universal on the passing of great conquerors, and characteristically it takes the passing of a single generation before the legends begin to appear and be recorded: analogous examples may be the legends concerning Genghis Khan[6] or Attila the Hun. In the case of the latter we have a historical account by which we can check the creation of the almost contemporaneous legend: in Norse saga Attila is murdered by his wife who is here called Gudrun, whereas in fact he died of a nosebleed in the presence of his wife who was really called Ildico.[7] Again, the story of Jesus as recorded by Mark about 69 CE was first written down some thirty years after Jesus' death on the cross.[8] One may imagine that Homeric saga arose in a similar way, but (as with Jesus) we have no independent historical source by which we can evaluate the ways in which the legend varies from what really happened. In the *Alexander Romance* we see history becoming saga before our very eyes.

It is consonant with this development that Alexander gathers overtones of Greek heroes like Achilles or Odysseus: Alexander himself encouraged contemporaries to regard him in this heroic mould. This is most apparent in the first-person narrative of the adventures (compare the *Odyssey*), and in the hero's military prowess in which he resembles Achilles – e.g. in the episode of the death of Porus (III.4) (though his clemency is in sharp contrast to Achilles' vengefulness). In general the epic quality of the narrative should not be exaggerated.

Early pieces of Alexander saga which seem to have contributed to the *Alexander Romance* or resemble it include the following. A papyrus of the second century CE has been found which contains part of a correspondence of Alexander and Darius closely resembling the exchanges in our text.[9] Another letter, of Craterus to his mother, describing the expedition to the Ganges (a fiction) is mentioned by Strabo (15.1.35: FGrH153F2). Part of a Hellenistic speech belonging perhaps to a version of the debate in Athens (Jacoby suggests it relates to the siege of Thebes) is in POxy 216 (FGrH153F8). Another second-century CE papyrus (POxy 1798) is part of an Alexander history, very likely of Hellenistic origin, which contains some small but interesting points of contact with the Romance, notably the statement that Philip was murdered in the theatre, not at its entrance (as in Diodorus and Justin). Another papyrus (PFreib 7–8; FGrH153F7) is part of a dialogue of Callistratus and Mnesippus about Macedonian affairs immediately after Alexander's death, and looks like a rhetorical exercise of similar type to the debate in Athens in the Romance. Berlin papyrus 13044[10] is a version of Alexander's debate with the Gymnosophists resembling the encounter in the Romance. The quantity of these remnants makes plausible the supposition that such compositions became numerous quite soon after the death of the conqueror, and were available to be drawn on in the composition of the Romance.

Enough has been said to indicate that there was a plethora of material in the centuries after Alexander which treated his career in a marvellous and legendary way, side by side with the historical accounts. If we have but one text (albeit with many variants) which purveys the fabulous career of the hero, compared with numerous historical accounts, that may be because the Romance acted as a kind of magnet for all this fabulous material: the Romance was composed by a process of accretion and is the work not of scholars like the histories, but of popular writers. The development of a text through successive redactions is a characteristic of popular works: other examples include *Apollonius of Tyre*, the medieval Greek *Digenis Akritas* and perhaps the Gospels.

II LIFE

Several of the recensions have similar titles: in L the work is the *Life of Alexander and his Deeds*; in ε it is the *Life of Alexander*; in [P] it is the *Life and Opinions of Alexander.* The historical importance of the figure of Alexander ensured that, for once, history could be told through an account of the hero's career. An important analogy to the Romance is thus the ancient *bios* or Life.[11] The writing of Lives as distinct works became customary as early as the fourth century BCE and was applied both to literary figures (Satyrus' *Life of Euripides, Lives of Homer*) and to political ones (which often took the form of encomia like Isocrates' *Evagoras* and Xenophon's *Agesilaus*). Xenophon's *Education of Cyrus* is a special case not least because of its considerable length and obvious non-historical elements,[12] while his *Memoirs of Socrates*, despite the dialogue form which they share with Satyrus' *Life of Euripides*, is another kind of attempt to portray a historical character in prose. The writing of *bioi* reached its apogee in Plutarch, who defined his purpose as the revelation of character rather than the comprehensive narrative of achievements. That is a more sophisticated view than the author of the *Alexander Romance* pretends to. The Romance is not an exploration of character but a narrative of actions, as is indicated by the second element of the title, 'deeds' or 'acts'. This expression prompts a comparison with the Acts – both canonical and apocryphal – of the Apostles. The point should not be pressed verbally, since the titles will have been fixed at the earliest when the Romance was written down and may belong to the second or third century CE when such Christian

Acts were also being composed. But the two elements do express the characteristic features of this text. We shall not go far wrong if we regard the *Alexander Romance* as a narrative about a historical figure, with a historical basis but with much additional material casting light on the hero's significance and making the story more exciting.

III FICTIONAL ELEMENTS

The central section of the Romance, containing the wonder-tales (more of them with each successive recension), takes as its starting point the remark by Aeschines that Alexander, after the death of Darius, 'withdrew to the uttermost regions of the North, almost beyond the borders of the inhabited world'.[13] To show how the historical foundation has been built on, let us examine the elements the narrative shares with the ancient fictional texts.

(1) One thing of which we can be fairly certain is that the *Alexander Romance* was composed in Egypt: it displays considerable knowledge of Egyptian data such as the topography of Alexandria, and shows great interest in the figure of the Pharaoh Nectanebo. Egyptian gods are the only gods who figure in the action (apart from some mentions of Heracles), and the culmination of the whole work is Alexander's deposition in his tomb in Egypt. Many Greek romances share an interest in or preoccupation with Egypt: one example is Heliodorus' *Ethiopica*. Egyptian religion also plays an important part in the Latin work, the *Golden Ass* of Apuleius.

An important article by J. W. B. Barns[14] has examined the Egyptian contribution to the development of Greek Romance. In this article he points to a number of features of Egyptian stories which are also characteristic of Greek novels. The traveller's tale is one very important element. Another is the appearance of a magician (as a hero, not a villain). Egyptian stories also often introduce historical characters. The first Greek romance is in fact a translation from Egyptian, the *Tale of Tefnut*.

All these features find parallels in the *Alexander Romance*: the introduction of historical characters (apart from the protagonists), notably Nectanebo, who as a magician seems to be treated very seriously, though there is perhaps some tension between the importance of Nectanebo's role as legitimator of Alexander's rule in Egypt and the slightly ludicrous tale of his adultery with Olym-

pias. In addition, the idea that a child may be fathered by a divine father on a mortal mother, though it is of course very common in Greek literature, is also found in Egyptian contexts. (It may be worth mentioning that the same story pattern occurs in the Gospels of Matthew and Luke. Matthew 1:18–22 is particularly interesting, as Joseph is on the point of divorcing his wife when he learns in a dream – like Philip – that his son will be of divine parentage.)[15]

It is perhaps hardly necessary to regard the appearance of omens and the supernatural, prominent as they are in the *Alexander Romance*, as anything specific to the novel. However, Alexander's love of disguises certainly belongs to the character of the cunning hero, and cases of mistaken identity are important also in the Greek novels. Alexander's visits to Darius and Candace in disguise, fiction though they are, find an interesting historical parallel in the visit of Majorian, as his own ambassador, to Genseric[16] – perhaps a case of life imitating art.

(2) The Candace episode, indeed, reads very much like a Greek romance or novella in miniature. The plot is suitably complicated by the disguise element. However, what is very striking is that there is no romantic interest (in the modern sense) in this novella. One expects that Alexander is going to take Candace as his bride but this never happens. In another account of this episode, by the sixth-century CE Antiochene chronicler John Malalas (194–5), Alexander is so impressed by the cleverness of Candace's trick with the portrait that he immediately undertakes to marry her. The omission of such a *dénouement* seems characteristic of the author of the *Alexander Romance*, who also passes up the opportunity to describe a romantic liaison between Alexander and the Queen of the Amazons, which featured in the vulgate historians. Such liaisons might be expected of protagonists even of historical narratives, as in the case of Cyrus the Younger and the queen of Cilicia in Xenophon's *Anabasis* (I.1.12). Achilles' love for the Amazon Penthesilea in the Epic Cycle is a relevant source for the motif.

(3) Alexander's cleverness is a characteristic feature of the Romance. He invents stratagems, interprets inscriptions (e.g. Nectanebo's statue, I.34) and omens, he reinterprets symbolic statements like Darius' gift of a whip, a ball and gold (I.38). The world is a palimpsest which only the wise can interpret; the one thing

Alexander cannot discover is when he is to die. . . . He invents a diving bell and a flying machine. This cleverness recalls the figure of Aesop in the *Life of Aesop*: in fact the episode of the flying machine, which only occurs in later recensions of the *Alexander Romance*, is probably derived from the Aesop story.[17] His military cleverness resembles that of Xenophon's Cyrus the Elder in the *Education of Cyrus*, a text with which the Romance has other features in common. Cyrus receives advance notice of his death from a kind of angel (8.3.2) as does Alexander; the *Education of Cyrus* ends with the disposition of Cyrus' empire on his deathbed;[18] and, like Alexander's, Cyrus' empire falls into strife and decline after the hero's death.

(4) The wonder-tale aspect of the Romance recalls the Egyptian model of travellers' tales, though this was from an early date a characteristic of Greek writing also. It would be foolish in categorizing this element to ignore such Greek models as the *Odyssey* or the book of Iambulus.[19] Craterus' letter to his mother, mentioned by Strabo (15.1.35) seems to be another of the genre, which became extremely popular in Greek writing, so that it was much mocked by Lucian.[20] But an interesting feature of the wonder-tales in the *Alexander Romance* is the extent to which they become part of a quest (rather like a medieval romance) – in this case a quest for immortality or an attempt to reach the land of the blessed. In this respect the Romance looks forward very strikingly to the Christian Saints' Lives with their quest for Paradise.[21]

IV PERSPECTIVES

In this connection it is worth drawing attention to the parallelism between the *Alexander Romance* and a number of early Christian texts which used the generic mix of works like the *Alexander Romance* to present their own worldviews. A study by Reiser[22] has detailed the many similarities between the *Alexander Romance* and Mark's Gospel, which range from syntactic features to aspects of narrative style including parataxis and repetition, absence of complex narrative, vagueness of geographical and chronological reference, ideal scenes and the miracles which accompany the deaths of Jesus and Alexander. Both texts thus exhibit the linguistic and stylistic features of popular literature in the service of a portrait of a unique figure. The question-and-answer session with the

Brahmans is not entirely unlike the question-and-answer sessions of Jesus and his disciples in the Gospels, though the roles of teacher and taught are reversed. Both types of text are drawing on the same kind of tradition, catering for the same kind of appetite for wondrous tales with a meaning, or pithy sayings (*chreiai*).

The apocryphal Gospels and apocryphal Acts show a similar relation to our text. The latter may often be entitled 'Deeds' ('Acts') or 'Life and Deeds', like our text. The Acts of Thomas, for example, contain an expedition to India and miraculous encounters.

Our examination of the different literary strands of the Alexander Romance has revealed rather little direct correspondence with the themes and motifs of the Greek novel as usually defined. Its affinities are rather, where it is not pretending to the condition of history, with folk-tales and travellers' tales – unsophisticated forms which address unsophisticated people and, characteristically, deal with the behaviour and standards of people of a like kind, people who are usually victims rather than protagonists of historical process. What is the great conqueror Alexander doing as a vehicle for the concerns of simple people? An answer may be discoverable in the paradox of Alexander's personality in the Romance.

V THE QUEST FOR IMMORTALITY: A FICTION OF EMPIRE

The leitmotif of the wonder-tales in the *Alexander Romance* is Alexander's quest to explore the furthest reaches of earth and to learn from the gods the hour of his death. This motif develops from the famous *pothos*, 'yearning', attributed to Alexander by Arrian and his sources – his desire to go ever further, to see and conquer ever more lands. In the later recensions his quest is amplified in the stories of his ascent, the construction of the diving bell and the discovery by his cook of the Water of Life, which Alexander is fated not to drink. In recension A the motif appears only in Alexander's encounter with Sesonchosis and in the admonition of the flying creatures to turn back (II.41, cf. II.38). The later versions may be influenced by the common topos of the search for Paradise in Saints' Lives; but the theme is central to the early versions also.

The related theme of the discovery of a happier land, which is exemplified by the life of the Brahmans, derives in part from

Utopian tales like that of the third-century BCE author Iambulus. But both this and the immortality theme demonstrate not only the extent of Alexander's achievement but its limitations. He cannot become immortal, and cannot even learn the day of his death; yet death in a horrible form comes upon him. His power as a conqueror cannot save him from death, and it will not even allow him to partake of the blessed life of the Brahmans. 'For my part I would like to stop making war, but the master of my soul does not allow me' (III.7). The contrast between the Brahmans, who need no graves but the ground where they lie, and are free, and Alexander, whose tomb will be built in Memphis, but who is doomed to die young and lose all his conquests, is at the heart of the Romance.

This contrast encapsulates the paradox of the Hellenistic world which Alexander's conquests created. Alexander is both the creator and the victim of his Empire. In one aspect Alexander is a hero like those of heroic legend, with almost superhuman military powers and a penchant for wisdom. Yet in another aspect he is like the protagonists of Greek romance, a genre which is often seen as portraying the peculiar situation of the individual in the newly expanded world of the Hellenistic kingdoms, and in which they are the victims of divine powers as vague and amorphous as Fortune, or the 'Providence Above' of the *Alexander Romance*.[23] So pronounced is this second aspect that it has even led some scholars to characterize this Alexander as an 'anti-hero'.[24] In my opinion this overstates the position, but he certainly has many features of the picaresque hero rather than the 'heroic' one.

Typical of this presentation of Alexander in the Romance is that his wisdom can only be expressed in terms of cleverness. Greeks often expressed wisdom as cleverness: Thales, one of the Seven Sages, was noted for the clever trick of buying up olive presses and renting them out at harvest time – hardly what we should call wisdom. The fact that Alexander's wisdom is only expressed in his tricks and disguises reduces him to the level of a folk-tale hero like Aesop,[25] even more than the often canny protagonists of romance. Disguise seems often to be the stratagem of a character who does not control the world he is trying to manipulate: Alexander's tricks align him with victims of empire like Rudyard Kipling's Kim[26] rather than its controllers.

Response to empire is the underlying theme of the Romance. Alexander's concern with immortality is a metaphor of his anxiety

about his imperial rule, and by its very extravagance of desire emphasizes the incommensurability of empire with the ambit of the average mortal. An intriguing parallel for this meditation on the problems of empire occurs in another adventurous tale of imperial rule, H. Rider Haggard's *She*. This is an account (like the wonder-tales in the *Alexander Romance*) of a quest for the secret of immortality, in which immortality becomes a metaphor for imperial rule. At one point the immortal Ayesha takes up the idea of becoming Queen of England and ruler of its Empire. The dream of immortality which captures the participants is countered by the narrator, Holly, who plays a role rather like that of the Brahmans in arguing that there is a higher good than length of days. The tale, inevitably, ends, like the *Alexander Romance*, in the puncturing of all such dreams in the violent death of She (though the hero Leo, and Holly, survive).

It is left unclear in the Romance whether Alexander learns the lesson the story teaches; but its truth is forced on him by the fact of his death, and he seems to admit the impracticability of unending conquest in his reply to the Brahmans. (That curious phenomenon, Alexander's smile, may be relevant here. Alexander smiles when he is caught out by the pygmies at II.44, and when the Brahmans tell him some home truths at III.7. This gentle and impassive gesture seems to indicate moments of self-knowledge, of however small a kind. So it is striking that he actually laughs at the moment of his death – though only in the γ-recension – and that this laugh is immortalized in the statue of him erected after his death in Alexandria.)

By the end of the story, the inevitable constraint of *Life* as of life means that death must obtrude, where romance would have a happy ending. The brute reality of death sets the historical conqueror Alexander face to face with the picaresque fictional character Alexander. It is the confrontation and interplay of these two roles in the same character that gives the Romance its poignancy. The essence of this particular text, both in terms of philosophical significance, and in terms of generic taxonomy, is to be found in the position it occupies between history and fiction.

NOTES

1 Polybius (1.14.6) defined διήγημα *per genus et differentiam* as History without Truth.

2 Averil Cameron, *Christianity and the Rhetoric of Empire*, Berkeley, 1991, 92 (narrative implies truth); cf. M. J. Wheeldon in Averil Cameron (ed.), *History as Text*, London, 1991. The Muses know how to tell many lies that look like truth: Hes.*Th*.27–8.

3 See my translation of *The Greek Alexander Romance*, Harmondsworth, 1991, 17; A. B. Lloyd, 'Nationalist propaganda in Hellenistic Egypt', *Historia* 31 (1982), 33ff.

4 The Hellenistic genre of tragic history aimed to arouse emotions with pathetic or tremendous narratives and wonder-tales: F. W. Walbank, 'Tragedy and history', *Historia* 9 (1960), 216–34. Cleitarchus is an example among Alexander-historians.

5 Felix Jacoby, *Die Fragmente der griechischen Historiker* II B, 117–53 (commentary in II D).

6 G. D. Painter in R. A. Skelton (ed.), *The Vinland Map and the Tartar Relation*, New Haven, 1965, 34ff.

7 C. M. Bowra, *Heroic Poetry*, London, 1966, 460.

8 Martin Hengel, *Studies in the Gospel of Mark*, London, 1985, 11 and n.70.

9 D. Pieraccioni, *Lettere del Ciclo di Alessandro in un Papiro Egiziano*, Florence, 1947.

10 U. Wilcken, 'Alexander der Grosse und die indischen Gymnosophisten', *Sitzungsber.d.Preuss.Akad.Berlin (phil.-hist.Kl.)* (1923), 150–83.

11 A. Dihle, *Studien zur griechischen Biographie*, Göttingen, 1970.

12 See my edition of Xenophon, *Education of Cyrus*, tr. H. G. Dakyns, London, 1992, introduction.

13 Aeschin.*in Ctes*.165.

14 J. W. B. Barns, 'Egypt and the Greek Romance', *Mitteilungen aus der Papyrussammlung der Österreichsichen Nationalbibliothek* n.s. 5 (1956), 29–36.

15 O. Weinreich, *Der Trug des Nektanebos*, Leipzig and Berlin, 1911; Raymond E. Brown, *The Birth of the Messiah*, New York, 1977.

16 Procopius *Bell.Vandal.*I.8.

17 See R. Stoneman, 'Oriental motifs in the Alexander Romance', *Antichthon* 26 (1992).

18 J. Tatum, *Xenophon's Imperial Fiction*, Princeton, 1989, 209–10.

19 Iambulus as recounted by Diodorus Siculus 2.55–60.

20 Lucian, *Icaromenippus*, for example.

21 A. G. Elliott, *Roads to Paradise: Reading the Lives of the Early Saints*, Hanover, NH and London, 1987.

22 M. Reiser, 'Der Alexanderroman und das Markusevangelium', in H. Cancik (ed.), *Markusphilologie*, WUNT 33, Tübingen, 1984, 131–63.

23 B. Reardon, *The Form of Greek Romance*, Princeton, 1991, 31.

24 J. Romm, 'Alexander as anti-hero: the late antique romance tradition', paper given at APA conference, December 1990.

25 *The Life of Aesop* in B. E. Perry, *Aesopica*, Urbana, 1952; see Niklas Holzberg (ed.), *Der Äsop-Roman*, Tübingen, 1992.

26 A suggestive discussion is Edward Said's introduction to the Penguin edition of *Kim*, Harmondsworth, 1987.

BIBLIOGRAPHY

Kroll, Wilhelm, *Historia Alexandri Magni recensio vetusta*, Berlin, 1926.

Merkelbach, Reinhold, *Die Quellen des griechischen Alexanderroman*, 2nd edn, Munich, 1977.

Pfister, Friedrich, *Kleine Schriften zum Alexanderroman*, Meisenheim am Glan, 1975.

Stoneman, Richard, *The Greek Alexander Romance*, Harmondsworth, 1991.

Stoneman, Richard, 'Oriental motifs in the Alexander Romance', *Antichthon* 26 (1992).

Stoneman, Richard, 'Romantic ethnography: central Asia and India in the *Alexander Romance*', *The Ancient World* (1993).

van Thiel, Helmut, *Leben und Taten Alexanders von Makedonien: der griechische Alexanderroman Rezension L*, Darmstadt, 1983.

Wolohojian, Albert Mugrdich, *The Romance of Alexander by Pseudo-Callisthenes* (translation of the Armenian version), New York, 1969.

8

NEW PAGES OF GREEK FICTION

Gerald Sandy

The fragments of Greek novels provide a valuable perspective on the prose fiction of classical antiquity. In addition to offering a more comprehensive understanding of the fully extant novels, they raise new questions and discredit some earlier answers.

New perspectives reveal unexpected sights. The fragmentary *Iolaus* and the remains of Lollianus' *A Phoenician Story*, for instance, undermine the persistent view that the Greeks wrote only idealized stories, the Romans only coarse, farcical tales rooted in low-life reality. The chronological progression of Greek fiction that Rohde laboured to deduce from inadequate evidence was frustrated less than twenty years after the publication of his seminal study by the publication of papyrus fragments of *Ninus and Semiramis* (Rohde 1876).[1] Similarly, Durham's plausible hypothesis that Achilles Tatius' bizarre novel was a systematic parody of Heliodorus' *An Ethiopian Story* crumbled completely in the year of its publication in the face of the hard evidence of a papyrus fragment of *Leucippe and Clitophon* that antedates the supposed object of its parody by some two centuries.[2] Even Petronius' Latin novel is not shaded from the glaring light of knowledge that has radiated from the expanded perspective of the fragments.

SOURCES

Photius

Without Photius' *Bibliotheca*, we would know scarcely anything of Antonius Diogenes' *The Wonders beyond Thule*, and Iamblichus' *A Babylonian Story* would consist of little more than the approximately four pages of narrative contained in three manuscript extracts that provide no hints of context. The Byzantine patriarch Photius composed the *Bibliotheca* near the middle of the ninth century. The title given by him to the compilation provides a good idea of its nature: *Inventory and Enumeration of the Books That We Have Read, of Which Our Beloved Brother Tarasius Requested a General Analysis* (Treadgold 1980: 4).

In the preface and postface Photius explains important principles of his compilation of summaries. For our purposes his most important statement of principle is that he has intentionally excluded books that Tarasius himself has read and books that are commonly included in the curriculum of the liberal arts and sciences. Thus almost by definition the works summarized by Photius did not occupy the top rung of books held to be worthy of reading in Byzantine intellectual circles near the middle of the ninth century.

Papyrology

Whereas Photius and his taste, moral sensibilities, criteria of choice and the inherently restrictive nature of his enterprise impose obstacles between readers and texts, papyrology in approximately the past one hundred years has greatly reduced the gap between the two groups. As Lesky averred, 'The traditional picture of no other genre in Greek literature was altered so completely by the papyri as that of the romance' (Lesky 1966: 857). The 'revolution' has continued. It is chronicled until 1971 in O. Montevecchi's useful papyrological handbook and thereafter more fully but selectively by R. Kussl, and in the near future we can expect still more details in the annotated critical edition of the fragments edited by S. Stephens and J. Winkler and in the third edition of R. Pack's inventory of published literary papyri being prepared under the supervision of P. Mertens by the Séminaire de Papyrologie de l'Université de Liège.[3] Some of the papyrus remains, such as *Ninus and Semiramis, Metiochus and Parthenope* and the *A Phoenician Story*, warrant discussion in their own right and I will return to them later in this chapter. At this point, however, it is appropriate to summarize the radical transformation that has occurred in the 'traditional picture' of ancient Greek fiction.

Erwin Rohde's chronological scheme, which linked the beginnings of Greek fiction to the heightened intellectual activity of the so-called Second Sophistic of the second and third centuries CE was the first element in the 'traditional picture' to be undermined by papyrology. His progression from Antonius Diogenes near the middle of the second century to Achilles Tatius three centuries later was a myth from the moment of its conception. Like Photius, he ignored Antonius Diogenes' mention of 'an earlier writer, a certain Antiphanes, who, he says, spent his time on marvellous tales of the same sort' (*CAGN*: 782); instead, Rohde seems to have been unduly influenced by Photius' preceding assertion that Antonius Diogenes appeared to antedate the other novelists whose works he reviews and that the 'wanderings, love affairs, capture, and dangers' experienced by Antonius Diogenes' protagonists served as models for the other novelists' (*CAGN*: 782).

Only seventeen years after the publication of Rohde's influential chronological scheme, two fragments of *Ninus and Semiramis* were published. A document on the back of the papyrus is explicitly dated to 100–1 CE. This *terminus ante quem* and palaeographical considerations suggest that the fragments belong to the period 100 BCE–100 CE.

Papyrus fragments have also mapped the East-to-West and West-to-East migrations of fictional narratives. The earliest documented example of Greek prose fictional narrative is in fact a Greek translation of the Demotic *Dream of Nectanebus*, both of which are preserved on papyrus.[4] Some twelve centuries later, in the late tenth or early eleventh century, the now fragmentary Greek novel *Metiochus and Parthenope* was to serve as the basis of the Persian poet Unsuri's poem *Vamiq u Adhra* (*Metiochus and Virgin* (Greek *parthenope* = virgin)), 372 lines of which were published in 1967.[5]

In my opinion, the most valuable and exciting contribution of papyrology has been to open a window on the richly varied range of Greek prose fiction. One can still, even in the most authoritative surveys, encounter generalizations that will lead the unwary to suppose that all ancient Greek novels were written by unsophisticated novelists for unsophisticated readers who craved sentimental stories of love and adventure. T. T. Renner has recently edited a papyrus fragment of the third or early fourth century CE that will serve to demonstrate that Greek novelists were capable of extending themes far beyond the range of the idealized sentimental love that has been held to be the norm for the genre since the time of P-D. Huet's *Traité de l'origine des romans* (1670). Renner summarizes it thus:

> The density with which incidents involving Aphrodite, love, travel, wild beasts, and acts of violence appear to be packed into this scanty fragment points clearly to romance as the genre to which the work belongs.
>
> (Renner 1981: 100)

Some of these sensational incidents and others not mentioned in the summary quoted above recall scenes in other Greek novels. Someone in the fragment has been 'eaten by beasts', a gruesome detail that has its counterpart in Iamblichus (*CAGN*: 791) and, potentially, Xenophon of Ephesus (4.6); and someone has 'stripped off' 'women's upper garments', presumably in an act of violence that is duplicated in the fragmentary *A Phoenician Story*. Thus the ancient Greek novel could sink to depths of sex and violence alien to the traditional image of the genre represented by such works as *An Ethiopian Story*.

Similarly, the conventional paradigm formulated by Huet in 1670 (and before him by Photius) becomes positively chimerical when one attempts to fit the epitome provided by Photius of the comical Greek novel known as *Lucius or the Ass* and two recently published fragmentary Greek picaresque novels, *A Phoenician Story* and *Iolaus*, into the traditional arrangement. The murder and mayhem and coarse humour that characterize these fragments are no less evident in the papyrus fragment described earlier. Thus one must recongize that the phrase 'ancient Greek fiction' encompasses great thematic diversity as well as a chronological span of some five or six centuries.

READERSHIP

For whom was ancient Greek fiction written? The conventional answer, based on the conventional but chimerical picture described above, is women, as is evident in the following formulations: 'The population outside the big cities, the women, people looking for romanticism'; and 'it is tempting to think of the novels as the first great literary form to have had its main support among women'.[6] Underlying this assumption as well, I suspect, is the undeniable fact that modern popular romance, as exemplified in the Harlequin Romance series, with which the traditional picture implicitly aligns ancient Greek prose fiction, is written, almost if not absolutely exclusively, by and for females.[7] A still more basic assumption, I believe, is that ancient Greek novels were popular in both senses of that word: widely read and pitched low to accommodate the largest possible number of readers. These assumptions warrant testing against the evidence available, both old and new.

The extant novels appear at first blush to confirm the traditional hypothesis. In Heliodorus' novel, for instance, the heroine Chariclea eclipses her mate Theagenes in physical bravery, cunning and religious conviction until he literally takes the bull by the horns in Book 9 (Sandy 1982: 60–5); and her radiating beauty strikes terror into the hearts of the Egyptian brigands who gaze at her near the beginning of the story. Photius' summary and the fragments of Iamblichus' *A Babylonian Story* convey a similar impression. The heroine Sinonis' jealous wrath keeps the 'hero' Rhodanes' friend Soraechus at a respectful distance from her when he is not trying to dissuade the 'hero' from committing suicide or she is not threatening to kill her imagined rival for Rhodanes' affection. The little that survives of the story about Calligone portrays her as menacing Eubiotus with the threat to 'strangle you with my own hands' (*CAGN*: 827). As well, according to Photius' summary of his novel, Antonius Diogenes dedicated the work 'to his learned sister Isidora' (*CAGN*: 781). Thus there is a prima facie case for supposing that the ancient Greek novel was intended for, and catered to, female readers.

I am not confident, however, that the sex of the intended readership can be discovered from the evidence currently available. The situation is better for trying to determine the popularity of ancient Greek prose fiction. As noted previously, Photius' choice of works to be summarized for his brother is predicated on their not being popular in Byzantine intellectual circles of the mid-ninth century. Mere acknowledgement of the existence of prose fiction during classical antiquity is notoriously scarce and with one possible exception contemptuous (Sandy 1982: 6). The reason for this contempt can perhaps best be seen in Macrobius' distinction between stories that merely gratify the ear, that is, entertain, and those that elevate the reader, as well as Plutarch's distinction between historiography and stories composed 'for the pleasure of listening' (Sandy 1982: 6). As Perry has explained more fully than anyone else, the force of learned tradition strongly resisted the use of prose for any purpose other than its conventional role of conveying information in works of history and philosophy and in technical treatises (Perry 1967: 44–95).

The papyrological record that has emerged from the sands of Roman Egypt bears out the impression that ancient Greek prose fiction was not widely read during classical antiquity. The statistics are readily available up to 1971 and nothing has appeared in the intervening years to contradict that impression: four papyrus fragments for each of the extant authors Achilles Tatius and Chariton and twenty-six papyrus fragments of works known only in fragmentary or abbreviated form.[8] In contrast to this total of thirty-four papyrus fragments of ancient Greek prose fiction, Demosthenes, who occupies one of the lower rungs of mainline Greek literary figures, is represented by ninety-four papyrus fragments. Similar discrepancies are evident in the papyrus record of other Greek writers and literary genres: Menander and New Comedy (74), Callimachus (60), anonymous orators (67). Most striking, perhaps, is the discrepancy expressed thus by Stephens:

> A comparison with texts of the Old and New Testaments from the second to the fourth century A.D., readers of which were, by Hägg's assessment, the same to whom romance would have appealed, shows a staggering difference (172).[9]

In other words, the targeted audience for ancient Greek novels appears to have been no less sophisticated or more 'popular' than the readership envisaged by the writers of other Greek literary forms.

HISTORICAL NOVELS

The statistical record available for the period up to 1971 does not of course tell the complete story. Papyrological publications of ancient Greek prose fiction have continued to appear during the past two decades. Some of the material is of little value except as an aid to improving existing texts. Some of it, however, has revolutionized the study of the ancient novel.

As we have seen, the revolution actually began with the publication in 1893 of fragments of *Ninus and Semiramis*. It is the earliest datable example of originally composed Greek fictional narratives that are linked overtly to historical events and figures.[10] Like it and Chariton's extant novel, *Metiochus and Parthenope* has a historical setting. This did not become clear until Maehler published a substantial fragment of the work in 1976 (Maehler 1976: 1–20).

The setting is the court of Polycrates, the historically attested tyrant of Samos. He, his daughter Parthenope, the philosopher Anaximenes of Miletus and Metiochus have gathered at a symposium. Metiochus' historically attested stepmother, Hegesipyle, is mentioned but not in attendance. Although all these figures are known from historical chronicles, the unknown author has not adhered strictly to the historical chronology that he could have found in Herodotus, where it is clear that Metiochus and the political events associated with his father Miltiades' expulsion from the Chersonese and flight to Samos belong to a period at least twenty years after the time of Polycrates and the philosopher Anaximenes of Miletus, the only one of the characters who does not appear in Herodotus. The most recent papyrus fragment has, however, rooted Parthenope more deeply in historical reality, for until its publication she was believed, on the basis of a Byzantine commentator, to be the legendary Siren of Naples rather than the daughter of Polycrates.

Maehler has reconstructed the fragments as follows. Metiochus and Parthenope, who have fallen in love with each other at some preceding point in the narrative, are distressed because Polycrates in the role of *magister bibendi* has set Eros (Love) as the topic of symposiac discussion. To mask his embarrassment, Metiochus ridicules the traditional notion of a perennially youthful Eros equipped with bow and arrows and the unsubstantiated belief that the passion in lovers' souls is like some holy spirit in the breasts of those who are religiously inspired. He then expresses the wish that he may never experience similar emotions and provides his own definition of love, ' "Love [is] a disturbance of the rational faculties caused by beauty and intensified by intimate contact" ' (*CAGN*: 815). At this point the philosopher Anaximenes urges Parthenope to join the debate. She, however, feels betrayed by Metiochus' claim never to have fallen in love and exclaims, ' "The stranger is talking nonsense, and [I disagree]" ' (*CAGN*: 815).

Maehler has recognized that the most immediate significance of this fragmentary novel is that it adds one more page to the documentation of the overtly historical novel. This association recalls Chariton's novel and *Ninus and Semiramis*, both of which present their stories of idealized, sentimental love in a straightforward, seemingly objective way. In a word, they are non-sophistic; that is, they do not exploit the playful combination of sentimentality and sophistication found above all in the novels of Achilles Tatius and Heliodorus (Anderson 1982).

Metiochus and Parthenope may, however, have been simultaneously historical and sophistic. What appears to be a heartfelt debate on the nature of love between two young, impressionable people touched directly and deeply by the subject may, in the larger (now lost) context, have been part of the kind of disingenuous intrigue exploited ironically by Heliodorus and given a wry, even cynical twist by Achilles Tatius.[11] Moreover, any mention of Eros in a symposiac setting is bound to recall Plato's *Symposium*, one of the best known and most exploited Platonic dialogues during the period of the Second Sophistic, which indeed our author seems to be echoing when Metiochus likens the passion in lovers' souls to the frenzy experienced by those who are infused with a divine spirit.[12] The philosopher Anaximenes may be coaching Parthenope from the sidelines in an elaborate scheme to deceive her father much as the Platonic go-between Calasiris counsels Chariclea in her deception of her foster-father in Heliodorus' novel.

As in *Ninus and Semiramis*, the blushing beginnings of love at first sight occur against a backdrop of clashing oriental armies in *Sesonchosis*. The papyrus fragments of this work purport to recount the military, political and emotional experiences of two conflated Twelfth Dynasty Egyptian rulers. The most recent commentator on one of the fragments remarks that the combination of 'military campaigns' and 'the presence of an erotic episode would seem to mark it as a work of transition between the historical romance and the love romance' (Ruiz-Montero 1989: 56). It is worthwhile considering at this point whether the fragments support the notion of the progressive fusion of historiography and erotic fictional narrative.

Because *Ninus and Semiramis* appears to be the earliest of the datable fragmentary and extant Greek novels and because one of its best-preserved fragments gives a straightforward account of Ninus disposing his troops against Armenian forces, there has been a tendency to suppose that Greek prose fiction developed from this putative pre-sophistic fusion of historiography and romantic biography into the sophistic emphasis on the emotional lives of hero and heroine seen, for instance, in Achilles Tatius' *Leucippe and Clitophon*. However, the pose that the author of a fictional narrative is an objective reporter of observed or researched facts over which he has no control rather than their (literally) omniscient creator is evident in both the so-called pre-sophistic (Chariton) and sophistic (Heliodorus) novelists (Morgan 1982: 221–65).

Antonius Diogenes' *The Wonders beyond Thule* is a vivid example of the sober historiographical pose maintained in the face of fantastic adventures. The author employs Alexander the Great, the historically attested Phila, a list of 'authorities' prefixed to each of the twenty-four volumes (books), dramatized eye-witness sources, his learned sister Isidora, a representative of the Arcadian League, hidden official documents and other authenticating devices to put the reassuring stamp of True History on his collection of fantastic tales, and the ruse was successful: Photius, seemingly oblivious of the implications of his conclusion that Antonius Diogenes was 'the father of fictional stories', infers that 'he belongs to a time not far removed from that of King Alexander' (*CAGN*: 782). It also fooled Porphyry, who near the middle of the third century used the novel as an 'authority' for his account of the childhood of the philosopher Pythagoras.

Even if one accepts detached, detailed military analysis as a valid criterion for classifying a fictional narrative as historical rather than erotic, the available evidence contains some surprises. *Ninus and Semiramis*, which appears at first glance to admit love as only an incidental component of its military preoccupations, can be broken down thus:

Love	War
fragment A: 191 lines	fragment B: 152 lines[13]

Whether or not love maintained the 20 per cent ascendency of this admittedly crude analysis throughout the complete novel is of course anyone's guess.

Photius' summary of Antonius Diogenes' novel runs to 247 lines. Twelve of these deal with love, that is, approximately 2 per cent of the total. This compares with the twelve lines referring to the love of Theagenes and Chariclea of the total of 145 lines of his summary of Heliodorus' novel, a ratio of approximately 8 per cent devoted to love. If all that survived of *An Ethiopian Story* was Photius' summary and a papyrus fragment of the detailed description of the siege of Syene in Book 9, we might be tempted to suppose that the work in its entirety focused on adventures and warfare, when in fact the accident of papyrus survival and Photius' predilection for what he calls a variety of occurring, hoped-for and unhoped-for incidents as well as incredible escapes from calamities would be responsible for a false impression (Photius 1959–91: vol. 1, 147).

The conclusion to be drawn from this material is that we have no reason to suppose that ancient Greek fiction developed from a fusion of gradually diminishing doses of historiography and ever-increasing injections of love until at some measurable point the erotic novel was synthesized. The various components, among them love and 'history', remained in a state of flux over a period of at least five centuries and were combined in varying proportions according to the taste and genius of individual authors.

PICARESQUE NOVELS

The two most extraordinary substantial fragments that have emerged from the sands of Roman Egypt are Lollianus' *A Phoenician Story* and *Iolaus*. Published within two years of each other, in 1969 and 1971, these two fragmentary works undermine the long-held view that the Greek tradition of extended, prose fictional narrative did not encompass the vulgarity and coarse farce of Apuleius' and Petronius' Latin novels.[14]

The fragments of the *A Phoenician Story*, which originally comprised at least three volumes (books), document one basic feature not otherwise attested in the classical period for any of the fragmentary or extant Greek novels: the title. *Phoenicica*, literally 'Phoenician things', that is, *A Phoenician Story*, is a type of title commonly associated with extant examples of the genre, as in Heliodorus' *Aethiopica* or Xenophon of Ephesus' *Ephesiaca*, but these and other familiar titles such as *Daphnis and Chloe* and *Leucippe and Clitophon* are generally derived from much later manuscripts or from Photius' Byzantine summaries (e.g. 'twenty-four books of incredible things beyond Thule by Antonius Diogenes'). The title of Lollianus' novel is at least as old as the fragments of the second century CE. More importantly, a common interpretation of the title of Petronius' farcical Latin novel is thus confirmed as a documented possibility. *Satyricon*, '[books] of satyr-like things', that is, *A Randy Story*, is a title that suits the contents. We shall return to the *Satyricon vis-à-vis A Phoenician Story*, but first a summary of the fragmentary Greek novel is in order.

The surviving narrative opens with festive dancing, from which a woman named Persis slips away to spend the night with her lover. He is probably Androtimus, the central male character in the subsequent fragments. He has with her his first experience of sex, for which he is apparently richly rewarded with jewellery in compensation for the loss of *his* maidenhood.

The most substantial fragments, labelled B1 recto and verso by the editor, a total of sixty-one partially preserved lines, describe the savage activities of a gang of robbers called 'the initiates'. They hold Androtimus captive and kill a boy known to him. One of the gang members, wearing only a loincloth, kills the boy, cuts out his heart, roasts it over a fire and parcels it out to his colleagues, who swear an oath over it and who as a consequence of dining on human heart appear to suffer indigestion to judge by Androtimus' complaints of 'belching and farting' and 'this sickening smell' and the reference to vomiting (*CAGN*: 812). This orgy of blood and guts is followed by singing, drinking and sexual intercourse before Androtimus' eyes and in the midst of corpses, whose clothing the robbers strip apparently in order to disguise themselves as they make their escape under cover of darkness.

The less well preserved *Iolaus*, also recorded on papyrus fragments of the second century CE, does not abound to the same extent as *A Phoenician Story* in cannibalism, human sacrifice and the flouting of sexual mores but it has no less significance for documenting the range of topics and especially forms exploited by ancient Greek novelists. Vulgarity is restricted to the four-letter word *beinein*, 'to screw', and the disguise adopted by an apparently false *cinaedus* is no more sinister than the deceits employed in the amorous intrigues of Greek New Comedy.

The plot, in so far as the editor has been able to reconstruct it from the severely truncated remains, may have been similar to that of Terence's play *The Eunuch*. Accordingly, Iolaus has persuaded an unnamed friend to be instructed in the practices of a *gallus* so that he can coach him (Iolaus) in gaining access to the women's quarters.

The most remarkable feature of the fragment is that it consists of nineteen lines of verse and a slightly altered quotation of Euripides embedded in a prose narrative.[15] This so-called prosimetrum form recalls the *Satyricon*, of course, and it is appropriate at this point to stand back from the fragments of the Greek novels and consider whether they shed any new light on the old issue of the *Satyricon* as a parody of the Greek novel.

R. Heinze formulated this hypothesis in 1899 and nothing of

substance has been added to it since that time (Heinze 1899: 494–519). Heinze anticipated that his views would meet resistance because he was unaware of any Greek novels antedating the *Satyricon* that might have served as the butt of its parody. The publication of fragments of *Ninus and Semiramis* eliminated that possible objection but, ironically, subsequent publications of fragments have seriously impaired the plausibility of the thesis.[16]

The cornerstone of Heinze's view is that the homosexual love affairs of the *Satyricon* are intended as parodies of the heterosexual ideal of Greek fictional prose. This presupposes that homosexuality is alien to the Greek novel, but that is far from the case, even in the canonical examples of the genre and possibly Antonius Diogenes, whom Photius calls 'the father of fictional stories'.[17] Once that cornerstone is removed, the other props of Heinze's theory, such as *ekphraseis* (detailed word-pictures), as at *Satyricon* 89.1, prove to be insubstantial, most of them deriving from epic poetry, which Petronius demonstrably uses as a frame of reference to emphasize the unbridgeable gap between the heroic world of Homer and Virgil and the illusory pretensions of his cast of criminal *poseurs*.

Less specifically, the debauchery of the *Satyricon* cannot possibly function as parody of Greek fictional prose if the supposed butt of the satire is no less debauched. *A Phoenician Story* features cannibalism, sexual promiscuity carried on openly before the eyes of onlookers and sexual deflowering. The same incidents occur in the *Satyricon*.[18] *Iolaus* includes transvestism, vulgar language, the prosimetrum form and literary pastiche, all of which are duplicated in the *Satyricon*.[19]

Pierre-Daniel Huet's *Traité de l'origine des romans* (1670) and Erwin Rohde's *Der griechische Roman* (1876) are responsible for the prevailing scholarly view that Greek prose fiction uniformly conforms to the norm enunciated by Photius at the end of his summary of *The Wonders Beyond Thule* by Antonius Diogenes, 'the father of fictional stories':

> It seems that he is earlier than those who have made it their business to write this kind of fiction, such as . . . Iamblichus, Achilles Tatius [and] Heliodorus . . . Dercyllis, Ceryllus, Thruscanus, and Dinias seem to have been the models for the romances about Sinonis and Rhodanes, Leucippe and

> Clitophon, Chariclea and Theagenes, and for their wanderings, love affairs, capture, and dangers.[20]

In this short survey I have attempted to dispel the notion that Greek prose fiction adhered to an idealized norm. The papyrological publications that have appeared since 1893 have annihilated almost every stereotype and systematized scheme of progressive development that Huet and Rohde formulated. The evidence on which they based their judgments did not exceed, indeed fell short of, that available to Photius near the middle of the ninth century. After eleven hundred years of blinkered stereotyping, it is time to appreciate the diversity of plot, tone and form achieved by Greek writers of prose fiction.

ABBREVIATIONS

CAGN	Reardon, B. P. (ed.), *Collected Ancient Greek Novels*, Berkeley: University of California Press, 1989.
Classical Paradigms	Tatum, J. (ed.), *The Ancient Novel: Classical Paradigms and Modern Perspectives*, Hanover: Dartmouth College, 1990.
POxy	Papyri Oxyrhynchus, Graeco-Roman Memoirs.
Pornography	Richlin, A. (ed.), *Pornography and Representation in Greece and Rome*, Oxford: Oxford University Press, 1992.
'Women Like This'	Levine, J. (ed.), *'Women Like This': New Perspectives on Jewish Women in the Greco-Roman World*, Atlanta: Scholars, 1991.

NOTES

1 The titles such as *Ninus and Semiramis* that I use throughout are with one exception to be explained later a modern convenience. I have adopted the titles used in *CAGN*.

2 Durham 1938: 1–18; Perry 1967: 348–9.

3 Montevecchi 1973: 391–2; Kussl 1991. Dr Stephens has kindly informed me that the critical edition edited by her and J. Winkler will be published by Princeton University Press in 1993. Professor A. Wouters kindly informed me of the undertaking at the Université de Liège.

4 Barns 1956: 29–36, *CAGN*: 655, n. 1 and 677, n. 38; *quod contra*, Koenen 1985: 171–94.

5 Hägg 1984: 61–92, 1985: 92–102, 1986: 99–131; Utas 1984–6: 429–41.

6 Hägg 1983: 90 and 95; see also Egger 1990: 85–6; Pervo 1991: 145–60; Lefkowitz 1991: 199–219; Montague 1992: 231–49.

7 Elson 1992: 212–30; Montague 1992: 231–49.

8 Montevecchi 1973: 360 and 391–2; see also Stephens 1990: 148–9.

9 Stephens 1990: 149; Hägg 1983: 90.

10 Hägg 1987 and 1988 has made valuable contributions to the understanding of the historical novel.

11 Achilles Tatius 2.35–8, Heliodorus 4.6–15. See Sandy 1982: 68–9.

12 So Maehler 1976: 17, citing Plato, *Symposium* 179b. See in general P. de Lacy, 'Plato and the intellectual life of the second century', in G. W. Bowersock (ed.) (1974), *Approaches to the Second Sophistic*, University Park: The American Philological Association, 4–10.

13 The two themes merge in the approximately fifty lines of fragment C where Ninus laments separation from his wife as a consequence of war.

14 Henrichs 1969: 205–15 (*editio princeps*) and id. 1972 (definitive publication); Parsons 1971: 53–68 (*editio princeps*) and id. 1974: 34–41 (definitive publication).

15 Haslam 1981: 35–45 has published another papyrus fragment of Greek prosimetrum fictional narrative.

16 Heinze remained unaware of the publication of the *Ninus and Semiramis* material in 1893 until his article had reached the proof stage.

17 E.g. Xenophon of Ephesus 1.14.7–2.1, 3.2 and 5.9.3; Achilles Tatius 1.7ff. and 2.34; Longus 4.11–12. Wehrli 1965: 136–9 argues that in Antonius Diogenes' novel Dinias' son Demochares is in fact a *puer delicatus*, that is, a young, pathic homosexual companion.

18 *Satyricon* 141 (cannibalism), 21–26.5 (sexual deflowering and voyeurism); see Sandy 1979: 367–76.

19 Transvestism: Satyricon 23.5; the other enumerated features occur throughout the *Satyricon*.

20 *CAGN*: 782. See too the beginning of Photius' summary of Iamblichus, 'These three writers [viz. Iamblichus, Achilles Tatius and Heliodorus] set for themselves almost the same goal in presenting love stories' (ibid. 785). Anderson 1982 has fully developed an alternative hypothesis.

BIBLIOGRAPHY

Anderson, G. (1982), *Eros Sophistes: Ancient Novelists at Play*, Chico, CA: Scholars.

Barns, J. W. B. (1956), 'Egypt and the Greek romance', in H. Gerstinger (ed.), *Akten des VIII. Internationalen Kongresses für Papyrologie*, *Mitteilungen der Papyrussammlung der Österreichischen Nationalbibliothek* n.s. 5, 29–36.

Durham, D. B. (1938) 'Parody in Achilles Tatius', *CP* 33, 1–19.

Egger, B. (1990), 'Women and marriage in the Greek novels: fiction and reality', in *Classical Paradigms*.
Elson, H. E. (1992), 'Callirhoe: displaying the phallic woman', in *Pornography*.
Hägg, T. (1983), *The Novel in Antiquity*, Oxford: Blackwell.
Hägg, T. (1984), 'The *Parthenope romance* decapitated?', *Symbolae Osloenses* 59, 61–92.
Hägg, T. (1985), 'Metiochus at Polycrates' court', *Eranos* 83, 92–102.
Hägg, T. (1986), 'The oriental reception of Greek novels', *Symbolae Osloenses* 61, 99–131.
Hägg, T. (1987), '*Callirhoe* and *Parthenope*: the beginnings of the historical novel', *Classical Antiquity* 6, 184–204.
Hägg, T. (1988), 'The beginnings of the historical novel', in R. Beaton (ed.), *The Greek Novel: AD 1–1985*, London: Croom Helm.
Haslam, M. W. (1981), 'Narrative about Tinouphis in prosimetrum', *Graeco-Roman Memoirs* 68, 35–45.
Heinze, R. (1899), 'Petron und der griechische roman', *Hermes* 34, 494–519.
Henrichs, A. (1969), 'Lollianos, *Phoinikika*', *ZPE* 4, 205–15.
Henrichs, A. (1972), *Die Phoinikika des Lollianos*, Bonn: Rudolf Habelt.
Koenen, L. (1985), 'The dream of Nektanebos', *BASP* 22, 171–94.
Kussl, R. (1991), *Papyrusfragmente griechischer Romane* (Classica Monacensia 2), Tübingen: Narr.
Lefkowitz, M. K. (1991), 'Did ancient women write novels?', in *'Women Like This'*.
Lesky, A. (1966), *A History of Greek Literature*, tr. J. Willis and C. de Heer, London: Methuen.
Maehler, H. (1976), 'Der Metiochos-Parthenope-roman', *ZPE* 23, 1–20.
Montague, H. (1922), 'Sweet and pleasant passion: female and male fantasy in ancient romance novels', in *Pornography*.
Montevecchi, O. (1973), *La papirologia*, Turin: Società editrice internazionale.
Morgan, J. R. (1982), 'History, romance, and realism in the *Aithiopika* of Heliodoros', *Classical Antiquity* 1, 221–65.
Parsons, P. A. (1971), 'A Greek *Satyricon*?', *Bulletin of the Institute of Classical Studies* 18, 53–68.
Parsons, P. A. (1974), '3010. Narrative about Iolaus', POxy 42, 34–41.
Perry, B. E. (1967), *The Ancient Romances*, Berkeley: University of California Press.
Pervo, R. I. (1991), 'Aseneth and her sisters: women in Jewish narrative and in the Greek novels', in *'Women Like This'*.
Photius (1959–91), *Bibliothèque*, ed. R. Henry and J. Schamp, Paris: Les Belles Lettres.
Renner, T. T. (1981), 'A composition concerning Pamphilus and Eurydice', in R. Bagnall (ed.), *Proceedings of the XVI Congress of Papyrology*, Chico, CA: Scholars.
Rohde, E. (1876), *Der griechische Roman und seine Vorläufer*, 4th edn 1960, Hildesheim: Georg Olms.

Ruiz-Montero, C. (1989), 'P.Oxy.2466: the Sesonchosis romance', *ZPE* 79, 51–7.
Sandy, G. N. (1979), 'Notes on Lollianus' *Phoenicica*', *AJP* 100, 367–76.
Sandy, G. N. (1982), *Heliodorus*, Boston: Twayne.
Stephens, S. A. (1990), ' "Popularity" of the ancient novel', in *Classical Paradigms*.
Treadgold, W. T. (1980), *The Nature of the 'Bibliotheca' of Photius*, Washington: Dumbarton Oaks.
Utas, B. (1984–6), 'Did Adhra remain a virgin?' *Orientalia Suecana* 33–5, 429–41.
Wehrli, F. (1965), 'Einheit und Vorgeschichte der griechisch-römischen Romanliteratur', *Museum Helveticum* 22, 133–54.

9

THE EPISTOLARY NOVEL

Patricia A. Rosenmeyer

I INTRODUCTION

The epistolary genre

Studies on the European epistolary novel often begin with the 'invention' of the genre claimed by Ovid (*Ars Am.* 3.346: *ille novavit opus*) for his *Heroides*, a series of fictional love letters in verse from abandoned heroines. While the tradition of epistolary correspondence between mythological lovers may have started with the Alexandrian poets, and Ovid's originality remains debatable, his work has become the undeniable archetype of the genre. In addition to single, unanswered letters, the collection includes three paired sets in which the male addressee responds, an exchange of voices interpreting the same event. These two basic forms of epistolary narrative re-emerge in works such as the *Letters of a Portuguese Nun* (one voice) and Laclos' *Liaisons dangereuses* (multiple voices).

The literary influence of the *Heroides* persisted throughout the Middle Ages and well into the eighteenth century. Less appreciated were the Greek authors of antiquity who experimented with epistolary form and convention in fictional contexts, embedding letters in other genres (e.g. Euripides' *Phaedra*), composing single letters for particular occasions (e.g. *Grk. Anth.* 6.227: Crinagoras), or writing letter collections united thematically (e.g. Philostratus' *Epistolai Erotikai*). But there is a difference between a fictional narrative described in a letter and a fictional narrative told through or by means of letters; in the latter case, epistolary form itself creates and manipulates meaning, and letters themselves spur further action. We will consider both types below, but will concentrate on one epistolary fiction (*Chion of Heraclea*) told through a series of univocal, unidirectional letters.

A multiplicity of literary uses complicates the definition of a 'fictional' letter. Hellenistic private letters preserved on papyri are unmistakeably real, but what about letters written with a view to eventual publication (e.g. Synesius), or those used for didactic purposes (e.g. Epicurus)? More complex are epistolary collections attributed to famous authors: some are clearly forgeries (e.g. Phalaris, Euripides); others are rhetorical inventions or school exercises which acquired in antiquity an aura of authenticity; yet others may be amalgamations of real and spurious letters (e.g. Isocrates, Plato).

Yet behind the awkward issue of authenticity lies a central feature of letter-writing: epistolary technique always problematizes the boundary between reality and fiction. Epistolary discourse entails the construction of a self based on an assumption of what might interest the intended addressee. Thus the slippery question of sincerity may be bypassed for a closer look at the rhetoric of epistolary self-representation. Every letter is an artefact purporting to be historically authentic. But better to ask not whether Ovid's Sappho writing to Phaon represents the 'real' poet of Lesbos, but rather what rhetorical effect Ovid achieves by representing her voice through the medium of a letter.

Epistolary fictions

Ovid's heroines advertised the unique advantages of epistolary discourse in Latin poetry; somewhat later, various modes of Greek epistolary fiction flourished, most visibly from the second to the fourth centuries CE.[1] Lucian (*c.* 120–80) composed four prose letters (*Epistolai Kronikai*) between Kronos and himself which suggest a miniature epistolary novel of social reform. In his novella *A True Story* (2.35), he rewrote literary history by quoting a letter from Odysseus to Calypso, expressing regret at having left her for Ithacan domesticity, and planning to return. Lucian's fictions, as well as characters and plots of Greek New Comedy, influenced three great epistolographers of the Second Sophistic: Alciphron, Aelian and Philostratus (active *c.* 170–220 CE).[2]

Alciphron wrote four books of letters in the voices respectively of fishermen, farmers, parasites and courtesans, i.e., fictional writers addressing fictional addressees; Aelian produced one shorter book of farmers' letters. Both writers cross boundaries of gender, class and time, constructing a window into the past by imitating the language and manners of fourth-century BCE Athenian society. Alciphron invents imaginative 'speaking names' for his epistolary greetings (e.g. parasites in 3.10: *Stemphylochaeron* (Olivecake-lover) to *Trapezocharon* (Table-killer)). While the works of Alciphron and Aelian are peopled with stereotypes (e.g. a money-hungry courtesan, a country bumpkin), we also find remarkable individuality of expression; consider one farmer's offer to geld a friend's unruly son (Aelian 10), or a women's festival degenerating into a rehash of the judgement of Paris, as rival courtesans compare buttocks (Alciphron 4.14). The variety of modes (e.g. elegiac, satiric) and rhetorical techniques (e.g. *ecphrasis*, *prosopopoieia*) is balanced by the homogeneity, whether rustic or urban, of an invented fourth-century world.

Most of the individual letters are unconnected, but some reveal proto-novelistic impulses by incorporating responses or multiple perspectives. Alciphron describes a convoluted love affair through the letters of one writer to the various people involved (4.3–5), or develops an erotic mini-plot in pairs (2.6–7, 24–5; 4.8–9), sometimes inspired by famous fourth-century personalities (e.g. 4. 18–19: Menander and Glycera). The letters between Menander and Glycera suggest a sophisticated epistolary *mise-en-abŷme*: Menander tells Glycera he has received a letter from Ptolemy, who has also written to Philemon, who transcribed a copy for Menander. Both poets are invited to Egypt, but Menander boasts that his invitation is more elegantly written than Philemon's. Thus far three letters have been mentioned, in addition to the one currently being written. Menander then summarizes for Glycera the king's message, sending the original letter along with his own. In her response, Glycera reads and reinterprets both Menander's and Ptolemy's letters to suit her own aspirations. We see how fluid the distinction is between epistolary writer and reader, and how two readers interpret the same letter differently. Since we are never directly shown Ptolemy's letter, we must choose between divergent interpretations offered by two internal readers.

Aelian also groups individual letters; he shows lovers pleading and being rejected (7–8, 11–12), or uses four letters together to depict an ongoing quarrel between neighbours (13–16); the misanthrope praises the impersonality of letter writing: 'at least I can communicate by messenger, not face-to-face' (14). The combined letter and response recall the paired letters of the *Heroides*, although the Greek authors choose historical or imaginative personae, not mythological figures.

Alciphron and Aelian write in the voices of their characters; their contemporary Philostratus writes in his own name on erotic themes to both women and boys. His 'discourses of desire'[3] may be read as fictional erotic autobiography in letters, and testify to the author's interest in the relationship between erotic and epistolary rhetoric. The individual letters, however, resemble brief sketches, and epistolary convention goes no further than the heading 'To So-and-so'; there is no sense of connection or development within the collection to tie the parts into a larger novelistic whole.

While the epistolographers wrote free-standing letter collections, Greek novelists inserted individual letters into larger fictional narratives. In Xenophon and Chariton, embedded letters occur primarily in erotic contexts: a married woman propositions the hero by letter and he writes back a rejection, instigating a chain of disasters; or love letters fall into the wrong hands with dire consequences for all. In Heliodorus, a cloth 'letter' embroidered with mysterious words accompanies the heroine on her journey; once read by the correct recipient, it allows the novel to conclude happily. Letters also play a role in Achilles Tatius, Iamblichus (where the missive is hidden in a camel's ear [cf. the letter-carrying rabbit in Hdt. 1.123–4]), and *Apollonius of Tyre*. In the *Alexander Romance*, the core of an earlier (*c.* 100 BCE) epistolary novel appears in the correspondence between Alexander and his enemies, Darius and Poros.

The preceding examples of epistolary fiction are relatively easily attributed to a specific author and date, although the chronology of the novelists remains uncertain. Another group of texts important for the development of the genre is not so neatly identifiable: the pseudonymous letters of famous men, condemned by Richard Bentley's brilliant 'Dissertation upon the epistles of Phalaris, Themistocles, Socrates, Euripides, and others' (London, 1697), in which he scornfully claimed that it would be 'no unpleasant labour . . . to pull off the disguise from those little pedants, that have stalked about so long in the apparel of heroes'. Scholars concur that these letters are later inventions, even if based on genuine collections no longer extant. But they interest us because, as far as it is possible to assign them a date, many originate in the first or second century CE, the same period which produced the epistolographers of the Second Sophistic and *Chion of Heraclea*, suggesting a substantial interest in epistolary forms at this time.

The impulse behind pseudonymous letters was the illumination of a particular historical figure: to write an 'apology' for his life or to praise his accomplishments for posterity, presenting historical events through the lens of his personal correspondence. This type of writing had its roots in rhetorical character sketches. Some of the collections preserved are univocal (e.g. Diogenes, Themistocles), while others include multiple writers (Hippocrates, the Socratic letters); most are the products of several authors.

The most famous pseudonymous collection is surely that of Plato, but the issues surrounding it are too thorny to be summarized effectively in this essay. Let us instead survey the letters of the Cynics, Socrates, and Themistocles. The cynic epistles include those of Anacharsis, Crates, Diogenes, Heraclitus and Socrates and his disciples. They are all of spurious, multiple authorship (although this does not preclude the inclusion of genuine material), and all depict their writers as advancing cynic views.

The ten letters of Anacharsis reveal a propagandistic bent, as the sixth-century Scythian 'noble savage', visiting Greece in search of wisdom, is transformed into a preacher of cynic doctrine. The fourth-century philosophers Crates and Diogenes may have written their own letter collections, but a large pseudepigraphic tradition quickly developed around their names, and our collections of thirty-six and fifty-one letters respectively come from a later period. Crates is represented as writing short pieces, with epistolary headings but no closures, exhorting his readers on a variety of cynic topics, and frequently quoting his mentor Diogenes. Letters 28–33 form an internal unit addressed to Crates' wife Hipparchia; he begins by encouraging her to join him on the road in pursuit of virtue, but finally congratulates her on their baby's birth and instructs her in the home-bound duties of motherhood. Diogenes is also shown writing to his pupil's wife (3), as well as to his own mother (34) and father (7, 30), attempting an explanation of the cynic lifestyle. His moralizing letters on the hard path to philosophy offer great variety in form and content, including invective and paraenetic modes and straight narratives. He also comments on epistolary practice itself: 'letters . . . are not inferior to conversation with people actually present' (3), and 'letters . . . preserve the memory of those who are no longer alive' (17).

The collection attributed to Heraclitus varies the pace by opening with an invitation to Heraclitus from the Persian King Darius, rejected in turn by the philosopher who is 'satisfied with little'. The letters, nine in number, criticize the evil ways of men, and Letter 8 includes an act of self-censorship: 'I would write these things, except that I must, above all, keep them secret', implying that letters always run the risk of interception.

Three pseudonymous collections in particular attract scholars searching under the rubric 'epistolary novel': the letters of Socrates and his disciples, of Themistocles, and of Chion. Let us consider the first two briefly before focusing on the third.

The thirty-five Socratic letters divide into two parts: Letters 1–7, supposedly from Socrates himself, and Letters 8–35, between the Socratic disciples. The first group is paraenetic in nature, philosophical and didactic in its discourse; the second group, written after the master's death, is more interested in historical detail, and the disciples act in keeping with what we know about them from other sources (e.g. Xenophon). Letters 8–35 are unified in their attempt to bring hedonistic and rigoristic Cynicism into harmony, and the letter-writers reappear throughout in smaller groupings and interconnections. The collection resembles an epistolary novel in that it presents a limited number of writers and addressees, joined by a bond of friendship with Socrates, with a common goal of remembering their teacher by recording his opinions for future readers. Letters 14–17 narrate the circumstances of Socrates' death, while Letter 21 is a consolation to Xanthippe for her loss. Speusippus dominates Letters 28–35, and we read his requests to Xenocrates to come to Athens and take over the Academy. In letter 34, Dionysius comments to Speusippus on the conventions of epistolary opening formulas, differentiating between the phrases 'do well' (*eu prattein*), 'greetings' (*chairein*), and 'enjoy yourself' (*hedesthai*). Although these writers are inconsistent in their use of a closing formula, it is clear that they were familiar with theories of epistolary style (e.g. Cicero).

Because the letters of Socrates and those of his disciples are so different in tone and purpose, it is difficult to ignore the internal division and call the whole work an epistolary novel. The twenty-one letters of Themistocles, however, come somewhat closer to that definition. They all purport to be from Themistocles, and are addressed to different people, some real and some fabricated, who would have been likely candidates for such a correspondence at that time in his career, i.e., during his exile from Athens and his subsequent escape to Persia. The collection reveals a mixture of solid historical evidence with imaginative invention, one which dramatizes Themistocles' political and philosophical outlook while building an artistic entirety. Objections have been made that the letters do not follow chronological order, and that certain inconsistencies within the collection, both of fact and of characterization, keep the work from forming a satisfying overall unit, a prerequisite for its identity as a novel. These arguments have been countered by a reconsideration of the sequences so as to read Letters 1–12 and 13–21 as distinctly ordered segments, a diptych as it were. We are left with the option of two series composed by the same author, or a larger whole that lacks artistic unity. All the letters justify or praise the character and actions of their hero, Themistocles, and although they are not strictly unified, and thus not wholly entitled to the designation 'epistolary novel', the work remains an intriguing historical letter collection, representative of a general contemporary interest in epistolary composition.

We are thus left with only one extant ancient Greek fictional work developed solely through an exchange of letters that cohere to form an undeniable artistic whole,[4] and it will be the focus of the rest of this essay.

II *CHION OF HERACLEA*

Chion of Heraclea is our prime surviving example of the ancient epistolary novel. The work contains seventeen letters from the young, aristocratic Chion, addressed variously to his parents, a friend, the tyrant Clearchus, and Plato. The bulk of the correspondence, however, is between Chion, studying in Athens, and his father, home in Heraclea. The letters depict the hero setting off somewhat unwillingly at his father's request to study philosophy with Plato, learning the value of personal commitment to an ideal such as political freedom; he returns home to sacrifice his life attempting to oust the tyrant from his city. The collection opens *in medias res*, and Chion's death, never explicitly stated, cuts off any possibility of a sequel.

Authorship and audience

Although some details have been fictionalized for artistic effect, the basic story reflects historical events recorded by numerous ancient sources.[5] In the mid-fourth century BCE, the city of Heraclea in Pontus was taken over by the tyrant Clearchus, who was killed twelve years later (353/2) by conspirators under the leadership of a man named Chion. We can thus accept a historical Chion, but we cannot defend the authenticity of the letters as productions of the same man. Chronological inconsistencies tell against that attribution: for example, Letter 3 shows Chion meeting Xenophon in Byzantium, which must have happened *c.* 400/399, but we are also told that Chion returned home five years later to kill Clearchus; this leaves an unexplained gap of over forty years. The language and style of the letters, and the absence of detail about Chion's experiences in Athens, appear to rule out authorship contemporary with the events. The evidence points to an anonymous author writing in the first century CE, combining a core of truth with layers of literary creativity. We cannot determine if the author found inspiration in an existing epistolary genre, although we have discussed above the prevalence of epistolary experimentation in this period; possible contemporaneous non-epistolary influences include the novels of Chariton and Xenophon, written perhaps for a similar readership.[6]

Knowing so little about the creation and reception of this collection, it is difficult to define its literary character or intent. Was it a rhetorical school exercise (*progymnasmata*), written in epistolary style from the perspective of a famous person? Was the novel meant primarily to entertain as an adventure story, to instruct readers in the value of a philosophical education for the practice of civic virtue, or perhaps to encourage rebellions against other cruel tyrants? The following discussion considers both the contents of the letters and the epistolary conventions shaping the work, differentiating it from other first- or third-person fictional narratives.

III THE CONTENTS OF THE LETTERS

Let us begin with an overview. The first letter introduces Chion consoling his parents for his absence. We are told very little at this stage, as the author, imitating a 'real' letter home, presumes the family knows why Chion visits Byzantium, what his final destination is, and what studies he will pursue. We gather between the lines that Chion's family is wealthy, having a servant to spare as a messenger. The next two letters find Chion still in Byzantium. Letter 2 is on behalf of the merchant Thraso, who is travelling to Heraclea, and whom Chion commends to his father's hospitable care. What appears to be a conventional recommendation manages also to inform us of Chion's own activities: Thraso acted as his tour guide around Byzantium, and Chion wishes to repay his kindness. The second letter's ending is linked closely with the beginning of Letter 3: both comment on the winds that delay Chion's plans to sail. Repeated references to the forced deferral of the journey add tension and a sense of the unexpected to the narrative.

Letter 3 is a lengthy description of a chance encounter with Xenophon, who was leading troops through Byzantium. The narrative includes a historical-biographical digression introducing the new character, a narrowly averted battle which Chion both participates in and chronicles, and praise of Xenophon's beauty and wisdom. Chion concludes, by more eagerly embracing his future as a student of philosophy, having seen the effects of such an education on Xenophon. Chion is enthralled by Xenophon's eloquence as he keeps his mutinous troops from sacking the city; here is proof that philosophy makes men useful citizens without enfeebling their potential for action. Chion gives an impression of youthful naivety as he praises Xenophon's physical beauty and gets caught up in the military excitement. The letter closes with a flashback to Chion's initial resistance to his father's plans for his education, and a statement of his present goals: he hopes to become a better man, not less brave (*andreios*) but certainly less rash (*thrasus*).

Letter 4 finds him finally on the way to Athens, although not without additional adventure. Chion reports how his crew refused to listen to his warnings of storms at sea, with the result that they barely escape alive, only to face further danger from hostile Thracians on shore. All ends well, obviously, or Chion would not have survived to write this letter home. The letter functions here as a witness to a living voice, but the unavoidable temporal gap between writing and receiving may at times cause a recipient to read the words of a dead man (e.g. Letter 17).

The next letter (5) marks Chion's arrival and initial meeting with Plato, quite understated after the fulsome hero-worship of

Xenophon. We now realize that Chion plans to study at the Academy. There is no physical description of the great man, nor information about Chion's immediate reactions; instead we (and Chion's father) are introduced to Plato the Socratic disciple, a wise man proclaiming a philosophy compatible with an active life. Chion quotes Plato's words, a sign that he is already under the philosopher's pedagogical spell, and says he is eager to become part of Plato's circle.

From Letter 6 to Letter 13, Chion studies in Athens, and we are told that five years pass by. The author hints that many letters have disappeared: some omissions are explicit (e.g. Letter 13 alludes to information in a letter not in our collection), while other missing pieces may be suggested by the relatively small number of letters written (eight in five years). By refusing to 'invent' letters to fill in the gaps, the author thinks to gain his readers's confidence. In the extant letters, Chion neither discusses daily routines nor debates deeper philosophical issues; this seems odd since his father, a former student of Socrates, would have an interest in the workings of the Academy. But what Chion does write reveals an 'image of his soul'[7] and developing views on friendship and duty.

Letter 6 announces the receipt of gifts from home, as Chion lists each item to check if all that was sent has indeed arrived. He asks his father not to send money, but rather local goods such as food and wine that remind him of home and allow him to entertain friends. For although Plato on principle refuses gifts, he can be 'tricked' into accepting meal contributions. We notice a focus on entertainment rather than on serious education (although intellectual discussion surely played a major part in the symposium), and a hint of homesickness, yet Chion never explicitly requests news of his family or city.

Letter 7, a confidential cover letter, and Letter 8, a formal recommendation, contrast sharply with the heartfelt praise of Letter 2. Letter 7 is both a devastating character sketch and a private warning: the man Archepolis, who recently abandoned philosophy for profit-making, is actually untrustworthy and reckless. After frequently insulting Chion, he has now demanded a letter of introduction for business ventures in Pontus, and Chion sends him to stay with his parents. Chion refuses to write a duplicitous letter, the literary model for which he finds in Homer: 'although he is unworthy, I will avoid the model of Bellerophon; I have given him another letter, in which I wrote nothing false.' The 'honest' letter is reproduced as Letter 8, a brief note resembling Pseudo-Demetrius' commendatory type (*systatikos*),[8] and the irony in reading it directly after the previous document is intense. Clearly the trusty servant carrying the one letter was meant to arrive before Archepolis with his official version. Chion asks his father to accommodate the guest, but to reveal at his departure how Chion knowingly returned good for evil, even if Archepolis is too stupid to learn from the experience. Both letters affirm Chion's views on friendship: a good man (*agathos*) helps both friends and enemies, and it is an advantage (*kerdos* – material or spiritual profit) to make every man your friend. Understanding these views to be the result of Chion's education, we perceive a certain maturation which will peak later in his sense of duty towards city and family.

Letter 9 continues the theme of friendship, as Chion writes for the first time to someone other than his father. Chion complains to his friend Bion that he receives no letters from him, and suggests two possible reasons (and solutions): either the messengers are at fault, in which case Bion should write more often so that some letters might arrive safely, or Bion himself is remiss, which is easily remedied by putting stylus to papyrus. Bion should 'write often as one remembering [their] friendship to another remembering it also'. The letter is perceived, as in the epistolary theorists, as a sign of friendship.[9] The bond forged while together must be sustained while apart, and ignoring a friend by not writing implies a low opinion of friendship.

Thus in four of the first nine letters, Chion writes about connections with his fellow man. Letter 9 shows an established long-term friendship, Letters 7 and 8 the undeserved decent treatment of a boor, and Letter 2 favours exchanged with an honest man. Chion's philosophy is to do good to others. Letter 10 picks up themes raised earlier in Letter 6, namely Chion's relationship to Plato and his friends.[10] But now philanthropy takes the form of convincing Plato that, in spite of reservations expressed earlier, money can be a good thing when used appropriately. Applying 'sincere and just argumentation' to turn cash into an honourable gift, Chion presses a talent on Plato for his grand-niece's dowry. Chion proudly informs his father of his generosity, ironically calling it a great profit (*kerdos*). But we note an undertone of boasting as he quotes the very words used successfully in debate with his teacher.

Chion has been in Athens for five years when his father calls him back, claiming longer absence will turn him into a stranger

(11). Chion admits feeling homesick (perhaps he writes what he thinks his father wishes to hear), but insists that another five years with Plato will make him even more virtuous and useful to his country. Explaining the decision to stay, he recalls his very first letter, when Chion asked his father to rejoice at his absence. It seems curious that the son can ignore his father's orders and act independently. He closes the letter with a condescending bit of humour: it is not the journey to Athens that makes one a good man, but the time spent studying there. Perhaps if Chion had written more about philosophy and less about generous gifts, his father might have had more confidence in the educational investment.

All this changes in Letter 12. Chion hears that Heraclea has fallen under the rule of Clearchus, and he now plans to sail as soon as the winter storms abate; even if he can do nothing to change the government, he still wishes to share the fate of his countrymen. This letter indirectly predicts the end of the correspondence, but allows that several months still remain for writing.

As Chion waits for good weather, Clearchus, suspecting his intentions, sends an assassin to Athens. In Letter 13, Chion describes vividly how he grabbed his assailant's knife and wrestled the man to the ground. This adventure parallels the military encounter in Letter 4, serving a similar purpose of retarding the main plot. Action narrative yields to reflection as Chion acknowledges his return might be perilous: 'living or dying, I shall be a good (*agathos*) man'. He closes the letter by asking his father to persuade Clearchus that he is no political threat, but merely a quiet student of philosophy. This subterfuge (if it is one – it is unclear if he has already decided to kill the tyrant) contradicts his insistence on honesty in Letter 7, but seems reasonable considering the goal, euphemistically termed 'performing a public service for my country'.

Letter 14 is written at Byzantium, as Chion sets out on his journey home; it is an explanation of his principles, and a strong attack on tyranny in general. He uses illness as a metaphor to describe Clearchus' rule, but he himself feels invulnerable, because philosophy has taught him that as long as the soul remains free, even the threat of death is endurable. A virtuous man must protect his city, and Chion plans not to be killed until he can die for the right cause: the slaying of the tyrant (now explicitly stated). Chion incorporates direct questions in his letter, as if conducting a

Socratic dialogue with himself (or his father). He encourages his father to continue misleading Clearchus as to his intent, and to write any further helpful information.

Chion's next letter (15) congratulates his father on calming Clearchus' suspicions, and offers additional justification for devious means to a noble end. He elaborates on the evils of tyranny, arguing paradoxically that a cruel despot is better than a mild one, since his cruelty makes the citizens hate him. Chion has also written to Clearchus, purposefully 'in an overwrought tone in order to make him despise me as a complete windbag'. He includes a copy for his father, reproduced as Letter 16. Letters 15 and 16 thus resemble 7 and 8: the first of each pair presents guidelines for the second, warning that the subsequent letter is not entirely straightforward. In retrospect, Letter 15 turns out to be the last written communication between Chion and his father.

The letter to Clearchus (16) is indeed verbose and convoluted. To allay the tyrant's suspicions, Chion invents a reason for writing, i.e., to defend himself against unjust accusations, and eulogizes a life of quiet study. He chronicles his early attraction to philosophy, depicting himself as wholly uninterested in politics, and mixes truth with deceit as he declares his code: 'to honor a just man, to requite an unjust man with good deeds, or, if this is impossible, with silence'. He turns again to Socratic dialogue, imagining the goddess Tranquillity debating with him the value of self-control and the danger of worldly affairs. Chion conceals his sense of duty beyond his individual sphere, to that of family and city. The letter is full of such wordy nonsense that we marvel at Clearchus' gullibility, but then he did not have the benefit, as we do, of comparing this message with the larger collection.

The final letter (17), addressed to Plato two days before the assassination, is written in a considerably more sober tone. Observing bad omens and visions, Chion realizes the end is near, and wishes Plato to know that he remains a worthy disciple. Eager to receive the posthumous glory (*kleos*) his deed will bring, he now actively seeks death. He claims to be in good spirits, closing with a formal epistolary valediction: 'Farewell (*chaire*), Plato, and be happy into a ripe old age; I think that I speak with you now for the last time.' With a prediction of silence imposed by death, the letters, and the novel, end.

Structure and themes

The epistolary collection forms a coherent whole. Six letters from Byzantium (1–3, 14–16), for example, frame the work, and unfavourable winds regulate much of the action (2, 3, 4, 12, 13). We find foreshadowing (violence in 4, 13 anticipates a violent end), parallelism (recommendations in 2, 7, 8; great men in 4, 5), recurrence (6 and 10 concerning Plato; 5 and 12 on travels to and from Athens), and a sustained focus (Chion's father as addressee). On the level of diction, many letters are written in a circular pattern, with word or phrase repetition at beginning and end (e.g. 1, 2, 4, 8); elsewhere, one particular word (e.g. profit, *kerdos*) reappears in different letters. The letters are composed or edited to create a consistent and carefully structured story.

Various themes connect individual letters, e.g. friendship, civic duty, the value of a philosophical education. Much of the novel deals with the tension between a quiet life and a capacity for action. Chion's intellectual maturation in Athens entails learning how to become a good citizen, while his return to Heraclea allows him to act on that knowledge. The letters may be read as entertainment, but they also challenge the reader to reconsider the relationship between personal lifestyle and obligations to a community. In this version, philosophy becomes the means by which the narrator learns best to fulfil his obligations.

IV EPISTOLARY FORM AND CONVENTION

So far the discussion could apply equally to any ancient Greek fiction (although the political emphasis is unusual), but what sets the work apart is its epistolary nature. Let us consider how epistolary form and convention make this novel unique.

Letter styles

Chion's letters closely resemble epistolary styles defined in the epistolary theorists. According to categories inherited by Pseudo-Demetrius (dated between the second century BCE and the third century CE) or Pseudo-Libanius (fourth to sixth centuries CE),[11] the following types are represented: Letter 1 is consoling, 2 and 8 commendatory: 3, 4, 5 and 13 reporting; 6 thankful; 7 vituperative; 9 friendly; 11 accounting; 14 and 16 didactic; and 15 apologetic.

Thus, in addition to working within a historical framework, our author also followed certain hand-book conventions of letter writing. Ancient theorists agreed that letters should not be overly long (Chion cuts himself short in 3, 4, 15); that a letter is written conversation with one who is absent (9 to Bion); that one should answer questions from previous letters (Chion often refers to his father's letters); and that a letter reflects its writer's soul (Chion hides his soul behind the obfuscating verbosity of 16). As we watch Chion develop intellectually, we also see his letters adapt themselves to the circumstances and moods of their addressees, another tenet of epistolary style.

All literary letters are self-conscious works of art and prone to rhetorical strategies, some specifically epistolary, others common to all fictional genres. What does epistolarity bring to this novel that other forms of narrative might not? Issues to consider are references to the act of writing, sending or receiving; clashes between the information required for the external and internal reader; and the absence of an external voice to verify or challenge the writer's single perspective.

Epistolary strategies

In the epistolary novel, attention is drawn to the difficulties of sustaining communication. The author, aiming for verisimilitude, frequently explains practical aspects of writing and sending letters. The servant Lysis delivers Letter 1, later travelling back to Heraclea with Letters 7 and 12. In the last example, Chion fearlessly hints at tyrannicide, since, as he says, Lysis is wholly trustworthy. In Letter 13, we again meet honest servants, and are informed that Clearchus takes no interest in letters, an observation which inversely suggests censorship of the mail under different circumstances. When servants are unavailable, Chion uses merchants *en route* to Heraclea: Thraso (2), Archepolis (7, 8), Simon (4). Chion admits that Letter 4 was written only upon discovering a ship about to sail; we are made to wonder how many adventures are left untold for lack of a messenger, causing gaps in the epistolary chronology.

In spite of these breaks, continuity is established whenever the writer becomes a reader by alluding to his father's letters. The epistolary experience, while predicated on an absent addressee, is inherently reciprocal and continuous. Chion answers his father's questions (11), records his views (15: 'I will follow your advice . . .'), recalls their conversations (3: 'you must remember when . . .') and quotes earlier letters (5: 'you wrote to me that . . .'). Allusions to other voices or texts are an important dimension of the genre. Unidirectional letters demand that we read through the prism of the recipient's voice, but preclude the balanced perspective produced by the presence of an external commentator (e.g. omniscient narrator) or several voices interacting (e.g. dramatic chorus). The univocal collection which reproduces only one side of the correspondence forces the external reader to depend entirely on Chion's words.[12] Doubled letters (7–8, 15–16) let us test his honesty by comparing metatextual statements to the effect that he will write a 'special' letter with the document itself. Letter 16 is particularly complicated because the author must explain how it found its way into the collection – Clearchus surely would not have returned the original. To include a copy for someone else's perusal is a perfect solution, and the technique resembles that of embedded letters in other ancient novels.

The goal of verisimilitude in Chion's letters is nowhere more evident than in the tension between internal and external levels of narration. This takes the form of what the reader expects the narrator to know (in his role as Chion) and actual narrative omniscience, or, from another angle, what Chion's correspondents already know and what external readers must be told. In other novels, information is disseminated by embedded stories, oracular commandments, an omniscient narrator or direct address to an ideal reader. The primary narrative complication of epistolary fiction is that the author must make the narrator/letter-writer speak to an addressee in order to communicate to us as readers. These multiple levels may provoke tension between the exigencies of fictive discourse (letter-writer to addressee) and the necessity to clarify the plot for an external audience (author to reader).[13] Thus many details remain obscure in Chion's first letter, to be revealed only gradually by casual reference, because the author could not justify an explanation of what the internal reader (Chion's father) obviously already knew. For an epistolary novelist, the initial withholding of information from the external reader is a generic necessity.

The author, self-consciously aware of the epistemological limitations imposed by epistolarity, guides his character's voice accordingly. In Letter 3, for example, Chion acknowledges he cannot report Xenophon's exhortation of the troops because he simply couldn't hear – but he could see the result, so it must have been a marvellous speech. In Letter 13, Chion describes an assault by Cotys, one of Clearchus' bodyguards, 'as I learned later' he quickly adds, saving the narrative from contamination by hindsight or improbable omniscience. Epistolary writing exhibits an immediacy unknown to other modes, revealing its origins as the communication of 'news'. The assumption is that a letter is written during or immediately after a newsworthy event; the reality is that the item is 'edited' as soon as it is written down, and already old by the time it reaches its recipient.

In our consideration of epistolary conventions, we must not ignore certain obviously literary characteristics of the novel. Most of the letter headings, for example, read 'to the same person' (*toi autoi*), which could be written only by an editor after the fact. In addition, we miss many mundane details such as those in Hellenistic private letters: gossip, family births and marriages, lawsuits. The collection has an earnestness about it which suggests that it was composed with a view to future reading, and that the pretence at 'genuineness' went only so far.

V THE EPISTOLARY NOVEL

The final question to ask of this letter collection is whether we are justified in calling it a novel. Without rehearsing the complex arguments about the applications of modern terminology to an ancient genre, let us consider briefly whether the individual letters together form a satisfying artistic whole. We identified the work as a historically inspired prose fiction composed solely of letters, arranged chronologically with a clear beginning, middle and end, and containing a number of unifying themes and concepts. Chion as 'hero' guides the plot, developing from shallow youth to dedicated good citizen, and we can identify villains, accomplices and friends. If our definition of a novel requires coherent structure, systematic development of plot and themes, and consistent characterization of the hero, the work certainly fulfils our expectations. History informs us that (unlike other ancient novels) the story concludes with the death of the protagonist, but only after he has accomplished the task he set for himself. Some would deny that the explicit moral point of the tale survives (i.e., self-sacrifice for one's country), since we know that Chion's heroism was rewarded by the slaughter of his family and an immediate transfer of power to Clearchus' successor. But the novel itself ends before doom descends, on a note of hope and martyrdom.

History draws the outlines of Chion's story, but epistolarity gives it form, encouraging the exposition of ideas as well as the description of events and the formation of the hero. Some of the letters explaining his views on tyranny approximate philosophical treatises, much against the grain of the epistolary theorists.[14] It is curious that although Chion puts great emphasis on being a man of deeds, he is represented using a mode more suited for communicating emotions and opinions than straight action narratives. It allows the novel more introspection and deeper character delineation than most ancient non-epistolary narratives achieve; instead of struggling only against external interference (e.g. pirates, robbers), the protagonist struggles also with his own opinions and decisions.

The epistolary novel progresses through personal communications, which we are invited to read over the internal reader's shoulder. As external interpreters, we partially relive the fiction of Chion's father's original reading, not knowing how the story will end. But on another level, the publication of the collection has altered our ability to read through the single prism of the internal, private addressee. The collection becomes public property, written and edited with a view to *kleos*, posthumous glory for its purported author. When the author writes in the voice of Chion, he automatically constructs a self, an occasion, a version of the truth; he decides what is worth telling and what is not. Based on a process of selection and self-censorship, the letter is a construction, not a reflection, of reality. What the epistolary narrator constructs in this novel is both true (historically accurate) and fictional (imaginatively elaborated upon), both private (ostensibly for Chion's father and friends) and public. The ability of the epistolary genre to blend its paradoxes so well with the framework of a historical novel creates the unique work known as *Chion of Heraclea*.

NOTES

1 Representative of later developments in the genre are 'Aristaenetus' (fifth century CE) and Theophylactus of Simocatta (seventh century CE).

2 On the question of Philostratus' identity and dates, see A. R. Benner and F. H. Fobes (eds), *The Letters of Alciphron, Aelian and Philostratus*, Cambridge, MA, 1949, 387–91.

3 For modern applications, see L. S. Kauffman, *Discourses of Desire: Gender, Genre, and Epistolary Fictions*, Ithaca, NY, 1986.

4 It is impossible within the scope of this essay to consider other examples such as the letters of Apollonius of Tyana, Phalaris, Isocrates or Hippocrates and Democritus. For further information on the latter correspondence, see W. D. Smith, *Hippocrates: Pseudoepigraphic Writings*, Leiden, 1990, and T. Rütten, *Demokrit: lachender Philosoph und sanguinischer Melancholiker*, Leiden, 1992, who dates an epistolary 'novel' containing letters between Democritus and Hippocrates to the first century BCE, perhaps antedating Ovid.

5 The references are collected in I. Düring, *Chion of Heraclea: A Novel in Letters*, Gothenburg, 1951, 9–13.

6 On probable readers, see D. Konstan and P. Mitsis, 'Chion of Heraclea: a philosophical novel in letters', *Apeiron* 23 (1990), 258.

7 A common concept in epistolary theories, e.g. Demetrius *De Eloc.* 227 (Malherbe 1988.18).

8 *Typoi Epist.*, type 2 (Malherbe 1988.30, 32). See also Pseudo-Libanius *Epist. Char.* (Malherbe 1988.66, 68, 74), and Julius Victor *Ars Rhet.* 27: 'Commendaticias fideliter dat aut ne dat' (Malherbe 1988.64).

9 For example, Cicero *Ep. ad Fam.* 2.1; Seneca *Ep. Mor.* 40.

10 Letters 6 and 10 were probably influenced by the thirteenth 'Platonic' letter.

11 Texts are found in A. J. Malherbe, *Ancient Epistolary Theorists*, Atlanta, 1988.

12 An aspect noticed by ancient theorists: 'A letter is one half of a dialogue' (Demetrius *De Eloc.* 223 (Malherbe 1988.12, 16) quoting Artemon).

13 On this fundamental problem, see J. G. Altman, *Epistolarity: Approaches to a Form*, Columbus, OH, 1982, 185–215.

14 Demetrius *De Eloc.* 230–1 (Malherbe 1988.18).

SELECT BIBLIOGRAPHY

Altman, J. G., *Epistolarity: Approaches to a Form*, Columbus, OH, 1982.

Benner, A. R. and Fobes, F. H., *The Letters of Alciphron, Aelian and Philostratus*, Cambridge, MA, 1949.

Düring, I. (ed. and tr.), *Chion of Heraclea: A Novel in Letters*, Gothenburg, 1951.

Kauffman, L. S., *Discourses of Desire: Gender, Genre, and Epistolary Fictions*, Ithaca, NY, 1986.

Konstan, D. and Mitsis, P., 'Chion of Heraclea: a philosophical novel in letters', *Apeiron* 23 (1990), 257–79.

Koskenniemi, H., *Studien zur Ideologie und Phraseologie des griechischen Briefes bis auf 400 n. Chr.*, Helsinki, 1956.

Luck, G., 'Brief und Epistel in der Antike', *Das Altertum* 7 (1961), 77–84.

Malherbe, Abraham J., *The Cynic Epistles*, Missoula, 1977.
Malherbe, Abraham J., *Ancient Epistolary Theorists*, Atlanta, 1988.
Müller, W. G., 'Der Brief als Spiegel der Seele', *A&A* 26 (1980), 138–57.
Penwill, J. L., 'The letters of Themistokles: an epistolary novel?', *Antichthon* 12 (1978), 83–103.
Stowers, S. K., *Letter Writing in Greco-Roman Antiquity*, Philadelphia, 1986.
Sykutris, J., 'Epistolographie', *RE* supplement 5 (1931), 185–220.
Thraede, K., *Grundzüge griechisch-römischer Brieftopik*, Munich, 1970.
Ussher, R., 'Love letter, novel, Alciphron, and "Chion" ', *Hermathenea* 143 (1987), 99–106.
Ussher, R., 'Letter Writing' in M. Grant and R. Kitzinger (eds), *Civilization of the Ancient Mediterranean*, 3 vols, New York, 1988, vol. 3, 1573–82.
White, J. L., *Light from Ancient Letters*, Philadelphia, 1986.

10

DIO AND LUCIAN

Simon Swain

Dio of Prusa (later known as Dio Chrysostom, 'the Golden Mouthed') was born about 45 and died after 110. Lucian of Samosata lived from about 120 to 180 or later. Both men were witnesses and contributors to the Greek social and cultural renaissance of the first three centuries CE which is known as the Second Sophistic. The name goes back to Philostratus, who in the mid-third century composed the lives of many of the so-called sophists, the cultural stars of the age. The men who earned or appropriated this title were those who dedicated their lives to word and speech and achieved empire-wide renown through their talents. Those who entered Philostratus' *Lives* were the extremely rich and the well-connected and 'nobly' born among them. In the *Lives* Philostratus found a place for Dio but not for Lucian. The reasons for this are to be found in the cultural and social personas our two authors adopted. The 'novelistic' texts that are the subject of this chapter – Dio's *Euboicus* and Lucian's *Toxaris*, *Lovers of Lies* and *True History* – all reflect these personas and show well enough the place of their authors in the cultural and social history of the time.[1]

Philostratus' 'proper' sophists (as he puts it) were those who were especially devoted to composing and delivering speeches on fictional subjects. We know in fact that sophists did use their rhetorical skills for practical and often explicitly political or civic purposes. Philostratus does not hide this 'real' activity, but he focuses on speeches which 'made use of the characters of poor men, rich men, heroes, and the particular subjects suggested by history' (*Lives*, 481). What he means by these broad categories is speeches where the speaker would take on the character of, say, a tyrant-killer (who might come under the category 'hero') and then narrate his adventures in the form of, say, a mock legal oration.

Lucian's works happen to include just such a speech. Dio also practised overtly sophistic rhetoric of this type. These speeches had to be entertaining and the characterizations had to achieve consistency. One can see how important a training in this type of rhetoric would be for successful novelistic fiction. Above all Philostratus liked fictional speeches which were based on real or plausible scenarios from Greek history. Here he reflects the general obsession of his time with the classical age. The sophists were men very much involved in the exercise and privileges of contemporary Roman power, but their cultural activity was mostly directed away from Rome towards a Greek past which is often (though not always) contextualized by the political actions of the free states of the classical Greek world, especially Athens. Dio and Lucian offer comparisons and contrasts with Philostratus' idea of a sophist. But both they themselves and their works of fiction can best be understood against the cultural background that the biographer describes so well.

Dio's *Euboicus* (*Euboean Speech*) divides into two parts. The first is a description of rural and urban life on Euboea as witnessed or heard of by Dio following his shipwreck on the south-east coast of the island. Dio stresses at the outset that the story he will narrate is a true one: 'I shall be speaking of the character and manner of life of men that I met in what is more or less the centre of Greece' (1). A huntsman (hence the alternative title, *Kunēgos*, 'Hunter') finds Dio and conducts him to his home. On the way he tells Dio about himself and his family (who are herdsmen and farmers as well as hunters), and especially of the occasion when he was summoned to the city (very probably Carystus) by a tax collector, the allegations made about him by hostile speakers in the assembly there, the interventions on his behalf by a 'mild' (*epieikēs*) man and a certain Sotades who had once suffered the same fate as Dio and had been rescued by the hunter, and finally the gifts made to him by the citizens. At this point Dio and the hunter arrive at the man's hut. Here Dio gets to know the family, including the daughter and her cousin who is in love with her. Partly as a result of Dio's promptings the marriage of the young couple is announced and Dio ends by noting that he went to the ceremony (1–80). At this point (81) he makes explicit the moral worth of his story, defending its length and asserting its value for those who wish to investigate the advantages and disadvantages of poverty (81).

He starts his investigation (81) with the formal rhetorical device of refuting the opinion of the playwright Euripides that the poor man does not make a good host (*Electra*, 424–5); the absence of the quotation itself makes it plain that some sort of new introduction has been lost before 81. Dio goes on to contrast the mean welcome one can expect from rich hosts (91–102). He follows this by discussing what sort of occupations the poor should and should not carry on, if they live in cities (103–24). After a further apology for the length of the speech and a further justification of the tale of the Euboean peasants on the grounds that it had showed how the poor could live respectably (125–32), Dio resumes the subject of urban activities with a virulent attack on prostitution and abuse of marriage (133–52). The work finishes abruptly.

The problem of the *Euboicus* concerns the relation of the first half to the second. The first half has long been admired as a charming, innocent evocation of pastoral life. This interpretation is sustained by the agreeable style Dio employs and by the easy progression of his story. The second half has a quite different 'declamatory' style which Dio uses to express his strident moral message. An initial approach to solving the problem of how the *Euboicus* fits together is to look at the interpretations of the ancient commentators, Philostratus and Synesius. Their readings reflect opposing views of stalwart heritage. Since classical times there had been a rigorous debate about the use to which language should be put. Rhetoric – the use of language to persuade or entertain – was condemned by the philosophers as empty and vain. Its exponents fought back. In the Second Sophistic period this debate was carried on quite as vigorously – if not more so – as before. Philostratus' Dio does double work as a sophist who is also a philosopher. Dio is indeed difficult to classify by the labels 'sophist' or 'philosopher', and in hedging his bets Philostratus was recognizing the varied output that is shown by the large surviving corpus of Dio's works – political orations, literary and art criticism, counselling, advice to emperors, sophistic fiction and more. The opinion of Synesius, the late fourth and early fifth-century Christian Neoplatonist, is that Dio had been a sophist but became a philosopher. According to Synesius Dio underwent some kind of conversion during the period of his exile by the emperor Domitian in the 90s. Before this he had indulged in sophistic activity, whereas afterwards his writings were strictly philosophical. Synesius' scheme is suspiciously tidy and has been rejected by one of Dio's most acute modern commentators, John Moles, who argues that the persona of the wandering cynic philosopher, which is frequently used in Dio's works, was adopted during his exile and was afterwards kept up as a convenient means of articulating his relations with the emperors Nerva and Trajan. In other words, Synesius took Dio's propaganda about himself too literally. Certainly it looks as though Dio wrote sophistic pieces after his exile (the lost *Encomium of Hair* celebrates the cleaning of his hair after a long period of unkemptness). Further, those speeches which relate Dio to his political activity in the Bithynian cities of Prusa, Apamea, Nicaea and Nicomedia, together with the testimony of Pliny the Younger, who governed Bithynia around the years 110–12, show a man dedicated to self-promotion and involved in bitter personal disputes with rivals. This Dio was more than capable of varying his persona between that of the elegant sophist (especially suitable under the emperor Vespasian who was hostile to philosophers) and that of the moral philosopher (particularly appropriate for dealing with Trajan).

The *Euboicus* shows both sides of Dio, in the first half the stylish story-teller and characterizer, in the second the direct, angry moralist and Cynic. However, there is a good deal of cross-over between the two parts and, though it is almost certain that the two pieces were separate in origin (the key evidence is the new introduction which must have stood before 81), as the work stands now they do belong together. Philostratus cites the *Euboicus* along with the lost *Encomium of a Parrot* as 'works where Dio was serious about things of no importance', a trait which he observes was typical of sophists. Synesius too was prepared to recognize Dio's virtuosity in fictional and humorous oratory, citing the lost works entitled *Praise of a Gnat*, *Tempe* (praise of the famous beauty-spot) and *Memnon* (praise of the famous talking statue), and even quoting a good deal of the *Encomium of Hair* in his own *Encomium of Baldness*. However, he makes a particular and forceful distinction between Dio's *Encomium of a Parrot* and the *Euboicus*. They do not, he asserts, show a common outlook on life (*prohairesis*). For Synesius the *Euboicus* was a work of extreme gravity. He saw Dio very much as a model for his own literary activity. His important speech 'On kingship', which he addressed to the emperor Arcadius, clearly harks back to Dio's orations on this subject addressed to the emperor Trajan (*Or.* 1–4). These are among Dio's most polished works and aimed to affect the emperor's conduct and policy. For Synesius the *Euboicus* was to be connected with them. First, it was clearly a work of philosophy, since the hostile reference to the emperor Domitian (12) and Dio's pose as an old man and a wandering exile showed it was composed during or after Dio's exile. Second, it fulfilled the promise Dio made at the end of his Fourth Kingship Oration to sketch the spirit of the truly moral man. Synesius identified this man as the hunter of Euboea.

Many modern interpretations of the *Euboicus* concentrate like Philostratus on the first half of the speech. Highet (1973) and Jouan (1977) in particular have associated Dio's plot with the plays of the New Comedy. Since comedy is one of the literary ingredients of the ancient Greek novel, it is sometimes claimed that the *Euboicus* is novelistic. That is not the case, since the main framing devices of the novel – rural location, timeless or past setting, the story of love between two teenagers – cannot be properly discovered in it. It is true that the setting of the first half of the work is rural. However, in the novels the central characters come from the city (that is true even in Longus), have their adventures in the unknown world of the countryside, and finally return in triumph to the urban world. Dio's hunter and his family – who remain anonymous – are genuine country dwellers and the description of the countryside (especially in 14–15) recalls the *locus amoenus* of philosophy rather than the elaborate descriptions (or *ekphraseis*) of the novelists. The time of the Euboean scenes in the *Euboicus* is the present. The love element in the story is brief, with none of the tribulations, separations, vows and other tests that must be endured by the novelists' heroes and heroines. Above all, it can scarcely be maintained that Dio is interested in achieving any deep individualizing characterization.

That is not to say that there is no contact with the major novels which, after all, come from much the same period as Dio. The literary ingredients of the novels – love elegy, historiography, travel literature, epic, as well as comedy – have all left their mark on the *Euboicus* (though, as Donald Russell's excellent new commentary (1992) makes plain, Plato is the most important linguistic source). But it is on the level of a shared cultural and ethical background that a particular link between the novel and the *Euboicus* can be maintained. One of the noticeable aspects of the novels is the insistence on chastity before marriage (especially for women) and on the inevitable progress of any proper love affair towards a life of conjugal bliss. Male friendship is of great importance in these texts, but homosexuality is a theme restricted to sub-plots. The sort of love sanctioned by Plato in works like the *Symposium* or the *Phaedrus* is, if not condemned outright, at least questioned. A key text in the morality of Dio's time is the *Dialogue on Love* by his contemporary, Plutarch. This work does not wholly condemn Platonic love, but it makes explicit its sexual consequences. Plutarch focuses on the inequality between the Platonic lover (an older, richer man) and his beloved (a beautiful youth); by contrast conjugal love is applauded for the spiritual and licitly sexual equivalence between the partners. It is precisely this reciprocity that we find taken for granted in many of the Greek novels. What is new here is not the valorization of happy marriage in itself; but the intensification of such values and their subjection to scrutiny and exegesis. The reasons for the change are not wholly clear; research currently focuses on the dominance among many of the elite of Stoic philosophical values with their accent on married love and also on the strengthening of familial interests among the elite as a result of the monopolization of public interests by the emperor. Whatever the causes, we certainly see a morality at work in the *Euboicus* which is also 'novelistic'. The first half of the work finishes with the charming celebration of a rural marriage whose loving partners Dio explicitly contrasts with the lies and deceits of the arranged liaisons of the rich (80). The last section of the work is a ringing condemnation of sex before and outside marriage.

It is interesting that Dio's recommendations about sex are, like those about the employment of the poor (103–24), quite so consciously programmatic. We must consider finally what this means. If we remember Dio's comments on the philosophical value of his work (cf. 1, 9, 128) and his explicit statement (129) that the figure of the hunter is an allegory for tracking down true knowledge, the strong sense of a programme or a manifesto will ultimately encourage us to follow Synesius in associating the *Euboicus* with the admonitory kingship orations, especially the first (rather than the fourth, as Synesius suggested). In this speech Dio during his exile learns true wisdom whilst wandering lost in the countryside among herdsmen and hunters. He presents what happened to him to Trajan as a 'story' (*Or.* 1.49ff., cf. *Euboicus* 1, 81). Herdsmen and hunters are earlier in the same oration models for the good king Trajan is being advised to become (*Or.* 1.17, 19: cf. *Or.* 49. 2). The *Euboicus* is not of course advice about the personal conduct of the emperor – there is nothing to suggest it was delivered before him – but rather about what should be done with the lower orders (cf. for the moral tone *Or.* 2.55ff.). Dio's attunement to contemporary sexual ethics supports the comparisons scholars have drawn between his advocacy of returning the urban unemployed to the country (*Euboicus* 107–8) and the 'emphyteutic' schemes (i.e., schemes to encourage the use of unworked land) which are found in the Empire at this time. Dio's aims are clear. He thought his kingship orations were 'useful' (*Or.* 57.11); the *Euboicus* is also 'useful for choosing public policy' (127). The emphasis in it on enforcing public morality (which Dio admits is Platonic in conception: 130–1) shows Dio championing a pastoral modality of power where the lives of the urban poor are to be supervised at work and at play. This is a conception of civic life only conceivable by so staunch a supporter of the monarchic ideal as Dio.

Lucian of Samosata offers many contrasts to Dio. He was undoubtedly one of the funniest and most sophisticated writers of antiquity and is probably the most widely known Second Sophistic author today. Although he was much read later, he was not referred to by contemporaries (with the exception of the great doctor, Galen). His absence from Philostratus' *Lives* is some indication of his untypicality. Lucian tells us in the semi-autobiographical work called the *Dream or Life of Lucian* that he did not have the extremely rich background and connections common to Philostratus' chosen few. It is quite probable that like the majority of those in the Greek East he was not Greek nor a descendant of Greeks. In his works he several times describes himself – not without some bitterness – as a 'barbarian' (*Double Indictment* 27, 34; *Scythian* 9). In other words, it is likely that he was one of the indigenous Semitic population of Samosata and that his family spoke Aramaic as well as Greek. He must have had a good early grounding in Greek culture, but it is noticeable that throughout his life he remained sensitive to criticism of his Greek (see *The False Critic*, *A Slip of the Tongue during a Greeting*), though it seems excellent to us. The persona which, as we shall see, he adopted in middle age, of a critical commentator on the culture of his contemporaries, observing its strengths and weaknesses, praising its good points and merits, and relentlessly exposing its vanities and pretensions, may have something to do with his background. The sophists we find in the pages of Philostratus were tightly rule-bound and incapable of self-criticism. It was Lucian's forte to know the rules and to know – when occasion demanded – how to break them slowly, deliciously and without mercy. Although he is for us a useful indicator of his times as well as a favoured author, he must have been someone that Philostratus wished had never existed.

Lucian did not always pose as the outside observer. He started his career as a sophist in order to acquire wealth and fame, then around the age of 40 took up the persona of the critical and parodic commentator. (It should be remembered that he never forgot the rhetorical techniques that had made him famous.) There are parallels (and contrasts) here with Dio. Lucian's early works are pretty standard sophistic fiction. Among them are *Praise of a Fly*, *Praise of One's Native Land*, *Slander* (containing a famous description of a painting of Slander by Apelles which was repainted from Lucian by Botticelli), two mock legal cases called *Tyrannicide* and *Disinherited Son*, and a pair of speeches relating to an historical figure, the sixth-century BCE tyrant Phalaris of Acragas. The latter show that Lucian's sophistic career was not without humour, for Phalaris, notorious for his cruelty, is defended by speakers who recommend that the bronze bull in which he roasted his victims should be accepted as an offering at Delphi.

Lucian made his money in the western half of the Empire (*Apology* 15). He came back east in the late 150s and then followed the expedition of the emperor Lucius Verus against the Parthians. Verus set up headquarters at Antioch in 163. It was here that Lucian wrote the *Dance*, a learned encomium of Verus' favourite art of pantomime, and two pieces of flattery, *Portraits* and *Defence of Portraits*, for Verus' mistress, Pantheia. It was also about this time (*Double Indictment*, 32: 'a man already about forty years of age') that Lucian abandoned the sort of rhetorical fictions that made his early career. In *Double Indictment* the personified Rhetoric complains in court that Lucian has left her and moved in with Dialogue; Dialogue then complains that Lucian had 'penned me up with Jest and Satire and Cynicism and Eupolis and Aristophanes' and 'finally one of those really old Cynic dogs, Menippus' (33). Lucian here refers to the birth of his famous comic dialogues, which blended the mockery of Old Comedy with cynic candour, sometimes following the prose and verse mix of the third-century BCE cynic satirist, Menippus of Gadara. Lucian was proud of what he considered to be his own invention. His targets in the comic dialogues are religion, superstition and contemporary philosophy. At *Fisherman* 20 Frankness (i.e., Lucian) tells Philosophy, 'I hate boasters, tricksters, liars, and poseurs'; this, together with the verdict at *Zeuxis* 2 that his works showed 'good vocabulary, conformity to the classical canon, biting intelligence, perception, Attic grace, good construction, and art', summarizes his own stance as a man whose complete mastery of the system was the key to his ability to parody it.

It seems probable that *Toxaris*, *Lovers of Lies* and *True History* belong to the second part of Lucian's life. They are not the trivial fare of the sophistic fictions of the first period. *Toxaris* (also known as *Friendship*) is the most difficult of these works to classify. It does not obviously debunk or parody anyone or anything. In the dialogue which frames the work a Scythian, Toxaris, and a Greek, Mnesippus, discuss the honour in which friendship (*philia*) is held today. Toxaris asserts that Greeks do not now value good friendship and challenges Mnesippus to compare examples of friendship from contemporaries. They decide that they will each tell five stories, which are claimed as true.

Mnesippus' first story concerns a wealthy Ephesian, Deinias, who abandons a faithful friend, Agathocles, while under the influence of flatterers; he eventually murders the mistress used by the flatterers to seduce him together with her husband and is exiled to an island where he is supported by his old friend. Like all the stories in the *Toxaris* – and unlike the ancient novel in general – the setting is the present. But as is usual in Second Sophistic authors stylistic reasons dictate that the Roman emperor is disguised, in this case under the name of the Great King (of Persia), while the Roman governor becomes a 'harmost' (originally a governor used by classical Sparta). The dramatic language (17: 'when he had promised to come to her, had come, was now inside, Demonax . . . sprang out as if from an ambush', etc.) is surpassed in the second tale of a rescue at sea during a storm (20: 'please put before your eyes the surge of the waves, the reverberation of the breaking water, the boiling foam', etc.); the friends of this story happily survive and are now studying philosophy. The third tale concerns a man who faithfully and honestly executes the will of a poor friend, the fourth a man who marries the unattractive daughter of his disgraced companion. The final and longest tale is about two more students; one falsely incriminates himself in order to be in prison with the other who has been wrongly arrested; when they are released he makes a wonderful law-court speech 'weeping moreover and imploring and taking the whole matter on himself' (34). 'That, Toxaris', says Mnesippus, 'is what Hellenic friends are like' (34).

Toxaris' stories of Scythians are far more imaginative, indeed fantastic. They live up to his claim that 'momentous occasions' reveal friendship more than the 'profound peace' that the Greek world now enjoys (36). The first tale concerns friendship shown in a war between the Scythians and the Sarmatians. The second story has two friends killed by a lion while hunting; the second friend neatly kills the beast before he himself dies. The third story is far more involved. Arsacomas with the help of his friends Lonchates and Macentes revenges himself on the Bosporan king, Leucanor, for the slight he had received when he proposed to marry Leucanor's daughter. After Leucanor's murder his half brother, Eubiotus, and his son-in-law, Adyrmachus, invade Scythia but are repulsed. Arsacomas gets his woman after she is kidnapped by Macentes. Toxaris claims to have taken part in the events. Of all the stories this has the most detail, including a digression on local customs. It has been linked with the so-called *Calligone* fragment, which seems to be part of a romantic novel set near the land of the Sarmatians. The fragment has a barbarian chief called Eubiotus addressing a Greek woman, Calligone; but, though Lucian's story looks as if it has been abridged from a longer one, the idea of a type of 'Scythian' novel is far-fetched and the particular comparison with *Calligone* is not particularly illuminating. As with all the stories, the source is unknown. Toxaris' fourth story concerns himself and his friend, Sisinnes. The latter becomes a gladiator to support them when they are robbed in the Pontic city of Amastris. The last tale features a man who in a fire saves his friend before his wife.

None of the stories shows any real characterization. The male-female love theme of the novels is not a major concern. The stories all concern obvious situations where male friendship can be proved – flatterers, difficulties in travel, wills, the marriage of children, false arrest, war, hunting, the slighted suitor, the arena, a fire. It is true that male friendship is important in the novelists, especially in Chariton, Achilles Tatius and Xenophon. It is also the worry of moralists and thinkers of the time like Plutarch (*On Having Many Friends*, *How to Tell a Flatterer from a Friend*, *On Brotherly Friendship*), Dio (*Or.* 74 *On Lack of Trust*), Musonius, Epictetus, Alcinous (Albinus) and Apuleius (in *On Plato*). And so Lucian's piece should perhaps be placed alongside collections exemplifying virtue rather than being viewed primarily as entertainment. The moral message is uppermost, something unusual but not implausible in this author.

Lovers of Lies is a rather different work and has more in common with the *True History*. The whole is an outright attack on credulity in the supernatural. Tychiades ('Son of Chance') asks Philocles 'why on earth are so many men fond of lying?' (1). He goes on to attack ancient liars like Herodotus and Ctesias (the fourth-century BCE historian of the Persian wars and of India who was famous for his lies) and 'Homer himself'. He then narrates to Philocles a series of stories he has heard at the house of Eucrates whom he has visited laid up in bed because of bad feet. These are told by Eucrates, his doctor and their philosopher friends. The tales are of magicians, cures, exorcisms, magic statues, a huge Gorgonesque demon who shows Eucrates the underworld, ghost stories and finally the famous story of the sorcerer's apprentice where Eucrates learns the spells of the Egyptian master, Pancrates; whether Lucian made this story up himself is unknown – it is clear that Pancrates is modelled on a famous Egyptian magician of Hadrian's time called Pachrates. It is plain that contemporary philosophers are as ever among Lucian's chief targets in *Lovers of Lies*. Tychiades finishes by saying, 'we have a potent antidote to this sort of nonsense – the truth' (40).

One of Lucian's parodic techniques is the piling on of details which are consistent with an initial claim. This is apparent, for example, at *Lovers of Lies* 24, where the huge Gorgo figure has dogs 'taller than Indian elephants, black, like them, shaggy with a coat filthy and squalid'. He outlines this method of composition at *Hermotimus* 73–4:

> Suppose one of those daring poets were to say that there was once a man with three heads and six hands, and suppose that you easily accepted this . . . he would immediately supply the appropriate details, how the man had six eyes, six ears, three voices coming from three mouths, each taking food, and thirty fingers, etc. . . . Who would disbelieve these details now, when they are consistent with the start of the story?

This is the method of composition that we see above all in the *True History*. The *True History* is again an attack on people's willingness to accept as fact what is fantasy and myth. Lucian had strong views on how to write (real) history. In his *How to Write History* he stresses that history should serve the truth (38ff.). Only when one has the facts can arrangement and style become the writer's concerns (47–51). *True History* rests on similar beliefs. The work is divided into two equal books and is narrated in the first person (a common means of suggesting truth; cf. Dio's *Euboicus*). The main adventures in Book 1 are Lucian's voyage to the far West, his meeting with Endymion, King of the Moon, the victory of Phaethon and the People of the Sun over the People of the Moon, Lucian's lengthy description of life on the moon, events after being swallowed by a huge whale, and the battle of the islands. In Book 2 Lucian escapes from the whale to visit the Island of the Blessed (where he spends less time parodying fantasy travel tales and trains his eye on some of his usual targets, philosophers, sophists and traditional religion), then visits the Island of the Damned, the Island of Dreams, and goes on to meet an assortment of odd and extraordinary creatures more in keeping with Book 1.

In the preface to *True History* (1.1ff.) Lucian says he is offering 'wit, charm, and distraction pure and simple . . . [and] some degree of cultured reflection', and stresses the 'novelty of his subject'. This reminds us of what he says in *Zeuxis* about his comic dialogues. He confesses that he is going to be lying openly. His targets are 'the old poets, historians, and philosophers who have composed long and fantastic yarns, whom I would mention by name, unless I thought they would be obvious to you as you read'. Those influences named by Lucian are Ctesias, Herodotus (branded a liar also by Plutarch in the *Malignity of Herodotus*), Iambulus (author of a lost work recording a voyage through Ethiopia and India), the *Odyssey* and Plato (probably with reference to the myth of the *Republic*). Also named is Aristophanes (1.29) who is however 'a wise man and a truthful one whose compositions are disbelieved for no reason'. Aristophanes is praised for being an honest fabricator. This is what Lucian says of himself too at 1.4:

> since I had nothing true to relate, never having had any interesting adventures, I turned to lying but of a far more honest kind than we see in the others. For in this one respect I shall at least be telling the truth, when I declare that I am a liar.

The attempt of older scholars to 'find' Lucian's sources rather missed the point of what Lucian implies, that he has used earlier authors not so much as sources but more as targets. This is a method that Lucian tells us of at *Fisherman* 6–7, where he says he wants his audience to recognize passages he has used, but also makes it plain that he has made what he found his own. His own technique is to eke out the details which his source or his own imagination invited a willing parodist to supply. Consider for example the battle of the islands at *True History* 1.40–2: we might think of Thucydides Book 7 and the famous battle scene in the Great Harbour at Syracuse; we might think of Herodotus' floating Egyptian island (2.156), and, since Lucian's crews have flames for hair, of what Homer says of Diomede and Achilles in the *Iliad* (5.4; 18.206). But when Lucian goes into detail about the huge length of the islands, the use of their forests as sails, the height of the crews, and their weapons, the hunt for parallels must be given up.

Lucian's *True History* is often classified as a novel; but, apart from anything else, it completely lacks a love element. However, it does at least parody the travel literature which Erwin Rohde, the father of modern-day scholarship on the novel, saw as an ingredient of the ancient romances. Moreover, the theme of curiosity which Lucian mentions at the beginning (1.5, *periergia*) invites comparison with the two comic novels of the second century, the anonymus *Lucius or Ass* and the *Metamorphoses* of Apuleius, which seem to parody the 'wisdom-seeking' literature of texts like the first century CE astrological and medical work of Thessalus of Tralles. Further, two novels known from summaries in Photius' *Library*, the *Babylonian History* of Lucian's contemporary and fellow-Syrian, Iamblichus, and the *Incredible Things Beyond Thule* by Antonius Diogenes, probably also of the second century CE, are comparable for the fantasy travel and magic elements in their plots. Antonius' work in particular probably had a scene on the moon. His relationship to Lucian is most likely one of being a fellow-parodist rather than a 'source', as was once thought. Among all classes in the ancient world science and rationalism competed always with the fantastic and the mystic. Like many of Lucian's other works the point of the *True History* is to combat such credulity and gullibility. Its success as literature and as entertainment depends on the fact that all parody must indulge its victims. In the *True History* Lucian has been particularly generous.

NOTES

1 Space does not allow discussion of the anonymous *Lucius or Ass*, an epitome of a work which is sometimes ascribed (notably by Perry 1967) to Lucian.

BIBLIOGRAPHY

Dio of Prusa, *Euboicus*

Anderson, G. (1976), *Studies in Lucian's Comic Fiction*, Leiden, 94–8.
Avezzù, E. (1985), *Dione di Prusa, Il Cacciatore*, ed. E. A. and F. Donadi, Venice.
Brunt, P. A. (1973), 'Aspects of the social thought of Dio Chrysostom and of the Stoics', *PCPS* 19, 9–34.
Foucault, M. (1988), *A History of Sexuality*, tr. R. Hurley, vol. 3 (*The Care of the Self*), London, 40, 228–32.
Highet, G. (1973), 'The hunters of Euboea', *GRBS* 14, 35–40.
Jones, C. P. (1978), *The Roman World of Dio Chrysostom*, Cambridge, MA and London, 56–61.
Jouan, F. (1977), 'Les thèmes romanesques dans l'*Euboicus* de Dion Chrysostome', *REG* 90, 38–46.
Moles, J. L. (1978), 'The career and conversion of Dio Chrysostom', *JHS* 98, 79–100.
Russell, D. A. (1992), *Dio Chrysostom: Orations VII, XII, XXXVI*, Cambridge.
Salmeri, G. (1982), *La politica e il potere: Saggio su Dione di Prusa*, Catania, 82–6.
Veyne, P. (1987), in Veyne (ed.), *A History of Private Life*, series editors Ph. Ariès and G. Duby, vol. 1, tr. A. Goldhammer, Cambridge, MA, 33–49.

Lucian of Samosata, *Toxaris*, *Lovers of Lies*, *True History*

Anderson, G. (1976a), *Lucian: Theme and Variation in the Second Sophistic*, Leiden, 23–66.
Anderson, G. (1976b), *Studies in Lucian's Comic Fiction*, Leiden, 1–33.
Bompaire, J. (1958), *Lucien écrivain*, Paris, 657–705.
Fusillo, M. (1988), 'Le Mirroir de la lune: l'"Histoire Vraie" de Lucien, de la satire à l'utopie', *Poétique* 19 (73), 109–35.
Hägg, T. (1983), *The Novel in Antiquity*, Oxford, 117–21.
Hall, J. (1981), *Lucian's Satire*, New York, 215–20, 339–54.
Jones, C. P. (1986), *Culture and Society in Lucian*, Cambridge, MA and London, 46–58.
Morgan, J. R. (1985), 'Lucian's *True Histories and the Wonders Beyond Thule* of Antonius Diogenes', *CQ* 35, 475–90.
Perry, B. E. (1967), *The Ancient Romances: A Literary-historical Account of their Origins*, Berkeley, CA, 211–35.

Swain, S. (1992), 'Antonius Diogenes and Lucian', *LCM* 17 (5), 74–6.

11

PHILOSTRATUS

Writer of fiction

Ewen Bowie

'You think that the Greeks will remember your words when you are dead. But those who are nobodies when they are alive, what can they be when they are not?'[1] With this epigrammatic letter, addressed to a Chariton who is most probably the novelist, Philostratus seems to dismiss his literary activity as worthless, and the text has been used to support the thesis that the writing of romantic fiction was despised by respectable creators of high literature. Whether or not it can sustain this weight, we should hesitate before concluding that it is the fictionality of Chariton's writing that the sophist expects his readers to find unacceptable. After all, if a librarian were required to keep all Philostratus' works on the same shelf, and were permitted only the categories of 'non-fiction' and 'fiction', the decision would be hard to make. In what follows I attempt a brief exploration of the territory of the fictional in Philostratus' writing, bearing in mind that the most important landmark in contemporary fictional writing as a whole was undoubtedly the romantic novel.

There are indeed two works where 'non-fiction' is preponderant, the *Gymnasticus* and the *Lives of the Sophists*, both works which give a historical account of two important features of contemporary Greek culture. But even in these, and especially in the latter, that account is often thick with anecdotes in which it is hard to know what is drawn from reliable tradition and what from the moulding of Philostratus' imagination.[2]

In another group of works fictionality operates on a different level. The *Letters* contain a few like that to Chariton with which I began, 'addressed' to dead men whose names will be recognized by Philostratus' readers: 67 to Philemon, 72 to an Antoninus who is probably Caracalla. We should no more read them as 'real' letters than we should read as 'real' the request to Julia Domna in 73 (which could indeed be a 'real' letter) to argue Plutarch out of his disapproval of sophists. But most are *Love Letters*, as the Suda and almost all manuscripts entitle the collection as a whole, manipulating common erotic themes and addressed in the main to an unnamed woman or boy. Those with named addressees (e.g. 45 to Diodorus) are no more likely than the rest to be intended to flatter or persuade real people. Their rhetorical elaborations of the predicaments, emotions and physical sensations of a lover stand close to the monologues given by the novelists to their heroes and heroines. One example will suffice.

> And what is this new sort of burning up? In my peril I beg for water: but nobody lays it to rest, for the extinguisher for this flame is most ineffective, whether one brought it from a spring or took it from a river. For the water itself is burned by love.[3]

Such facility in the creation of verbal responses appropriate to particular situations occasions no surprise in a man who himself delivered *Discourses* and *Declamations* as a practising sophist.[4] The former might involve anecdotes which could be fictional, the latter required the sophist's speech to assume and exploit a set of circumstances which to him and his audience were equally unreal, whether based on an episode in classical Greek history or on an imaginary and improbable legal dispute. We have only one or perhaps two of Philostratus' *Discourses*, and none of the *Declamations* attested by the Suda. But some of the latter, like the letters, might have blended fiction and love, since we know of several declamations by other sophists which did: Onomarchus' speech for a man in love with a statue,[5] Choricius' pair which plays off the speech of a young man claiming as his prize for valour the right to marry the pretty girl he loves against that of his miserly father who has lined up a rich but ugly bride for him.[6]

Third in this group would stand the first of the two sets of *Pictures*, if we could be sure they were by this Philostratus. Here we find deployed another rhetorical skill that is also much exploited in the more sophistic novels, detailed and evocative description of a scene or object. The *Pictures* purport to describe a set of paintings in a gallery at Naples, chiefly mythological in subject, and naturally Philostratus chooses scenes and techniques of rendering them with which his readers will be familiar from the paintings that decorated their public and private buildings. That he is actually describing a set of paintings that he saw is a possible but unnecessary conclusion, and it would cohere better with his other literary activity to suppose that here too is a set of fictional entities.[7]

Such incursions into the fictive are of course very different in intent and in effect from that of a writer of extended narrative fiction. But that Philostratus made them should deter us from overestimating the gap that separates his literary activity from that of the novelists. Once the remaining two works are considered that gap will be seen to be quite narrow.

The shorter work (though longer than *Daphnis and Chloe*) is the dialogue *Heroicus*, *Of Heroes*. Its major speaker had been born into the élite of his city Elaeous on the Thracian Chersonnese, but had been robbed of most of his ancestral estates when orphaned; now he is contentedly cultivating the one that is left, chiefly planted with vines, across the Dardanelles from Troy. His interlocutor is a Phoenician storm-bound on a sea-voyage that had already lasted thirty-five days since Phoenicia and Egypt. Soon the vintner discloses that his farming is aided by the hero of Trojan legend, Protesilaus. They move to the *locus amoenus* of the vineyard and once he has combated the Phoenician's scepticism by cataloguing documented discoveries of gigantic skeletons (interpreted as those of mythological heroes) the vintner gives a detailed account of the activities and appearance of a ghostly Protesilaus. Stories of miraculous powers of reward and punishment exercised by Protesilaus and other heroes finally convince the interlocutor, whose role thereafter is to assure the vintner how exciting his stories are and to ask for more. Some space is devoted to the assault on Telephus' kingdom of Mysia, omitted by Homer, and a number of other corrections and supplementations of Homer's account are offered without any clear structure, until two-fifths of the way through the work (c. 26) the vintner settles down to describing the appearance, character and achievements of the major Greek and Trojan heroes, including a sustained rehabilitation of Palamedes. This sequence – obvious enough for our medieval manuscripts to pick out the section on each hero by writing his name in the margin as a subtitle – is punctuated by appetite-whetting anticipations of The Truth about Achilles, a narrative on a much larger scale that eventually begins at c. 45, about three-quarters of the way through the dialogue. This section on Achilles also tells us more than Homer about Patroclus and Neoptolemus before we are given an account of cult offered by Thessalians at Achilles' tomb and stories of sailors who have heard Achilles and Helen singing to each other of their mutual love on an island in the Black Sea. This move away from information gleaned from the ghost of Protesilaus prepares for a tempestuous ending, an account of an Amazon raid on the island's reputedly rich shrine, a raid which ended in disaster when a divine madness drove their horses to trample and savage them and a supernatural storm destroyed their ships.

There are two levels of fiction here. First the frame. Both the vintner from the Chersonese and the Phoenician sailor are anonymous and unlikely to bear any relation to individuals in Philostratus' own world. But of course the fictional dialogue had a long and respectable ancestry in Greek prose, and although most writers maintained Plato's normal practice of giving speakers the names of historical characters who might plausibly be supposed to have met on some such occasion to discuss such topics, his later and less common technique of using unnamed speakers was also taken up. It was a form of fiction common in imperial Greek writing, and Philostratus will probably have known the dialogues of Lucian and Athenaeus, certainly those of Plutarch and Dio. Indeed Dio's *Euboean Tale*, not itself a dialogue, may have been one of Philostratus' sources for the idea of a cultivated traveller brought face to face with a contented rustic living in tune with nature.

The second level of fiction lies in the material that provides the bulk of the work, the accounts of Homeric heroes' appearance, character and actions that supplement and sometimes correct the narrative of the Homeric poems. This caters to the same sort of reading public that pored over commentaries on the Homeric poems to resolve omissions, uncertainties and contradictions in the poet's story. Like such commentaries, it assumes that behind the surviving poems there lies a set of historical characters and events about which more can be discovered. But here, in calling a fictional witness who claims privileged access to these, Philostratus invites readers to treat his solutions to questions about the Trojan war as his own creations. The possibility that there had been such an encounter, that there was a peasant in the Chersonese who communed with the ghost of Protesilaus, that this ghost could indeed offer a keen Trojan war-correspondent a series of journalistic scoops – all this permits the reader a self-indulgent *frisson* of satisfaction. With one part of her mind she knows that it is all Philostratean illusion, with another she can toy with the notion that this source might really provide extra information that only the privileged readers of this work can share.

It is partly to corroborate this second inclination that Philostratus frames his narrative of the Homeric heroes in material of a rather different stamp. His opening with tales of gigantic skeletons, some at least of which a reader will have found 'attested' in other texts and some of whose reputed find-spots she will perhaps have visited, helps to erode the scepticism not only of the fictional interlocutor but of the real-life reader too. His closing tale of a hero's punishment of a sacrilegious attack fits a pattern widespread in Greek religious thought and could be accepted as credible even by highly educated pagans of the second and third centuries CE.

The combination of a claim to a reliable channel of information and framing in plausible material shows that Philostratus has some interest in presenting his fiction as truth. The first technique is used in various forms to achieve a similar end by some of the romantic novelists and, much closer to Philostratus in his subject matter, by the Dictys story, which we know from fragments to have circulated in Greek as well as in the Latin version preserved in manuscripts. Nearest among the former is Iamblichus' claim to have derived the story of his *Babylonian Tale* from a 'Babylonian' captured in Trajan's Parthian wars. More remote but still analogous are Longus' presentation of the story of Daphnis and Chloe as a local exegete's interpretation of paintings seen in a shrine of the nymphs by the narrator while hunting on Lesbos, and Achilles Tatius' presentation of his story as told to the narrator by one of its principals, the love-sick Cleitophon of Tyre, in the shrine of Astarte at Sidon (both, of course, Phoenician cities). Achilles' opening shares what may be only a superficial similarity with the *Heroicus* in having the interlocutor a sailor and the narrator in effect the chief participant in the reported action (since the vintner is simply a mouthpiece for Protesilaus). A variant on these techniques of authentication was to be found in Antonius Diogenes' *The Incredible beyond Thule*: this story, he claimed, was written down by one of its leading actors, Deinias, on tablets buried in his and his beloved Dercyllis' grave at Tyre, there to be discovered during the city's siege by Alexander the Great.[8] This is surely related to the opening claim of Dictys' Trojan narrative that its author was taken to Troy by Idomeneus and Meriones for the express purpose of compiling a history of the war. Wooden tablets bearing this history were buried beside him in his grave in Crete and discovered when it was opened in the thirteenth year of the Roman emperor Nero. Nero commissioned a Greek translation of the original Phoenician and lodged it in his library; from this our Latin text claims to have been translated. Philostratus is doing something similar to these in the *Heroicus*, a similarity he may wish to draw to our attention by identifying his sailor as Phoenician.

The framing of the far-fetched by the credible also has a number of analogies in the novels, though it can take different forms and none of these is so manifestly close. One is to anchor the narrative in an explicit and familiar historical context: the family of Hermocrates after the Athenian defeat at Syracuse provides Chariton with his heroine Callirhoe, the court of Polycrates ties the story of Metiochus and Parthenope to historical 'reality'. More generally the novelist may adopt the historiographic pose so well analysed in Heliodorus by John Morgan.[9]

In some significant elements of his technique, then, Philostratus in the *Heroicus* stands close to the novelists. Other details exemplify some shared interests. Such is the recurrent insistence on the heroes' physical beauty, with especial attention to their hair-styles (e.g. Menelaus 29.5, Hector 37.3, Aeneas 38.3). There are also occasional erotic episodes, like Agamemnon's lust for Cassandra (31.4) and an Amazon's for a captive youth; or Achilles and Polyxena falling in love at the ransoming of Hector's body, so that she deserted to kill herself on Achilles' tomb, a 'correction' of tradition (51.2–6), and finally Achilles and Helen sharing an immortal love on the White Island (54). Yet other details show preoccupations similar to those of the sophistic novelists: the pictorial creation of vivid and memorable scenes, like the ship fired and allowed to drift out to sea at dawn in commemoration of the drowned Locrian Ajax (31.8–9).

There are also, of course, features common to many types of literature, like the short speeches employed to give a further dimension to heroes' characters: Idomeneus, Ajax and Agamemnon at Aulis (30.2–3), or the contrary recommendations and ensuing dispute of Palamedes and Odysseus after a solar eclipse (33.6–14). Finally there are elements that set Philostratus apart from the novelists, attributable sometimes to the difference in subject matter, sometimes to different habits of writing. The heroes are quick with repartee, a facility that ranges them with Philostratus' sophists rather than with novelistic characters. Thus at 33.44:

> Once Achilles said to him: 'Palamedes, you seem rather uncultivated to the majority, because you don't have somebody to attend you.'
>
> 'Then what are these, Achilles?', he said holding out both hands.
>
> And when the Achaeans offered him wealth from the division of spoils and urged him to be rich, he replied: 'I will not take it: for I urge you to be poor and you ignore me.'

Such exchanges are clearly influenced by the sort of intellectual and particularly philosophical biographies we have in Lucian's *Demonax* and Philostratus' own *Lives*, but they are not confined to the proto-Cynic Palamedes. Even Achilles spits *bons mots*:

> 'What wound was it, Achilles, that gave you most pain?'
>
> 'That inflicted by Hector.'
>
> 'But you were not wounded by Hector', said Ajax.
>
> 'Oh yes I was', said Achilles, 'in the head and in the arms: for I consider you my own head, and Patroclus was my arms.'

The *Heroicus*, then, lures the reader through a landscape where some of the illusions will be familiar from incursions into the romantic novel but many will not. But illusions they are: this can hardly be doubted. For the remaining and longest work the boundaries between fact and fiction are much more contentious.

A Severan reader encountering *The Stories of Apollonius of Tyana* in a library or bookshop would have been prudent to suspend judgement about genre and factuality until much of the work had been read. Its scale alone must have puzzled. The title (if original) might suggest biography. But most biographies were in one book – more often the thirty or so modern pages of Lucian's *Alexander* or Diogenes Laertius' *Plato* than the seventy of the latter's *Epicurus*. The eight books of the work on Apollonius (344 Teubner pages) might rather recall the proto-novelistic *Cyropaedia* of Xenophon, a historical monograph like those of Thucydides or historians of Alexander,[10] or the genre that has debts to all of these, the ideal novel (both Chariton's and Achilles' are in eight books).

The narrative proper only begins (at 1.4) after a triad of oblique openings redolent of a sophistic prefatory discourse or *prolalia*. The first gives a brief sketch of the archaic sage Pythagoras. The second notes Apollonius' resemblance to Pythagoras and adumbrates a defence against the charge that his powers were those of a *magos*. The third sets out as the writer's goal an account accurate in chronology and characterization, based on oral and written sources, including letters of Apollonius. It is in this connection that Philostratus claims (1.3) to have used not only a work by Maximus of Aegeae on Apollonius' residence there as a young man, and a four-book work by Moeragenes, dismissed with such venom that it must have been the standard work Philostratus sought to supersede, but a hitherto unknown memoir drafted by one Damis of Nineveh, brought to his attention by Julia Domna. We later read in more detail (1.18–19) how Apollonius resolved to travel to Mesopotamia and India to consort with *magoi* and Brahmans, and *en route* at Nineveh acquired Damis as a disciple. Damis joined him for the duration of his travels and compiled a notebook of tit-bits (*ecphatnismata*) which professed to include all that Apollonius had said, even casual remarks, and to combat any suspicion that he had invented this journal written in mediocre Greek ('for Damis had been educated among people who did not speak Greek') he reports an anonymous criticism of it and Damis' spirited defence.

From this point the narrative is constructed around a series of exchanges of Apollonius with Damis and with others that display his formidable moral and intellectual strength. He has many sides: the ascetic philosopher who blends Socratic and cynic with predominantly neo-Pythagorean stances; the encyclopedic sage who knows that eunuchs can feel sexual desire (1.33, 36) and can discourse on animal behaviour (2.14–16); the philhellene who secures the rights of descendants of Eretrians transplanted to Cissia by Dareius (1.23–4);[11] the literary scholar who knows obscure poems composed by one Damophyle of Perge (surely bogus) in the tradition of Sappho (1.30) and later criticizes Dio of Prusa's rhetorical style (5.40). In Book 2 the journey to India introduces the staples of ethnography and paradoxography – mountains, rivers, strange plants and diet – and Apollonius talks philosophy and aesthetics with the Indian king Phraotes who is fluent in Greek. Book 3 takes him to a Brahman community presided over by the sage Iarchas, then quickly back to the Mediterranean. Book 4 starts with visits to Greek cities of Ionia and Achaea in which Apollonius combines the sharp reforming tongue of a stoic or cynic philosopher with a readiness to offer political advice characteristic of a sophist.[12] Thence to Italy, where he corresponds with a Musonius Rufus supposedly in exile and survives confrontations with Nero and his praetorian praefect Tigellinus. The fifth book first takes him to Spain, then Egypt, again linking him with prominent historical figures. In Spain these are Vindex and Galba, while at Alexandria Apollonius, Dio of Prusa and the Stoic Euphrates advise Vespasian in his choice between monarchy and democracy and Apollonius gives his blessing to the imperial rule he has recommended. A journey to Ethiopian sages replays some of the Indian themes while establishing that the Indian Brahmans were superior. Then for the finale in Book 8 Philostratus offers a confrontation with Domitian much more serious than that with Nero, involving a major trial scene and Apollonius' miraculous escape from prison. He ends with the conflicting stories of his death or apotheosis.

I have cited more detail from the first book than the remaining seven because it is in reading it that the reader will form his preliminary judgement of the character of the work. He may of course revise that judgement, and as different sorts of material are brought in by Philostratus some revision would certainly be appropriate. How would he assess it once the colophon of the last roll had been reached?

Some features might have inclined a reader to see the work as novelistic, though none of these is unique to the novel. Scale has already been mentioned, pointing to novels, *Cyropaedia* and perhaps Alexander-histories. More diagnostic of the novel might be the form of the title – not *The Life of Apollonius* but *The Stories of Apollonius of Tyana*, like a novelist's *The Story of Chaereas and Callirhoe*.[13] Even more indicative is the elaborate construction of convincing 'testimony' constituted by the journals of Damis (cf. above, 185–6). Of course real historians have prefaces which discuss their handling of their sources, and again histories of Alexander present a closer analogy, appealing to contemporary accounts by companions (cf. Arrian *Anabasis* 1.1.1) or claiming to be based on diaries. But 'Damis' more closely resembles the 'witnesses' claimed by the novels and might suggest to the reader that both he and the material that he authenticates partake of the fictional.[14] A third feature linking the *Apollonius* with both novels and Alexander-histories is the vast extent and variety of the hero's travels.

These adumbrations would be countered by some marked

differences from the novel. Three stand out, and of these the first two can be briefly stated. First, between Cadiz and the Ganges there are no pirates or brigands to threaten Apollonius' travels. Even Longus gets pirates into his pastoral dreamworld, and Philostratus would not have been short of *bons mots* with which Apollonius in his present incarnation might brow-beat pirate kings. But Philostratus distances him from that novelistic *topos*. Instead pirates are given a second-order cameo appearance in Apollonius' account to the Brahman Iarchas of a previous incarnation: as an Egyptian helmsman he had deceived pirates into letting his ship escape (3.24). The double-dealings with pirates and the role of a non-Greek helmsman of a merchant ship can be read as a parody of the novelistic topic,[15] while the over-the-top detail that he lived in a wretched hut on Proteus' island of Pharos adds to the attractions of a humorous reading.

Second, there are none of the independent sub-plots to which the novelists resort in varying degrees. Everything narrated in some way involves the central character. This is not odd in a hagiographic work, but its difference from the practice of the novelists would soon be observed. It is a related feature that although the novels are episodic, they have a unity which is a property of their narrative structure, whereas the *Apollonius* has only the unity imposed on it by the consistency of a central character, and its shape is that of a life rather than a plot.[16]

The third and most important difference concerns the power at the heart of the novels, *eros*. Philostratus' hero is no lover but an ascetic sage, his constant companion not a beautiful girl whom he worships as the object of his desire but a middle-brow Hellenized Syrian whom he often puts down as the target of his repartee. Philostratus gives him a vow of chastity at an early age and vehemently rejects charges of an erotic peccadillo (1.13). Writing for a readership familiar with Plato's *Phaedrus*[17] Philostratus could well have chosen to sound some erotic overtones in Apollonius' didactic relationship to Damis, or in Apollonius' pursuit of wisdom and truth, but he does neither.[18]

When *eros* intrudes it is wholly negative. At 1.10 Apollonius divines the sinful state of the richest man in Cilicia who has been offering prodigal sacrifices to Asclepius at Aegeae: he turns out to have conceived a passion for his stepdaughter and to be flagrantly cohabiting with her. Philostratus follows this tale and its moral (1.11) with that of how the ephebic Apollonius aroused the lust of a Roman governor who was 'a violent man and sexually depraved' (1.12). Apollonius sends him packing ('You are out of your mind, you scum') and within three days he has been summarily executed for conspiring with Archelaus of Cappadocia against Rome. Both these incidents were probably already in the tradition, since they are credited to Maximus of Aegeae, but Philostratus' decision to select from what was presumably a fuller narrative by Maximus shows his interest in establishing early in his work the polarity between Apollonius of Tyana and such characters as Apollonius of Tyre. Apollonius' contempt for sexual passion reappears when he asserts eunuchs' susceptibility to it at 1.33, an assertion borne out by the incident narrated at 1.36.

Another negative example decorates the sessions with Brahmans: Apollonius drives out a demon who for two years had possessed an 18-year-old youth (3.28). The demon was the ghost of a man who had died in battle, and whose wife (whom he still loved) had married another man after three days: disgusted with heterosexual passion he had become infatuated with the boy. A pendant, the famous 'Bride of Corinth', varies the themes of the Greek journeys of Book 4. A handsome pupil of Demetrius the Cynic (hence appropriately given the name Menippus) was about to marry a rich Phoenician woman who had fallen in love with and seduced him. His conquest is seen as diminishing his claim to be a philosopher – 'in other respects his philosophy was securely founded, but he was susceptible to sexual passion' (4.25). Apollonius can tell that she is an *empousa* (he has had experience of one *en route* to India, 2.4), one of those vampires who 'experience lust, and they lust for sex, but above all for human flesh, and they use sex to entice those on whom they wish to feast'. Apollonius challenges, unmasks and (it is implied) dismisses the vampire at the wedding itself. Vampire and riches vanish into thin air. Philostratus avers that the outlines of the story are widely known, but that he has taken the details and the link with Menippus from Damis. These details, like the implicitly Damian ghost in India, should be treated as Philostratean invention, and together the stories present *eros* both heterosexual and homosexual as a dangerous power to be feared and mistrusted. Unlike Apuleius in his *Metamorphoses*, where such images are balanced by diverse positive examples, Philostratus never invites us to see a benign element in *eros*. His only positive example is the love of Polyxena for Achilles, the subject of one of the five questions Achilles' ghost agrees to answer in the miniaturized *Heroicus* of 4.16; and although represented as noble, this love drives her to suicide on his tomb.

The same perspective is maintained in the second half of the work, though there it is given less prominence. Travelling up the Nile they encounter an Egyptian youth Timasion who is a replay of Menippus. In Naucratis, the sex-capital of literary Egypt, he had rejected the advances of his stepmother: Apollonius is supernaturally aware of his story, praises his virtuous conduct (especially impressive because Timasion conceded that he was a fan of Aphrodite) and welcomed him to his following (6.3). Further on, in Ethiopia, just south of the obligatory cataracts of the Nile, a satyr's ghost (*phasma*) has been plaguing village women and has killed two whom it especially desired: Apollonius uses wine to cure it of its lust, tricking it into drinking itself to sleep (6.27). Again sexual desire involves a desire to kill. Philostratus seeks to corroborate the reality of satyrs and their lust by citing a story of one of his contemporaries in Lemnos whose mother was said to be visited by a satyr. No word here of the lady's murder: Philostratus seems to be taking up a popular belief but developing a version for his Ethiopian sequence which casts *eros* in the worst possible light. A few pages later (6.40) the futility of *eros* is brought out by the story of the youth in love with the Aphrodite of Cnidos, a well-known tale whose association with Apollonius Philostratus can only expect his readers to take as a *jeu d'esprit*.[19] Apollonius' characterization of normal sexual relations here (with which the young man's passion is contrasted) is their only favourable recognition in the whole work.

It is hardly surprising, then, that some pertinent *erotica* are omitted. The affair between Titus and Berenice, given due coverage by Philostratus' contemporary Cassius Dio of Nicaea (66.15.3–4), cannot be mentioned. It would have cast a cloud over the sunny picture we are given of Titus (6.29–33). More telling is the total silence on a passion Apollonius allegedly felt for Alexander Peloplaton's mother, a society beauty whom the *Lives of the Sophists* reports as rejecting all lovers except the handsome sage (2.5,570). That anecdote was admittedly written later than the *Apollonius*, but it cannot be held that it was unknown to Philostratus when he wrote it, since he somewhat mendaciously refers to the *Apollonius* for the story's refutation. Rather the character and narrative constructed by Philostratus for Apollonius could not tolerate anything but a wholly negative view of *eros*, even a view presented for refutation.

Philostratus' handling of *eros* in the *Apollonius*, then, so different from that of the *Heroicus*, would check any reader's inclination to assimilate the work to a romantic novel. Instead it would reassert the work's status as a laudatory biography of an ascetic philosopher endowed with supernatural powers and claiming a special relationship with the divine. When the *Apollonius* was written, probably in the second decade of the third century, the only obvious pagan model for such a work would be biographies of Pythagoras, precisely the guru whom Philostratus delineates in his opening sentences and on whom his Apollonius most models himself. Similarities between the *Apollonius* and the later lives of Pythagoras by Porphyry and Iamblichus suggest that several details in the former are drawn from earlier Pythagorean biography. A Christian reader can of course see many similarities with the Gospels, but these are not so close as to require the supposition that Philostratus knew of and drew upon them.[20]

A feature which the *Apollonius* shares with works on Pythagoras and on Jesus of Nazareth is that it concerns a figure in whose historicity many readers believed. By the time Philostratus wrote many local traditions were already well established, associating Apollonius with miracles in mainland Greece, Ionia, Cilicia and Syria.[21] That of Apollonius' vision at Ephesus of Domitian's simultaneous murder in Rome was famous enough to be written up by Cassius Dio (67.18). Some readers might know the previous literary works to which Philostratus refers and from which he must draw much: that on Apollonius' youth by Maximus of Aegeae; Moeragenes' work in four books which seems already to have represented Apollonius as both a philosopher and a man with supernatural powers (*magos*); and a collection of letters of Apollonius to cities and individuals whose dominant theme seems to have been vituperative correction of the addressee's moral failure and degeneracy.[22] All this establishes a presumption shared by writer and reader that there is a set of historical facts concerning Apollonius on which Philostratus may draw. He may select well or ill, he may elaborate without warrant, but he and his readers would agree that his story has a historical core. In this respect too it clearly both differs from the novels, whose attempts to integrate themselves with historical events are never more than an author's ploy, and resembles the *Heroicus*, where Homer's account of the

Trojan war forms a historical core and the ghost of Protesilaus plays the role of Damis.

The *Apollonius* emerges as a literary hybrid, something *sui generis* that resists reduction to other genres. But if the principal stock is would-be-historical biography and the novelistic features have been grafted on, what is the point of these grafts? I do not imagine that I can track down Philostratus' literary objectives. We can only speculate on possible attractions, and in doing so we must remember the general enthusiasm for experimenting with literary form that marks Greek literature of the period.[23]

At the most basic level Philostratus may simply wish to expand the story. The motive for this might be partly to create a monumental tribute to Apollonius, partly to establish his work as definitive and clearly fuller (as well as more correct) than the four books of Moeragenes. The expansion to eight books results in the scale which I have earlier suggested might be read as a novelistic feature. But what material should be exploited to achieve this expansion, and how can it be presented as a historically reliable accretion? Without texts of Maximus and Moeragenes any identification of Philostratean additions is inevitably speculative. Moeragenes is attested by Origen to have narrated confrontations between Apollonius, the Stoic Euphrates and an Epicurean,[24] but the exchanges with Demetrius, Musonius and Dio of Prusa are a development of this element in the tradition that we can probably lay at Philostratus' door. He could have found many models in *Lives* of philosophers. So too the sequence of confrontations with temporal powers – Roman governors, oriental monarchs and finally the evil emperors Nero and Domitian and the good emperors Vespasian and Titus. These developments not only consolidate the image of a high-principled philosopher speaking his mind fearlessly but establish Apollonius as an important political actor on a historical world stage rather than a small-time wizard in the shadowy local traditions of the Aegean and Syria.

The exchanges with Vardanes and Phraotes, with the Indian Brahmans and the Ethiopian Gymnosophists, have the advantage not only of generating more entertaining copy but of extending Apollonius' power and manifest traces of Hellenism even wider than the power of Rome. Although the Indian journey has often been defended as historical, in my view it is a fiction, and the only doubt is whether it was already in the tradition by the time of Moeragenes.[25] If it was, Moeragenes had already embarked on a development which assimilates Apollonius to globe-trotting couples in novels and to Alexander the Great, and Philostratus needed simply to take this further, and should probably still be seen as the inventor of the Ethiopian trip. The point of stressing the Ethiopian Naked Sages' inferiority to Brahmans might then be to devalue the Ethiopian world created by Heliodorus.[26] If neither the Indian nor the Ethiopian travels were in Moeragenes, then Philostratus' decision to invent them is more momentous. But he may have reckoned the colour they imparted to be more that of Alexander-history than of the novels: so much might be argued from the explicit reference to Alexander at several points in the Indian travels (2.9–10, 12, 24, 42–3). In that case he would be developing a fictitious account which did not consistently parade its fictionality by alluding to the novels but dissimulated it by aping historical writing.

In this context it is appropriate to pay a final visit to Damis. If some of the prima facie novelistic features might not have evoked novels at all, and if Philostratus sets out chiefly to construct a monument to Apollonius grander and longer-lasting than the *heroon* built for him at Tyana by Caracalla, then why does he play the apparently novelistic card of an allegedly privileged source? Again part of the answer may be that it is not specific to the novel – witness the Dictys story. Another may be that Philostratus was pleased with the literary effect of such elaborate construction of convincing 'testimony' in the *Heroicus*. But neither the writer of the Dictys nor Philostratus in casting the *Heroicus* expected to be taken *au pied de la lettre*. Their works may not be read as Fiction, but they will be read as fiction. If I am right to maintain that Damis was invented, and invented by Philostratus, did his introduction not risk exposing his construction as something as insubstantial as the riches offered to Menippus by his vampire bride at Corinth? That risk was there, but perhaps he thought it worth taking. Over and above the patterns and themes that he may have drawn from the novelists he may have learned a deeper literary lesson: the pleasure of playing with the ontological status of a narrative.[27]

It is a corollary of our uncertainty about the seriousness with which Philostratus wheels on Damis that he seems to block our attempts to discern what he draws from this 'source'. Sometimes we are given clear indications that something is 'derived from' Damis, or is drawn from other traditions, or represents

Philostratus' own investigations ('I have discovered', e.g. 1.25, 4.22).[28] At others we are left uncertain, and Philostratus wilfully complicates the status of his narrative by introducing events with 'they say', where 'they' are not some unspecified oral or written sources but Apollonius, Damis and their companions of the moment. Thus in Spain, after reporting the phenomenon of tides and the topography of the isles of the blest with a 'they say' which is apparently unspecific (5.2–3), Philostratus proceeds to note trees that 'they say that they saw' (5.5) and to tell us that 'they say that they also sailed up the river Baetis' (5.6).[29] Yet the only eye-witness who can claim to have 'seen' is Damis, unless we are to suppose a group of ethnographic letters of Apollonius rather different from those that 'survive'. Philostratus is teasing us. He repeatedly gives his narrative ethnographic colour, and 'they say that they saw' is a discernably ethnographic formula. He does not scruple to use it despite the confusion it creates as to the source of the material, and he must know it will again strain our belief in Damis.

With some justification, Philostratus may hope to have his wedding cake and eat it. The sober and sceptical reader who wants a good but credible story will welcome the apparently reliable source that Philostratus claims Damis to be; the more sophisticated connoisseur of literary technique will interpret the 'notebooks' of Damis as a covert admission of fictionality. My conclusion is close to that I offered for the *Heroicus*. It leaves Philostratus as a borrower from and even a contributor to the techniques of fiction, and perhaps suggests that he saw Chariton not as a member of a despised club but as a rival in his own.

NOTES

1 Philostratus *Ep.* 66. I attribute to the second of the Suda's Philostrati, whose literary activity falls in the period 213–38 CE, the *Lives of the Sophists*, *The Story of Apollonius*, the *Gymnasticus*, the *Letters*, the *Heroicus* and the first set of *Pictures*. The authorship of the last two is contested. For the problem (and different solutions to it) see G. Anderson, *Philostratus*, London: Croom Helm, 1986, 291–6, G. W. Bowersock, *Greek Sophists in the Roman Empire*, Oxford: Clarendon, 1969, 2–4, K. Münscher, *Die Philostrate*, *Philologus Suppl.* 10 (1907), 515–57, F. Solmsen, 'Some works of Philostratus the Elder', *TAPhA* 71 (1940), 556–72 and 'Philostratos (9)-(12)', in *RE* 20(1), Stuttgart, 1941, cols 124–34. On the attribution of the letters to the writer of the *Lives* and the *Apollonius* cf. F. H. Fobes, in A. R. Benner and F. H. Fobes, *The Letters of Alciphron, Aelian and Philostratus*, Cam-

bridge, MA: Heinemann, 1949, 387–94. My chapter was not able to take account of the recent and thorough investigation of the *Apollonius*: J-J. Flinterman, *Politiek*, Paideia & *Pythagorisme*, Groningen: Styx Publications, 1993.

2 The reliability of the *Lives* is debated, but even if much can be defended (as by S. C. R. Swain, 'The reliability of Philostratus' *Lives of the Sophists*', *Classical Antiquity* 10(1) (1991), 148–63), a residue of fiction remains.

3 For the rhetorical question cf. e.g. Longus 1.14, 18; for the conceit of fire and water, id. 1.23.2. For the *Letters*' treatment of love see now A. Walker, 'EROS and the eye in the *Love-letters* of Philostratus', *PCPS* 38 (1992), 132–48.

4 For the difference between the informal and usually prefatory discourse and the full-blown declamation see D. A. Russell, *Greek Declamation*, Cambridge: Cambridge University Press, 1983, 77–84.

5 Philostr., *Lives of the Sophists*, 2.18.598–9.

6 R. Foerster and E. Richtsteig, *Choricius*, Leipzig: Teubner, 1929 (repr. Stuttgart, 1972).

7 For a bibliography of the prolonged debate over whether the set of pictures is real or invented see Anderson, *Philostratus*, 277 n.4; more fully E. Kalinka and O. Schönberger, *Philostratos: Die Bilder*, Munich: Heimeran, 1968, 26–37; and most recently Philostrate, *La Galerie de Tableaux*, tr. A. Bougot, revised and annotated by F. Lissarrague, with a preface by P. Hadot, Paris: Les Belles Lettres, 1991.

8 See the scholiast on Photius *Codex* 94 (Iamblichus); Longus, preface 1–3; Achilles Tatius 1.1–3; Photius *Codex* 166, 111a20-b31. Note too the claims of the *History of Apollonius King of Tyre*, version b c. 51, and of Xenophon's *Ephesian Tale* 5.15.2.

9 J. R. Morgan, 'History, romance and realism in the *Aithiopika* of Heliodoros', *Classical Antiquity* 1 (1982), 221–65.

10 The sort of length seems common in Alexander-histories, though the precise total of eight books can be claimed only tentatively for Chares of Mytilene (Jacoby *FGrH* 125) and with certainty for the work of Dio of Prusa *On the Virtues of Alexander* (Suda s.v. Δίων, Δ 1240).

11 For further marks of hellenism see Anderson, *Philostratus*, 129–30.

12 For many other details in which Apollonius resembles sophists of the *Lives* cf. Anderson, *Philostratus*, 125–7.

13 For a more detailed discussion of this point see E. L. Bowie, 'Apollonius of Tyana: tradition and reality', in H. Temporini and W. Haase (eds), *Aufstieg und Niedergang der römischen Welt*, ii.16.2, Berlin and New York: de Gruyter, 1978, 1665 with n.48.

14 See Bowie, 'Apollonius of Tyana', 1653–71. Anderson, *Philostratus*, 155–73 attempts to reinstate a real Damis and to establish the existence of some written source claiming to be by that Damis, but he seems to concede that that source need not be by a companion of Apollonius called Damis.

15 The closest analogy is at Heliod. 5.20–2.

16 I owe this point to John Morgan.

17 For knowledge of the *Phaedrus* in writers of the second and early

third century see M. B. Trapp, 'Plato's *Phaedrus* in second-century Greek literature', in D. A. Russell (ed.), *Antonine Literature*, Oxford: Clarendon Press, 1990, 141–73.

18 It is true that Philostratus uses *eran* of non-sexual admiration (e.g. 1.20 Damis is Apollonius' *erastes*, 4.1 of Apollonius' relationship with Smyrna), but this is a common Second Sophistic use of the verb.

19 Cf. Lucian, *Pictures*, 4, Ps-Lucian *Love Stories* 15–16; note too its use as a topic for declamation Philostr., *Lives of the Sophists*, 2.18.

20 So rightly Anderson, *Philostratus*, 144; for the convergences see G. Petzke, *Die Traditionen über Apollonius von Tyana und das Neue Testament*, Leiden: Brill, 1970. On the relation of the *Apollonius* to biographies of Pythagoras see Anderson, *Philostratus*, 136–7 with nn. 7–9 and p. 301 (re-establishing the case for identifying the *doxai* of Pythagoras brought by Apollonius from the cave of Trophonius at Lebadeia with the *Life of Pythagoras* attributed to him by the Suda).

21 See especially M. Dzielska, *Apollonius of Tyana in Legend and History*, Rome: 'L'Herma' di Bretschneider, 1986, with my review in *JRS* 79 (1989), 252–4.

22 On these works and Philostratus' relation to them see Bowie, 'Apollonius of Tyana', 1671–9, and on Moeragenes D. H. Raynor, 'Moeragenes and Philostratus: two views of Apollonius of Tyana', *CQ* 34 (1984), 223–8 and M. J. Edwards, 'Damis the Epicurean', *CQ* 41 (1991), 563–6.

23 Still fundamental is B. P. Reardon, *Courants littéraires grècs des iième et iiième siècles après J-C.*, Paris: Les Belles Lettres, 1971, 'Le nouveau', 233–405.

24 Origen *contra Celsum* 6.41=ii.110.4 K.

25 See Bowie, 'Apollonius of Tyana', 1674–6.

26 This would of course require an early third-century date for the *Aithiopika*: others hold that the evidence favours the second half of the fourth century.

27 Within the known novels the game nearest to this is played by Antonius Diogenes, with a preface which at one part claimed numerous sources and in another aligned him with writers of fiction: see Photius *Codex* 166, 111a30–40.

28 Anderson, *Philostratus*, 155–73 offers a thorough analysis and is right to protest against wholesome foisting upon Damis of material not explicitly attributed to him by Philostratus.

29 Anderson, *Philostratus*, 161–2 weakens his argument by failing to distinguish these different senses of 'they say'.

BIBLIOGRAPHY

Anderson, G., *Philostratus*, London: Croom Helm, 1986.

Bowersock, G. W., *Greek Sophists in the Roman Empire*, Oxford: Clarendon Press, 1969.

Bowersock, G. W., Introduction to C. P. Jones' translation of Philostratus' *Life of Apollonius*, Harmondsworth: Penguin, 1970, 9–22.

Bowersock, G. W., 'Philostratus and the Second Sophistic', in *The Cambridge History of Classical Literature*, Cambridge: Cambridge University Press, 1985, 655–8.

Bowie, E. L., 'Apollonius of Tyana: tradition and reality', in Temporini H. and Haase W. (eds), *Aufstieg und Niedergang der römischen Welt*, ii.16.2, Berlin and New York: de Gruyter, 1978, 1652–99.

Dzielska, M., *Apollonius of Tyana in Legend and History*, Rome: 'L' Herma' di Bretschneider, 1986.

Edwards, M. J., 'Damis the Epicurean', *CQ* 41 (1991), 563–6.

Eitrem, S., 'Philostrats Heroikos', *Symbolae Osloenses* 8 (1929), 1–56.

Flinterman, J-J. *Politiek*, Paideia & *Pythagorisme*, Groningen: Styx Publications, 1993.

Jones, C. P., 'The reliability of Philostratus', in G. W. Bowersock and C. P. Jones (eds), *Approaches to the Second Sophistic*, University Park, PA: A.P.A., 1974, 11–16.

Kalinka, E., and Schönberger, O., *Philostratos: Die Bilder*, Munich: Heimeran, 1968.

Philostrate, *La Galerie de Tableaux*, tr. A. Bougot, revised and annotated F. Lissarrague, with a preface by P. Hadot, Paris: Les Belles Lettres, 1991.

Lo Cascio, F., *La forma letteraria della Vita di Apollonio Tianeo*, Palermo, 1974.

Mantero, T., *Ricerche sull' Heroikos di Filostrato*, Genoa, 1966.

Meyer, E., 'Apollonius von Tyana und die Biographie des Philostratos', *Hermes* 52 (1917), 371–424=*Kleine Schriften*, vol. 2, Halle, 1924, 131–91.

Münscher, K., *Die Philostrate*, *Philologus Suppl.* 10 (1907), 469–558.

Raynor, D. H., 'Moeragenes and Philostratus: two views of Apollonius of Tyana', *CQ* 34 (1984), 223–8.

Reardon, B. P., *Courants littéraires grècs des iième et iiième siècles après J-C.*, Paris: Les Belles Lettres, 1971.

Solmsen, F., 'Some works of Philostratus the Elder', *TAPhA* 71 (1940), 556–72.

Solmsen, F., 'Philostratos (9)-(12)', *RE* 20(1), Stuttgart, 1941, cols 124–77.

Speyer, W., 'Zum Bild des Apollonius von Tyana bei Heiden und Christen', *JAC* 17 (1974), 47–63.

Swain, S. C. R., 'The reliability of Philostratus' *Lives of the Sophists*', *Classical Antiquity* 10(1) (1991), 148–63.

Walker, A., 'EROS and the eye in the *Love-letters* of Philostratus', *PCPS* 38 (1992), 132–48.

Part IV
OTHER TRADITIONS

12

EGYPTIAN FICTION IN DEMOTIC AND GREEK

John Tait

Stories written in the Egyptian Demotic script and in the stage of the Egyptian language known as Demotic survive from Roman-period Egypt in considerable numbers (above all from the second century CE). Of many, we have only a small fragment or fragments, but a few are rather better preserved. Most of the material stems from two large discoveries made in the Faiyum, both apparently in a temple context. For Ptolemaic Egypt (332–30 BCE), we have sufficient evidence of a narrative tradition. Yet the very beginnings of Demotic literature remain obscure. Stories in Greek (whether translations of Egyptian texts into Greek, or Greek compositions in the Egyptian manner) are attested from both Ptolemaic and Roman periods. However, narrative fiction flourished in ancient Egypt for many centuries before the Demotic script was developed for the writing of documents (in the seventh century BCE), and subsequently came to be used for literary purposes.

THE EGYPTIAN TRADITION

It is likely that, almost as soon as the Hieroglyphic script was created at the beginning of Egyptian dynastic history, the cursive Hieratic script, based upon natural or arbitrary simplifications of the Hieroglyphic signs, was quickly devised for everyday use. It was widely employed in the later Old Kingdom (perhaps from the middle of the third millennium BCE onwards) for documentary purposes: for example, accounts and letters. Whether any fictional literature at all was committed to writing in the Old Kingdom is doubted by many. There is no question, however, that, early in the Middle Kingdom (that is, early in the second millennium BCE), narratives, together with wisdom (instructional) literature, circulated among the Egyptian elite, and the royal court should probably be included in this audience. Some of the stories that survive from this period in a relatively well-preserved state are now widely regarded by Egyptologists as works of considerable literary sophistication. Modern scholarly views of them vary, sometimes, for example, seeing them as primarily a vehicle of court or state propaganda, and sometimes as deliberately enshrining or reaffirming generally accepted attitudes towards Egyptian institutions and culture. From then on, it is reasonable to see Egyptian narrative fiction as belonging to one single literary tradition, lasting well into the Roman period (perhaps into the third century CE). However, the evidence for this tradition is not itself continuous. To a large extent, copies of texts tend to survive in greater quantities from periods of greater prosperity and central control, and survival is very much a matter of chance. Occasionally we possess the remains of small private collections of papyri, but we know little of larger libraries. There is no doubt that some texts from the Middle Kingdom survived, copied and recopied, into the New Kingdom (*c.* 1550–1000 BCE). For example, the story of *Sinuhe*, dating from the earlier Twelfth Dynasty, became a school set text of the New Kingdom, principally as a model of classical 'Middle Egyptian' language and orthography.

In the New Kingdom, a new and relatively up-to-date form of the language (confusingly referred to in English as 'Late Egyptian', although it does not belong to what is often called the Egyptian 'Late Period') came to be written. This always appears in Hieratic script, Hieroglyphs being reserved for religious, formal or decorative purposes. A considerable literature survives in Late Egyptian, including a number of well-preserved narratives. These show a wide variation both in style and in language. This suggests that two broad statements might perhaps be ventured: first, that fiction was not confined to one single social context or purpose in the New Kingdom; and, second, that stories were being composed or committed to writing over a considerable period of time.

In terms of narrative literature, the transition from the New Kingdom to the Late Period (*c.* 1000–332 BCE, although this term is sometimes used to cover a narrower period) presents greater problems than those encountered concerning the break between the Middle Kingdom and the New. A few hints have been detected that possibly not all the classical – Middle Egyptian – literature had perished (these chiefly concern verbal echoes of particular phrases). However, our present evidence must suggest that in general Middle Kingdom texts probably did not survive in written form after the New Kingdom, and the endurance of various themes and techniques may have been a matter of oral tradition. Much religious literature did survive. However, the New Kingdom stories known to us seem to have disappeared by the Late Period. The publication of Papyrus Vandier in 1986 provided the first example of a narrative written in Hieratic later than the end of the New Kingdom (the manuscript might perhaps have been written after the middle of the first millennium BCE); its language, however, is arguably close to that of Demotic stories. Posener has pointed out a parallel between the New Kingdom tale of The Doomed Prince and a passage in Diodorus Siculus, but he seems to have had in mind the survival of a folk-story motif, rather than the survival of the actual text. Although some New Kingdom non-narrative literature was used in scribal training in the later New Kingdom, we must assume that the narratives did not achieve classic status.

DEMOTIC

We have no direct evidence for the very earliest stages of the emergence of Demotic. It is assumed to have been a natural development from the rapidly-written form of documentary Hieratic current in the North of Egypt. It presumably won its position as the new cursive script used throughout the country because the Saite (Twenty-sixth) Dynasty (664–525 BCE) chose to maintain its own city of origin, Sais in the Delta, as its administrative capital. The elimination of a rival form of cursive used in the Theban area is also not surprising, in view of the general decline of Thebes in the Late Period. The first uses of the script were surely documentary. How quickly it followed the example of Hieratic in beginning to be used for literary purposes is not yet certain. Our earliest evidence for narratives written in Demotic is probably provided by the fragmentary papyri from North Saqqâra. These texts do not form a coherent archive, but are an accidental collection of material that had been discarded as rubbish, and had by chance been swept together into the same dump. Only a small proportion of the papyri is literary in character. To judge from their handwriting, they clearly were not all written within a narrow span of time. Unfortunately there is no absolutely certain indication of their date, although those better-preserved examples that are without doubt fictional narratives (texts 1–4) perhaps belong in the second half of the fourth century BCE – they can hardly be later than the early Ptolemaic period.

GENERAL FEATURES OF DEMOTIC NARRATIVES

Demotic narratives are apparently all of fairly modest length. This matter is naturally difficult to judge in the case of fragmentary material. However, the columns of text are sometimes numbered in Demotic papyri. This tells us, for example, the exact extent of the First Setna Story. An English translation of the complete text (including the lost opening) might perhaps run to about 5,600 words. The first of the Saqqâra Demotic papyri contained at least sixteen columns (it seems likely that this column-numbering referred to a single text), which would (at the least) make the narrative perhaps three times as long as the First Setna Story. However, we have no indication that texts of vastly greater length were composed. The chief structural means by which stories were made more extensive than a simple anecdote is the device of a story-within-a-story. This was sometimes handled with considerable subtlety, and narratives of some complexity could be constructed.

It is generally agreed that Demotic narrative literature is essentially expressed in prose (and that the occasional inclusion of, for example, hymnic material in texts of a hybrid nature is exceptional). This particularly contrasts with the position in Middle Kingdom literature, where large portions of literary texts are usually analysed as metrical.

The stories all appear to have certain features in common. One of the most striking is the very extensive use of direct speech. Texts probably always had a narrative framework: that is, entire texts do not seem to be presented in the form of a first-person account (although a few examples are known of narrative material presented in the guise of brief letters). However, major portions of many texts take the form of a story-within-a-story. Even apart from this general feature, a large proportion of the contents of texts is set in direct speech. This must have given scope for virtuosity on the part of those who read the stories aloud. The material recording direct speech seems to present the most variety (and ingenuity). Hand in hand with this goes – in modern eyes – a certain poverty in the style of purely narrative passages. These employ a large number of set phrases and even whole sentences ('The moment that Pharaoh heard these words, he opened his mouth to the ground in a great cry. He said . . .'). Some of these recur in a wide range of texts, although it cannot be said that the phraseology of all Demotic narratives is uniform. Many texts include the repetition of whole passages. This is evidently a device exploited for deliberate effect, and not a 'weakness' of style. When similar events recur, the same words are used to describe them, normally without any attempt at curtailment on the subsequent occasions. A character may have cause to give a report of a conversation in which they have previously taken part, and therefore to repeat fairly lengthy statements, which in fact the story's audience has already heard. Usually, there appears to have been no desire to achieve any elegant variation in phraseology, and such modifications as do occur seem to have been haphazard. Events that recur in the stories in any case recur for effect, and thus the repetitions often serve a particular purpose in the narrative.

Certain themes appear again and again in Demotic narratives. Stories concerning the exploits of magicians are relatively common in the literature. These, however, probably form a separate genre of their own, and we may guess that incidents involving magicians were not incorporated as episodes in other kinds of texts. Although only a proportion of texts focus upon the exploits of Egyptian kings, the king and the royal court lie at the heart of many narratives, and most texts refer to the court at some point. Often, texts concern priests. This is hardly surprising, as in the Ptolemaic and Roman periods the priesthood roughly constituted that portion of the population that was literate in Demotic.

SOME PROBLEMS

Only a small proportion of Demotic stories have so far been published or studied. Many, especially in the case of fragmentary material, may simply not have been recognized. It is naturally easier to identify and to work upon texts that resemble those already known. Certainly, our papyrus collections contain many unpublished fragmentary texts that are evidently narrative, but whose general nature is as yet obscure. The range and variety of Demotic stories may eventually prove to be far wider than is at present evident.

No Demotic literary text survives entirely complete. Many texts are evidenced only by small fragments – perhaps only a part of one column, as damaged rolls were often torn up for use as scrap paper. Even when a papyrus roll has survived because it was hidden or stored, the outer layers – normally the beginning of the text – are particularly vulnerable. In the case of all the better-preserved texts, the opening words either are lost or at least present severe problems. The conclusion of the First Setna Story (papyrus of the first century BCE) does survive, and the text ends with a colophon which includes a kind of title: 'This narrative of Setna Khaʿemwese with Naneferkaptah and with Ihwertet his wife and Merib her son is a complete text' – there follows a date and scribal signature, not entirely legible. The Second Setna Story (papyrus of the second or early third century CE) ends with a simple colophon 'This is the completion of this book; it is written' (the final phrase often stands alone to mark the end of a text – *ʿOnchsheshonqy* provides a good literary example – and the colophon need not be supposed to have been accidentally left incomplete).

There is a problem involved in trying to determine what attitude the Egyptians themselves took towards narrative fiction in the Ptolemaic and Roman periods. The texts probably were written down by, and circulated among, priests, and we have no indication of any other audience. However, we cannot assume that for this reason they must have enjoyed a high prestige. The situation may also have been a little different in the Roman period from that in the Ptolemaic. As E. Tassier has recently pointed out, we have no good evidence for the use of narrative texts (or literature, in any strict sense) in the education of Demotic scribes. One possible explanation is that narrative fiction came relatively late upon the scene in the history of Demotic, and that, as Tassier suggests, during the centuries when Demotic remained a documentary script, other means of instruction had found more favour – word lists, grammatical paradigms, lists of names, etc. Even if it were conjectured that Demotic literature had had a longer history than that evidenced by the Saqqâra papyri, it would be rather improbable to suppose that it had been used for literary purposes from the first. Therefore an entirely new style of scribal training might well have become established in the meantime.

The text often referred to by the misleading title of the *Demotic Chronicle* is not in the strict sense a narrative. It is cast in the form of a series of cryptic explanations of a series of even more cryptic oracular statements. The aim of these is to comment on the course of Egyptian history and on the merits of Egyptian kings from the Twenty-eighth Dynasty (404–399 BCE) onwards. Neither beginning nor end is preserved, but in what survives the author pretends to be writing in the reign of king Teos/Tachos (362–360 BCE) of the Thirtieth Dynasty, so that previous history is treated as lying in the past, but subsequent events are supposed to be the subject of genuine prophecy. The text is generally accepted to be a composition of the earlier Ptolemaic period, and the surviving copy also will have been written at a similar date (third century BCE). The text deserves particular mention here, because of its relevance to the general question of anti-Greek feeling in Demotic literature – and Professor J. H. Johnson has suggested that it may, like other Egyptian prophetic texts, have been set within a narrative framework, now lost. She has also argued that the text contains very little anti-Greek feeling (although plainly it envisages the end of Greek rule of Egypt). Although it reveals more obvious dislike of the Persians, its chief purpose, she suggests, is to comment on the nature of Egyptian kingship. The unique manuscript of this text also contains other quite different material, some of which is documentary. A single column is preserved of the beginning of a story. We thus for once know its opening words ('It happened one day in the time of Pharaoh Amasis, Pharaoh said to his courtiers . . .'), which may perhaps be typical of Demotic narratives. The story follows a traditional Egyptian motif: a king demands to be diverted by hearing a new work of literature, and a priest obliges. The framing narrative appears (to us, at any rate) frivolous, in that Amasis' need for entertainment is occasioned by a hangover, but the text may eventually have taken on a more serious tone.

Fragments of apparently straightforward mythological narratives are known. Of course, in the nature of fragmentary material, it is impossible to be sure that the myth was not set in a further narrative framework. A considerable number of fragments of the myth of *Horus and Seth* are preserved. This is the only 'story' that certainly survives in manuscripts from the Middle Kingdom, the New Kingdom (one example, and the only one that is not fragmentary) and the period of Demotic literature. However, the fragments do not bear witness to a continuous tradition of one written text; and the Demotic material itself seems to represent more than one quite different version. An unpublished fragment from North Saqqâra (fourth century BCE) deals with an otherwise unknown episode, in which both Horus and Seth are crowned by Thoth on the instructions of the sun god Rêʿ, and it recounts Isis' reaction to each coronation. Published and unpublished material from Berlin of Ptolemaic date reveals a very different handling of the myth. Mythological narratives are perhaps a special case. However, all Demotic stories present the problem that we cannot easily judge whether the traditions of individual texts, and of whole types of text, were handed on in written, literary form, or survived in a continuous tradition of oral story-telling.

CYCLES OF DEMOTIC STORIES

Two 'cycles' of texts are known. Their common feature is that they each concern one character (or group of characters), and they each have a preference for a particular kind of subject matter. In other respects they seem to be very different in nature. It is reasonably clear that not all Demotic stories belonged to such groupings, and it does not appear probable that a very high proportion of them did so. The cycles could well have been a late development in the literature. It is easy to suppose that already existing motifs and episodes – or even whole stories – could readily have been drawn into an expanding cycle. It is notable, however, that the individual texts are presented as entirely self-contained. There do not appear to be references to events in other texts, and, in a sense, the reader does not need to know more than a bare minimum about the characters – and we may perhaps safely assume that the original audience did have this information.

The *Setna Stories* have in common that they are built around the adventures of a single character, Setna Khaʿemwese, who is represented as an antiquary, and as a rather second-rate magician. He is explicitly based upon the Khaʿemwese (the element 'Setna' derives from a priestly title) who was a son of Ramesses II of the Nineteenth Dynasty; he lived in the first half of the thirteenth century BCE, and did in fact take an interest in, for example, the monuments of the Memphite necropolis. The stories seem to display considerable similarities in their themes. Setna encounters a great magician of the past, and is both discomforted and enlightened by his superior magical skills and his superior moral stature. The episode recounting a visit to the underworld in the Second Story (papyrus of the second or early third century BCE) reveals to Setna that the rich may be punished there, and the poor rewarded. It clearly has a serious purpose. It incorporates both Egyptian and Greek ideas, the latter merely as incidental details. In the First Story (papyrus of the first century BCE), Setna greedily and selfishly steals a magical book from the tomb of a long-dead magician. He is eventually persuaded to return it by a nightmare episode (no doubt induced by the magician), in which his selfishness leads to his humiliation.

The *Inaros* (*Petubastis*) texts (papyri of the early Roman period – chiefly second century CE) are very different. Papyri are assigned to this cycle if they deal with the exploits of the family of 'Inaros'. Who this Inaros may have been supposed to be remains a problem. Some of the texts seem to have in mind a historical setting in the mid-seventh century BCE (the period of the second of the three historical kings 'Petubastis', although this character appears in only a small number of the surviving texts). However, names and the historical realities of other Dynasties have been interwoven; and some texts show no sign that any precise political situation was envisaged. If the wealth of unpublished material at Copenhagen is taken into account, the nature of the plots seems extremely varied. However, the chief characters appear always to be warriors. For this, it is difficult to find any parallel in earlier Egyptian stories. It has often been suggested that the cycle took the Homeric poems as its model. The extent and significance of Homeric influence on the plots and general style has been much discussed, and even flatly denied. Some of the stories plainly pursue traditional Egyptian themes. It is plausible to suggest that only a few general ideas for plots have been borrowed – and Homer need not have been the precise source.

FRAMING NARRATIVES

In the Egyptian literary tradition, the device of enshrining non-narrative material within a story was well established. In Demotic, *'Onchsheshonqy* (a single papyrus of the first century BCE) is an example of a wisdom or instructional text set within a story that in every way resembles Demotic narratives. There are, however, indications that the story and the instructions were composed together, and that the text does not, therefore, consist of two separate works subsequently combined. The text has a substantial introduction, which recounts the circumstances that (purportedly) led to its composition. 'Onchsheshonqy, a priest, finds himself imprisoned indefinitely for having failed to reveal promptly his knowledge of a plot against the king, in which his own benefactor at court has been an active participant. Despairing of being able to carry out in person his duty of educating his son, 'Onchsheshonqy writes down his advice on potsherds – as the king has denied him papyrus. At this point, the text proceeds to reproduce 'Onchsheshonqy's supposed composition, which chiefly comprises a series of brief, single-sentence commands, prohibitions and proverbial remarks. The manuscript comes to an end with a curt scribal signature, 'It is written', without resuming the narrative. It has often been suggested that possibly a narrative conclusion did exist, but the scribe chose to omit it. As Professor H-J. Thissen has pointed out, we should not too readily assume that the story had a happy ending. 'Onchsheshonqy's instructions may have gained authority from their fictional author's tragic plight.

The core of the fragmentary text known as *Bocchoris and the Lamb* (papyrus dated to 4 CE) is a series of disheartening prophetic utterances made by a lamb (an animal appropriate in the Egyptian tradition of prophecy), which dies when its task is complete. The predictions are written down by a character Psinyris, who immediately conveys them to the king (Bocchoris of the Twenty-fourth Dynasty – late eighth century BCE). The king is forced to recognize that the disasters predicted will occur in his own reign, and he instructs Psinyris to arrange an elaborate burial for the lamb. The earlier substantially surviving portion of the text concerns a separate episode in Psinyris' life, although the mention of a book 'of the days that have [happened in Egypt and those which] are to happen in Egypt' suggests that there was a close connection with the lamb's prophecy. An even more fragmentary text, which has no accepted modern title, is concerned with the funerary rites of Psammetichus I (papyrus of the first century BCE). In the framing story, a priest appeals to the king, because he has been turned away from temples where he had expected to receive a share of priestly income. To gain the king's sympathy, the priest recounts how he had written funerary texts for a king Psammetichus.

The *Myth of the Sun's Eye* (*Mythus*) (papyrus of the second century CE) is a text of a unique type, as far as our present knowledge goes. The myth concerns the withdrawal of the goddess Tefnut (the 'Sun's Eye' of the modern title of the text) southwards from Egypt, apparently to Kush, and the sun-god Rê''s wish for her to be persuaded to return. In the Demotic version, the god

Thoth is entrusted with this mission, which he undertakes in disguise. Much of the text comprises long speeches made by Thoth in an attempt to appease and flatter the goddess, who is inclined to fits of dangerous rage. Thoth's subject matter is very varied, including much 'philosophical' reflection on the value of Egyptian life, culture and religion. It includes a series of animal fables. Some of this material is unknown elsewhere, while some is simply a version of matter familiar from other traditions, including Aesop. The text is also remarkable for the fact that a Greek translation (papyrus of the third century CE) survives, albeit in a fragmentary state. It is the only example of a text that is extant in both Demotic and Greek. There can be no doubt that the Demotic was the original version. The overall plot is based upon an Egyptian myth. The text expresses throughout Egyptian religious and cultural ideas. The Greek version is a brave attempt at a plain translation, sometimes resorting to simplifications and to omissions, perhaps wherever the Greek threatened to make little sense. The general view is that the aim of the Greek translator was not so much to reproduce the details and the flavour of the original, as to produce a text that could be read without great appreciation of the religious and other ideas it contained. However, as far as can be judged from what survives, he was in no way trying merely to excerpt passages that he found to his taste. If this general view is correct, it still does not in itself establish the audience for whom the Greek version was intended.

TEXTS IN GREEK (AND COPTIC)

Our first substantial evidence of Greek interest in Egyptian tales is to be found in Herodotus' *Histories* (completed in the later fifth century BCE): in Book 2 numerous Egyptian traditions and tales are reported, which have received extensive modern discussion. Herodotus' informants are generally thought not to have been among the Egyptian elite, and there is no reason to suppose that he had access to written texts. The earliest indisputable surviving example of the literature often called Graeco-Egyptian (all of which is preserved on papyri found in Egypt) comes from the second century BCE, and such material was produced at least until the third century CE. The Greek translation of the *Myth of the Sun's Eye* – the only instance in which we can compare Demotic and Greek versions – has already been mentioned above. A few other texts survive with an Egyptian flavour. They are frequently argued to be translations of lost Demotic originals. This is a very difficult matter to prove. Perhaps only blatant mistranslations could settle the matter, and no totally decisive indications have been found.

The *Dream of Nectanebo* (UPZ i.81, second century BCE) perhaps has the strongest claim to be an actual translation; for example, some Egyptian terms appear in 'transcription', rather than in Greek guise. In this narrative, king Nectanebo receives in a dream a warning that his failure to ensure that the building of a shrine should be completed has come to the attention of the goddess Isis. Nectanebo makes apparently appropriate arrangements, but, just as the papyrus breaks off, a fresh episode seems likely to sabotage the project – and thus no doubt to threaten Nectanebo's tenure of the throne. The story has links with the *Alexander Romance*. It has often been compared with the material in the *Demotic Chronicle*. Its central theme may very well have been the traditional Egyptian one that the king's relationship with the gods is essential to Egypt's prosperity. Nectanebo also plays a role in the *Praise of Imouthes-Asclepius* (POxy.xi.1381, second century CE). Part of the text – in the form of a narrative introduction – is well preserved. It is hard to believe that the contents could have been a straightforward translation from Demotic, and this is virtually unthinkable in the case of the *Narrative about Tinouphis*, in a mixture of Greek prose and verse (P. Turner 8, second century CE), despite the Egyptian names and the 'prophet' (presumably an Egyptian priest) mentioned in the text.

The appeal of 'historical' narratives perhaps needs no special explanation. The *Amenophis Story* (POxy.xlii.3011, third century CE) and the *Sesonchosis Story* (POxy.xv.1826, late third/fourth century CE; xxvii.2466 + xlvii.3319, third century CE) are both more likely to have been composed in Greek than in Demotic. However, the unpublished texts in the Carlsberg collection at Copenhagen have shown that a wider range of Egyptian kings were the subject of Demotic stories than once seemed to be the case. The *Oracle of the Potter* (various papyri of second and third centuries CE, including POxy.xxii.2332, late third century CE) is generally taken to be an adaptation, if not an actual translation, of Egyptian material. It is remarkable that it makes a clear allusion to the lamb of the *Bocchoris and the Lamb* text. In the narrative, a potter has his wares removed from his kiln and broken, because of his alleged impiety. He is taken before 'king Amenophis'. He justifies himself on the grounds that the breaking of his pots signifies the future destruction of Egypt, and in particular of Alexandria. The Egyptian nationalistic feeling of the text is clear, although the text was doubtless adapted and reinterpreted many times.

Coptic was the language and script of the Egyptian (Coptic) church, and Coptic literature is almost entirely Christian. The earliest material comes from the fourth century CE, and the latest (poetry based on Arabic models) from the fourteenth; the last examples of other kinds of text were produced in the eleventh century. Martyrologies in particular have evident links with the Egyptian narrative tradition. However, nearly all Coptic literature is translated or adapted from Greek texts, so the question of any direct or specific Egyptian legacy is problematic. The most substantial example of a hagiographic work that might be termed narrative, and which was certainly written in Coptic is the *Life of Shenoute* (died probably in 466 CE), by his disciple Besa. Of course, the Copts will not have regarded this, or any of the other works mentioned here, as 'fiction'. The *Apocalypse of Elijah* (and related texts) is extremely unlikely to have been an original composition in Coptic (and a small fragment of an early Greek version is preserved, virtually settling the question). It has similarities to Graeco-Egyptian texts. Two stories do survive: the *Alexander Romance* is a translation from Greek, but the *Cambyses Romance* was probably composed in Coptic. The latter deals with Egyptian resistance to Cambyses' invasion of Egypt (the name of the aggressor at one point startlingly changes to Nebuchadnezzar). The text makes notable use of speeches and letters. These two works will not have circulated in the Coptic church as entertainment, but because they were open to Christian reinterpretation.

The chief problems that are debated concerning all this material – oral versus written traditions, literature as an expression of nationalistic feeling, foreign influences, ethnicity and social standing of authors and audience – have changed little over the last hundred years. Fortunately, in the case of both Egyptian and Greek evidence, there is a real hope that fresh material may help to clarify the position.

BIBLIOGRAPHY

This bibliography is highly selective. As far as individual Demotic and Greek texts are concerned, references are given only to those that are best preserved, or have been most discussed.

Earlier Egyptian literature

I Collected translations

(Those items marked with an asterisk contain Demotic material. Most of these works include general discussions and introductions to each text.)

*Bresciani, E., *Letteratura e poesia dell'antico Egitto*, 2nd edn, Turin: Einaudi, 1990 (1st edn 1969).

*Brunner-Traut, E., *Altägyptische Märchen*, 8th edn, Düsseldorf: Diederichs, 1989. (The first edition of this work was by G. Roeder, *Altägyptische Erzählungen und Märchen*, Jena: Diederichs, 1927; it had a slightly different scope, and remains of interest.)

*Budge, E. A. W., *Egyptian Tales and Romances: Pagan, Christian and Muslim*, London: Butterworth, 1931. (Although the philological side of Budge's translations is out-of-date on matters of detail, the range of his material, including Arabic texts, and his approach to it are still of value.)

Lefebvre, G., *Romans et contes Egyptiens de l'époque pharaonique: traduction avec introduction, notices et commentaire*, Paris: Maisonneuve, 1949.

*Lewis, B. (ed.), *Land of Enchanters: Egyptian Short Stories from the Earliest Times to the Present Day*, London: The Harville Press, 1948 (translations of Egyptian tales, including Demotic (by B. G. Gunn), Coptic, and Arabic).

*Lichtheim, M., *Ancient Egyptian Literature*, 3 vols (vol. 1: *The Old and Middle Kingdoms*; vol. 2: *The New Kingdom*; vol. 3: *The Late Period*), Berkeley: University of California Press, 1973–80.

*Maspero, G., *Les Contes populaires de l'Egypte ancienne*, 4th edn, Paris: Guilmoto, 1911 (translated as *Popular Stories of Ancient Egypt*, tr. C. H. W. Johns, London: Grevel, 1915). (Maspero, perhaps even more than Budge, had an instinctive feel for this material, and much of his comment is still of value.).

Pritchard, J. B. (ed.), *Ancient Near Eastern Texts Relating to the Old Testament*, 3rd edn, with supplement, Princeton: Princeton University Press, 1969 (the Egyptian material is translated by J. A. Wilson).

Simpson, W. K. (ed.), *The Literature of Ancient Egypt: An Anthology of Stories, Instructions, and Poetry*, tr. R. O. Faulkener, E. F. Wente and W. K. Simpson, New Haven: Yale University Press, 1972 (new edition 1973).

II Text edition

Posener, G., *Le Papyrus Vandier* (Bibliothèque générale 7), Le Caire: IFAO, 1986.

Demotic

Two plans to publish comprehensive bibliographies of Demotic literature have been announced in recent years. See J. Mertens and E. Tassier, 'Proposal for a bibliography and description of Demotic literary texts', *GM* 101 (1988), 45–55; J. Mertens, 'Bibliography and description of Demotic literary texts: a progress report', in J. H. Johnson (ed.), *Life in a multi-cultural society: Egypt from Cambyses to Constantine and Beyond* (Studies in Ancient Oriental Civilization 51), Chicago: The Oriental Institute of the University of Chicago, 1992, 233–5 (Ch. 24); and K-Th. Zauzich, 'Ein Index der demotischen Literatur', *Enchoria* 8, Sonderband (1978), 45–6. In 1992, Mertens reported that, of 535 Demotic literary texts that he and his colleague had so far noted, 136 were narratives: this total included both published and unpublished material – and, of course, much of it was highly fragmentary. In the meantime (apart from consultation of the bibliographies of the works cited below), further literature may be located in the *Lexikon der Ägyptologie* entry 'Papyri, Demotische', compiled by Professor E. Lüddeckens (the bulk of the material there is naturally documentary), and in the 'Demotische Literaturübersicht' compiled by Professor H-J. Thissen, which has appeared regularly in *Enchoria* from it first volume onwards.

I Studies and surveys

Barns, J. W. B., 'Egypt and the Greek romance', *Akten des VIII. Internationalen Kongresses für Papyrologie* (Mitteilungen aus der Papyrussammlung der Österreichischen Nationalbibliothek, n.s. 5), Vienna, 1956, 29–36.

Bresciani, E., 'I testi letterari demotici', *Textes et langages de l'Egypte pharaonique: Hommages à Jean-François Champollion* (Bibliothèque d'étude 64), 3 vols, Cairo: IFAO, 1974, vol. 3, 83–91.

Posener, G., 'Literature', in J. R. Harris (ed.), *The Legacy of Egypt*, 2nd edn, Oxford: Oxford University Press, 1971, 220–56 (Ch. 9).

Reymond, E. A. E., 'Demotic literary works of Graeco-Roman date in the Rainer Collection of papyri in Vienna', *Festschrift zum 100-jährigen Bestehen der Papyrussammlung der Österreichischen Nationalbibliothek: Papyrus Erzherzog Rainer (P. Rainer Cent.)*, Vienna: Hollinek, 1983, 42–60.

Spiegelberg, W., *Die Novelle im alten Aegypten: ein litterar-historisches Essay*, Strassburg: Trübner, 1898 (chiefly of historical interest, and notable as the only early study of this kind to deal with Demotic material).

Spiegelberg, W., 'Die demotischer Literatur', *ZDMG* 85 (1931), 147–71.

Tait, W. J., 'Handlist of published Carlsberg papyri', in P. J. Frandsen (ed.), *The Carlsberg Papyri I: Demotic texts from the collection* (Carsten Niebuhr Institute Publications 15), Copenhagen: Museum Tusculanum Press, 1991, 129–40.

Tait, W. J., 'Demotic literature and Egyptian society', in J. H. Johnson (ed.), *Life in a Multi-Cultural Society: Egypt from Cambyses to Constantine and Beyond* (Studies in Ancient Oriental Civilization 51), Chicago: The Oriental Institute of the University of Chicago, 1992, 303–10 (Ch. 37).

Tassier, E., 'Greek and Demotic school-exercises', in J. H. Johnson (ed.), *Life in a Multi-cultural society: Egypt from Cambyses to Constantine and Beyond* (Studies in Ancient Oriental Civilization 51), Chicago: The Oriental Institute of the University of Chicago, 1992, 311–15 (Ch. 38). (Deals with the status of literary texts in late-period and Graeco-Roman Egypt.)

Thissen, H-J., 'Graeco-ägyptische Literatur', *Lexikon der Ägyptologie*, vol. 2, 873–8.

Volten, A., 'The papyrus-collection of the Egyptological Institute of Copenhagen', *Archiv Orientální* 19 (1951), 70–4.

Zauzich, K-Th., 'Neue literarische Texte in demotischer Schrift', *Enchoria* 8, Teil 2, (1978), 33–9.

Zauzich, K-Th., 'Einleitung', in P. J. Frandsen (ed.), *The Carlsberg Papyri I: Demotic texts from the collection* (Carsten Niebuhr Institute Publications 15), Copenhagen: Museum Tusculanum Press, 1991, pp. 1–11.

II Texts: Editions and discussions

The North Saqqâra papyri

Smith, H. S. and Tait, W. J., 'New Demotic literary works from Saqqâra', *First International Congress of Egyptology, Cairo: Abstracts of Papers*, Munich: Im Auftrag des Beirats, 1976, 115–16.

Smith, H. S. and Tait, W. J., *Saqqâra Demotic papyri 1* (Texts from Excavations 7) [Excavations at North Saqqâra, Documentary Series 5], London: Egypt Exploration Society, 1983.

The Demotic Chronicle

Johnson, J. H., 'The Demotic Chronicle as an historical source', *Enchoria* 4 (1974), 1–17.

Johnson, J. H., 'The Demotic Chronicle as a statement of a theory of kingship', *JSSEA* 13 (1983), 61–72.

Johnson, J. H., 'Is the Demotic Chronicle an anti-Greek tract?', *Grammata demotika: Festschrift für Erich Lüddeckens zum 15 Juni 1983*, Würzburg: Gisela Zauzich, 1984, 107–24.

Kaplony, P., 'Demotische Chronik', *Lexikon der Ägyptologie*, vol. 1, 1056–60.

Spiegelberg, W., *Die sogenannte demotische Chronik des Pap. 215 der Bibliothèque Nationale zu Paris, nebst den auf der Rückseite des Papyrus stehenden Texten*, Leipzig: Hinrichs, 1914.

Setna texts

Bresciani, E., 'Chaemwese-Erzählungen', *Lexikon der Ägyptologie*, vol. 1, 899–901.

Doresse, J., *Des hiéroglyphes à la croix: ce que le passé pharaonique a légué au Christianisme* (Uitgaven van het Nederlands Historisché-Archaeologisch Institut te Istanbul 7), Istanbul, 1960 (see 56–66).

Gressmann, H., *Vom reichen Mann und armen Lazarus*, Berlin: Reimer, 1918.

Griffith, F. L., *Stories of the High Priests of Memphis: The Sethon of Herodotus and the Demotic tale of Khamuas*, 2 vols, Oxford: Clarendon Press, 1900.

Spiegelberg, W., *Die demotischen Denkmäler* [Cairo], vol. 2: *Die demotischen Papyri*, Strassburg: Schauberg, 1908, (See vol. 1, 88 (a brief entry referring the reader to Griffith's edition, above, of the First Setna Story); 112–15; 145–8; and the relevant plates in vol. 2.)

Tait, W. J., 'P. Carlsberg 207: two columns of a Setna text', in P. J. Frandsen (ed.), *The Carlsberg Papyri I: Demotic texts from the collection* (Carsten Niebuhr Institute Publications 15), Copenhagen: Museum Tusculanum Press, 1991, 19–46.

Inaros (Petubastis) texts

Bresciani, E., *Der Kampf um den Panzer des Inaros* (*Papyrus Krall*), (Mitteilungen aus der Papyrussammlung der Österreichischen Nationalbibliothek (Papyrus Erzherzog Rainer) n.s. 8), Vienna: Prachner, 1964.

Bresciani, E., 'La corazza di Inaro era fatta con la pelle del grifone del Mar Rosso', *EVO* 13 (1990), 103–7.

Kitchen, K. A., *The Third Intermediate Period in Egypt*, Warminster: Aris & Phillips, 1973 (2nd edn, with supplement, 1986). (See 455–61, 'Notes on the background of the story-cycle of Petubastis'. The inclusion of the text 'Naneferkasokar and the Babylonians' in the cycle has proved to be mistaken; the reading of the name 'Petubastis' is not compelling in P. Berlin dem.13640 (the edition by Spiegelberg was in *Studies Presented to F. L. Griffith*, London: EES, 1932, 171–80 – not *Festgabe Büdinger*), and more of the same text has now come to light: see K-Th. Zauzich, 'Einleitung', in P. J. Frandsen (ed.), *The Carlsberg Papyri I: Demotic texts from the collection* (Carsten Niebuhr Institute Publications 15), Copenhagen: Museum Tusculanum Press, 1991, 1–11)

Ray, J. D., 'Two inscribed objects in the Fitzwilliam Museum, Cambridge', *JEA* 58 (1972), 247–53. (The first part of the article deals with a limestone tablet, inscribed in the Ptolemaic period with (among other matter) what may be a quotation from an Inaros text – thus perhaps providing evidence for the existence of these texts before the Roman period.)

Schwartz, J., 'Le "cycle de Petubastis" et les commentaires égyptiens de l'Exode', *BIFAO* 49 (1950), 67–83.

Spiegelberg, W., *Der Sagenkreis des Königs Petubastis, nach dem Strassburger demotischen Papyrus sowie den Wiener und Pariser Bruchstücken*, Leipzig: Hinrichs, 1910.

Tait, W. J., *Papyri from Tebtunis in Egyptian and in Greek* (Texts from Excavations 3), London: Egypt Exploration Society, 1977 (texts 1–4).

Volten, A., 'Der demotische Petubastisroman und seine Beziehung zur griechischen Literatur', *Akten des VIII Internationalen Kongresses für Papyrologie* (Mitteilungen aus der Papyrussammlung der Österreichischen Nationalbibliothek n.s. 5), Vienna, 1955, 147–52.

Volten, A., *Ägypter und Amazonen: eine demotische Erzählung des Inaros-Petubastis-Kreises aus zwei Papyri der Österreichischen Nationalbibliothek* (*Pap. Dem. Vindob. 6165 und 6165A*) (Mitteilungen aus der Papyrussammlung der Österreichischen Nationalbibliothek (Papyrus Erzherzog Rainer) n.s. 6), Vienna: Prachner, 1962.

'Onchsheshonqy

Glanville, S. R. K., *The Instructions of 'Onchsheshonqy (British Museum Papyrus 10508)* (Catalogue of the Demotic Papyri in the British Museum 2), London: British Museum, 1955.

Lichtheim, M., *Late Egyptian Wisdom Literature in the International Context: A Study of Demotic Instructions* (Orbis biblicus et orientalis 52), Göttingen: Vandenhoeck & Ruprecht, 1983.

Smith, H. S., 'The story of 'Onchsheshonqy', *Sarapis* 6 (1980), 133–57 (deals chiefly with the narrative introduction).

Thissen, H-J., *Die Lehre des Anchscheschonqi (P. BM 10508): Einleitung, Übersetzung, Indices*, Bonn: Habelt, 1984.

Bocchoris and the Lamb

Zauzich, K-Th., 'Der Schreiber der Weissagung des Lammes', *Enchoria* 6 (1976), 127–8.

Zauzich, K-Th., 'Das Lamm des Bokchoris', *Festschrift zum 100-jährigen Bestehen der Papyrussammlung der Österreichischen Nationalbibliothek: Papyrus Erzherzog Rainer (P. Rainer Cent.)*, Vienna: Hollinek, 1983, 165–74.

Text concerned with the funerary rites of Psammetichus I

Erichsen, W., *Eine neue demotische Erzählung*, Wiesbaden: Steiner, 1956.

Smith, M. J., 'Did Psammetichus I die abroad?', *Orientalia lovanensia periodica* 22 (1991), 101–9.

The Myth of the Sun's Eye

Bresciani, E., 'L'Amore per il paese nativo nel mito egiziano dell'Occhio del Sole in demotico', *CRIPEL* 13 (1991) (Mélanges Jacques Jean Clère), 35–8.

De Cenival, F., 'Les nouveaux fragments du mythe de l'œil du soleil de l'Institut de Papyrologie et de l'Egyptologie de Lille', *CRIPEL* 7 (1985), 95–115. (Other articles devoted to this new material have appeared, chiefly in *CRIPEL*).

De Cenival, F., *Le Mythe de l'œil du soleil: translittération et traduction avec commentaire philologique* (Demotische Studien 9), Sommerhausen: Gisela Zauzich, 1988.

Smith, M. J., 'Sonnenauge, Demotischer Mythos vom', *Lexikon der Ägyptologie*, vol. 5, 1082–7 (in English).

Spiegelberg, W., *Der ägyptische Mythus vom Sonnenauge in einem demotischen Papyrus der römischen Kaiserzeit*, Sitzungsberichte der königlichen Preussischen Akademie der Wissenschaften, 1915, 876–94. (Comment.)

Spiegelberg, W., *Der ägyptische Mythus von Sonnenauge (der Papyrus der Tierfabeln – "Kufi"), nach dem Leidener Demotischen Papyrus I 384*, Strasburg: Schultz, 1917. (Text edition.)

Tait, W. J., 'A duplicate version of the Demotic *Kufi* text', *Acta Orientalia* [Copenhagen] 36 (1974), 23–37.

Tait, W. J., 'The fable of Sight and Hearing in the Demotic *Kufi* text', *Acta Orientalia* [Copenhagen] 37 (1976), 27–44.

Varia

Zauzich, K-Th., 'Demotische Fragmente zum Ahikar-Roman', *Folia rara W. Voigt . . . dedicata*; ed. H. Franke, W. Heissig and W. Treue, Wiesbaden: Harassowitz, 1976, 180–5.

Zauzich, K-Th., 'Der Streit zwischen Horus und Seth in einer demotischen Fassung (Pap.BerlinP15549 + 15551 + 23727)', *Grammata demotika: Festschrift für Erich Lüddeckens zum 15 Juni 1983*, Würzburg: Gisela Zauzich, 1984, 275–81.

Material in Greek

Frazer, P. M., *Ptolemaic Alexandria*, 3 vols, Oxford: Oxford University Press, 1972 (see esp. vol. 1, 675–87).

Haslam, M. W., 'Narrative about Tinouphis in Prosimetrum', *Papyri Greek and Egyptian Edited by Various Hands in Honour of Eric Gardiner Turner* (Graeco-Roman Memoirs 68), London: EES, 1981, 35–45.

Koenen, L., '[theoisin ekhthros]: Ein einheimischer Gegenkönig in Ägypten', *Cd'E* 34 (1959), 103–19.

Koenen, L., 'Die Prophezeiung des "Töpfers" ', *ZPE* 2 (1968), 178–209.

Koenen, L., 'The prophecies of a potter: a prophecy of world renewal becomes an apocalypse', *Proceedings of the XIIth International Congress of Papyrology* (ASP 7), Toronto: Hackert, 1970, 249–54.

Koenen, L., 'A supplementary note on the date of the Oracle of the Potter', *ZPE* 54 (1984), 9–13.

Koenen, L., 'The dream of Nektanebos' *BASP* 22 (1985), 171–94.

Lloyd, A. B., *Herodotus, Book II: Introduction (Commentary 1–98, 99–182)*, 3 vols, Leiden, Brill, 1975–88 (see esp. *Introduction*, Ch. 3, 'Sources', 77–140).

Lloyd, A. B., 'Nationalist propaganda in Ptolemaic Egypt', *Historia* 31 (1982), 50–4.

Posener, G., 'On the tale of the Doomed Prince', *JEA* 39 (1953), 107 (with reference to Diodorus i, 89).

West, S., 'The Greek version of the Legend of Tefnut', *JEA* 55 (1969), 161–83.

Coptic

Baumeister, T., *Martyr invictus: der Martyrer als Sinnbild der Erlösung in der Legende und im Kult der frühen koptischen Kirche: zur Kontinuität des ägyptischen Denkens* (Forschungen zur Volkskunde 46), Münster: Regensberg, 1972.

Bell, D. N., *Besa, the Life of Shenoute: Introduction Translation and Notes*, Kalamazoo: *Cistercian Publications*, MI 1983.

Jansen, H. L., *The Coptic Story of Cambyses' Invasion of Egypt*, Avhandlinger utgitt av Det Norske Videnskaps–Akademi i Oslo 2, Historisk–Filosofisk Klasse, 1950, no. 2.

Mueller, D., 'Romances', in A. S. Atiya (ed.), *The Coptic Encyclopedia*, vol. 7, New York: Macmillan, 1991, 2059–61.

Orlandi, T., 'Literature, Coptic', in A. S. Atiya (ed.), *The Coptic Encyclopedia*, vol. 5, New York: Macmillan, 1991, 1450–60.

Perez, G. A., 'Apocryphal literature', in A. S. Atiya (ed.), *The Coptic Encyclopedia*, vol. 1, New York: Macmillan, 1991, 161–9.

13

THE JEWISH NOVELLAS

Lawrence M. Wills

In addition to the 'canon' of five Greek and two Latin novels, there are also a number of indigenous novelistic works produced throughout the Graeco-Roman period which flesh out our knowledge of the background of the genre. They have attracted a great deal of scholarly interest, both in their own right, and also because they sometimes predate the larger novels, thereby granting us insights into how the genre might have developed. Among these indigenous writings one finds a large number of Jewish novellas. Although they do not reflect the length of the *Alexander Romance*, nor the typically Greek love theme of the *Ninus Romance*, they span the earliest centuries of the explosion of novelistic development, and exhibit some of the important elements of the genre: entertaining plots, an increasing number of women characters, internalizing psychological focus, interest in domestic settings and values (such as the containment of sexuality) and the manipulation of emotion. Further, because we possess a large number of variant recensions of some of these novellas, which can often be placed in a chronological order, the typical development of novelistic themes and techniques can be studied in detail.

Jewish novelistic literature can be divided into three groups:

1 *National hero novellas*, rousing adventure stories which champion the exploits of the ancient heroes of the Jews. The best preserved examples are by Artapanus, who wrote in Egypt in about 200 BCE. Sections of his works on Abraham, Joseph and Moses have been preserved, the last of which has been likened to the *Ninus* and *Alexander* romances.[1] Artapanus glorifies his subjects from Biblical history in unexpected ways, as when he states that Moses was not only a teacher of Orpheus and

benefactor of humanity, but also a general in the Egyptian army who initiated the animal cults in Egypt.

2 *Novellas*, which treat figures who were unimportant (and sometimes even unknown) to Jewish history, such as Esther, Daniel, Tobit or Judith, in the books by those names, or Aseneth, Joseph's wife, in *Joseph and Aseneth*. Presenting a semblance of historical verisimilitude to create atmosphere, they nevertheless contain incorrect and patently unbelievable historical figures: 'Darius the Mede' in Daniel, 'Nebuchadnezzar, king of the Assyrians' in Judith, and Esther as the Queen of Persia. It is, to be sure, difficult to be certain how these texts were understood, but it is likely that they were read as fictions, and even in some cases as satires or farces.

3 *Historical novellas*, which treat historical figures from the recent past in a way that, however implausible to us, was probably received as factually true, such as Third Maccabees, and the *Tobiad Romance* and *Royal Family of Adiabene* contained in Josephus' *Antiquities* (12.4.1–11 §§ 154–236 and 20.2.1.–4.3 §§ 17–96 respectively).

The number and variety of Jewish novelistic works provide a rich source of information on the broad spectrum of popular literature, but the subcategory that is the most interesting for a comparison with Greek and Roman novels are the five novellas proper of category (2). Whereas both the non-Jewish and Jewish indigenous works capture a sense of ethnic pride and competitiveness, such as we might expect among the once proud but now subjugated nationalities of the Hellenistic world, the Jewish novellas go further, reflecting in some ways a significant refinement of technique. The sense of a threat is increased, the point of conflict is sharpened and the scope of the action is limited and turned inward upon one or two protagonists who bear the burden of their extended family, and by extension, of Jews in general.

Although the Jewish novellas share some traits with much older Biblical narratives (especially the Joseph story of Genesis 37–50), there is a significant break in the continuity between the two epochs. The production and editing of prose narrative is more or less continuous in Israel from about 1000 to 400 BCE, but at the end of that period there occurs a hiatus. From 400 to 200 BCE there is a 'Dark Age' of Hebrew prose narrative, where we find at best only fragments (preserved, in fact, only in later collections).

When this Dark Age of prose narrative ends in the second century BCE, the new literary productions are often in the form of novellas, which reflect the vastly different situation of Jewish social life. Alexander the Great's conquest of the ancient world, which at first made only superficial inroads into Jewish society at large, by the second century BCE had wrought significant changes throughout the sizeable Diaspora population. A large entrepreneurial and administrative class arose, which had been trained in Jewish schools to be able to read and write. It is only natural that developments in literature would reflect these changes. The Jewish novellas may result from a process similar to that which produced Greek novels. Several scholars have suggested that the canonization of Greek culture and tradition in the fifth century, the establishment of a body of sacred tradition certified to be 'true', gave rise to an opposite impulse as well, the experimentation with that which is by common consent held to be 'false', that is fiction, and this process eventually led to the development of the novel: Herodotus' love of variant versions of stories, for example, or Xenophon's embellishment of the life of Cyrus in his *Cyropaedia* (Nagy 1990: 52–67; Reardon 1991: 59–69; Flory 1987: 49–79). Jews had also canonized their own tradition in the fifth century, and though there is a quiescence that follows, it is broken by the play of fiction. Stories based on Biblical and Persian narrative models, probably originally oral, are gathered, extended and refined, addressing the needs of a new class of at least partly literate, urban, entrepreneurial Jews. Although these novellas are not derived forms of the Greek or Roman novel, nor of the indigenous romances such as *Ninus* (since they predate both groups), they are nevertheless related by the common aesthetic developments of the late Hellenistic period.

The Jewish novellas are structurally quite different from each other, but this is mainly because they have evolved from very different source narratives. It is, in fact, the *changes* that are introduced into the sources that reveal most clearly the common direction and ethos of the Jewish novellas. The Jewish novellas constitute perhaps our best laboratory for discerning the process by which indigenous narratives of various kinds were transformed into popular literature, as can be seen from a brief survey of them.

We may begin with Daniel, since it has the clearest developmental history, and at one stage can be precisely dated. The Book of Daniel as it appears in the Hebrew Bible can be easily divided into the court narratives of Chapters 1–6, narrated in the third person, which portray the adventures of the wise courtier Daniel and his three friends in the courts of the great ancient Near Eastern monarchs, and the apocalyptic visions of Chapters 7–12, recounted in the first person. The two halves were probably not written by the same author. The second half, the apocalyptic visions, refer to events of the Maccabean Revolt of 167–164 BCE; the persecution of the pious Jews and the resulting sectarian consciousness is much in evidence. This is not the case, however, in the stories of Daniel 1–6. Here, the separate episodes depict threats and conflicts of life at court, but in each case end happily, usually with a repentant king. Thus Daniel 7–12 provides us with a firm dating for the visions, 167–164 BCE, while the narratives of Daniel 1–6 give every indication of having been composed before the Maccabean Revolt, in about the third or early second century BCE.

There is very little that is novelistic about the visions; it is the court narratives of Chapters 1–6 which attract our attention. These six adventurous stories present a threat to the Jewish heroes serving in the royal courts of Babylon, Media and Persia. The steadfastness of the heroes is their salvation; in each case the cloud of danger passes over as they are miraculously saved by God. These legends all focus on the king's court as the stage of the dramatic action, and the courtier as the protagonist who must negotiate this unforgiving terrain. They are examples of the court legend, a common genre of narrative art in the ancient world, attested not only among Jews, but among other cultures as well.[2] The splendid international *Story of Ahikar* and the Egyptian *Onkhsheshonq* also make use of this plot structure. It is a charming and lively genre, which, under the right conditions, might naturally lead to novelistic embellishments (as in the case of the later versions of *Ahikar*). This sort of development was only partially accomplished in Daniel 1–6, however. The collection of the legends into one longer work satisfies a certain need for extension of the adventure element in the written medium, but the stories remain essentially as they were: short, separate, originally oral narratives of court adventures. As interesting as the process of collection is – the creation of a new written corpus from independently circulating legends – it is still 'primitive' in terms of novelistic development. Such collections of 'saints' legends' are not uncommon in the history of literature, even in the ancient world.[3]

Still, the collection reveals some novelistic tendencies, a sort of experimentation with the possibilities of what the written medium might provide to a new class of more literate Jews. Daniel 1 may very well have been written as an introduction to the corpus, and reflect a more novelistic approach than the remainder. Here we are introduced to Daniel and the three companions and are told how they came to be in the court of Nebuchadnezzar. This chapter reflects a narrowing of the dramatic focus to everyday concerns. The other chapters contain life-or-death issues of prophecy, confession and the threat of martyrdom, while Daniel 1 focuses on how to remain kosher. Other chapters also received novelistic touches. Chapter 2 includes a private prayer of Daniel and his three companions, analogous to the prayers and dramatic monologues in the Greek novels, and an attempt is made to weave separate chapters together by reviewing in Chapter 5 the events of Chapter 4.

Such innovations as these, however, only touch the surface of this collection; other changes in the Daniel tradition were more radical. The apocalyptic visions of Daniel 7–12, added (as noted above) during the Maccabean Revolt, temporarily shift the tone of the resultant document in an entirely new direction, a direction that is not novelistic. But some time later, probably long after the rebellion was over, other stories were added which once again push Daniel along a trajectory that would lead to the novella: Susanna was added at the beginning of the corpus and Bel and the Dragon at the end (or so it appears from the varying evidence of the Greek versions). Individually, these narratives are similar to the legends in Daniel 1–6. Bel and the Dragon is a court narrative, a humorous, even satirical treatment of idolatry. Here Daniel uncovers fraud in the great temple of Bel, and in a separate episode, cleverly kills the dragon (or snake) which many worship. For his temerity he is thrown into the lions' den, much as in Daniel 6, but again escapes unharmed. The humour of the story, as well as its irony ('Surely', says the king at one point, pointing to the dragon, '*this* is a living god!') greatly extend its entertaining function.

Susanna is more of a novelistic innovation in the Daniel tradition. In this story, a beautiful young woman, the wife of a leading Jewish citizen, is being secretly watched by two elders. When they discover their shared obsession, they concoct a means to force her to have sex with them. They run in upon her as she is bathing, and demand that she accede to their wishes, or else they will accuse her of lying with a young man. Although caught in a horrible dilemma, she nevertheless decides that she must abide in God's law and not agree to their wicked plan. They do accuse her, but she is ultimately acquitted through the intercession of Daniel, and the elders are executed. The same structural pattern is present as in Daniel 3 and 6 and in Bel and the Dragon: the innocent righteous person is persecuted and nearly executed, but is ultimately vindicated, as the guilty parties are led to their death. In this case, however, the setting is not the highest court in the land, but the local, self-governing Jewish court, and the innocent person is not a courtier, but a pious and vulnerable *mater familias*. Erotic themes are also introduced, as when the wicked elders observe her bathing, or when the courtroom audience see her veil removed. In one version she is actually stripped during the trial as a ritual scourging of the adulteress. In Susanna, then, some of the main themes of novelistic literature are introduced, and although the new corpus of Greek Daniel remains a mixed grouping of narratives and visions, it has been brought much more into the orbit of novelistic literature (Steussy 1993).

While Daniel is the clearest of the novellas in terms of its process of development, the others still reveal some growth and evolution. Esther, for instance, a court narrative like Daniel 1–6, Susanna, and Bel and the Dragon, may have evolved from a somewhat simpler version of the story, which depicted Mordecai and Esther with somewhat different emphases (Clines 1984; Fox 1991a: 254–73 and 1991b; Wills 1990: 153–91). In the present version in the Hebrew Bible, the figure of the courtier Mordecai has been upstaged by his cousin and adopted daughter, Esther. The focus on the female protagonist is significant for a consideration of the development of the novella. The setting for the drama has shifted, in comparison with the court narratives, from the king's male-dominated court to the full run of the palace, and, not least, into the harem. The 'harem intrigue' element has a background in Persian literature,[4] but as it moves into its new context in Jewish novellas, the queen is no longer simply a foil for the protagonist, she *is* the protagonist.

The structure of Esther is more complex than at first appears, and for all its bombastic revenge theme, it is also a literary gem. An enjoyment of the story requires an arch view of the 'seriousness' of the situation, in keeping with the traditional Jewish interpretation of it as the reading for an uproarious and inebriated Purim celebration. The core of the book is a double-stranded plot concerning

Esther on one hand and Mordecai on the other. The villain Haman, furious at Mordecai's insubordination, has concocted two plans of revenge for his nemesis: he has set a date for an empire-wide pogrom against Mordecai's people, the Jews of Persia, and he has also arranged to execute Mordecai on a gallows. The tension created by Haman's dual threat finds an effective denouement in separate scenes, focusing on Mordecai and Esther respectively. In the first, Mordecai's prior loyalty to the king is recounted in the court at precisely the right time, causing Mordecai to be publicly honoured, and thus saved from Haman's clutches. In the second, Esther lays plans to expose Haman's plot against all the Jews of Persia. The two threats in the plot thus find their reversal in a chiastic pattern: threat to Jews/threat to Mordecai/rescue of Mordecai/rescue of Jews. At the centre of this chiasm, Chapter 4, the two strands intersect in a way that signals a growth in the characters and in their relationships. Mordecai begins the scene by upbraiding a complacent, even petulant Esther, who prefers to cover over all threat to her people, but the complicated interchange between them, intentionally retarded by the introduction of an intermediary who bears their messages back and forth, finally brings about a change in her, as she rises to meet her responsibilities. She decides to risk her life before the king, and organizes all the Jews of Persia by reversing her filial role and giving orders to Mordecai (Berg 1979; Fox 1991a and 1991b; Loader 1978). This more serious scene of encounter and personal growth can be contrasted to the broad farce in the final resolution of Haman's threat. At her banquet for Haman, Esther declares to the king that there is a plot afoot against her people, and unmasks Haman as the perpetrator. The king, who has imbibed at many a good banquet in this book while being heedless of important state developments, now rises in anger and steps into his garden. Haman throws himself on Esther's couch and begs for mercy, but the king, reentering the room, sees him and bellows, 'What? Will Haman attack my wife within my own quarters?' Only now, through this absurd gesture, is the threat ultimately removed.

Although this level of humour and satire, focusing on a female protagonist, can be considered novelistic, it is the additions to Esther found in the Greek version which especially push it in the direction of novella. First, at the beginning of the book is added the dream of Mordecai, which intimates in symbolic fashion everything that is about to occur. Second, the contents of Haman's decree to destroy the Jews, lacking in Hebrew Esther, are recounted, as are the contents of the king's later decree rescinding the order. They are both composed in a very ornate, rhetorical Greek prose, far more elevated than any other passage in the Greek Bible. Third, after Esther's central interchange with Mordecai, she retires to her room to utter a heartfelt prayer to God. Taking off her beautiful royal gown, she puts on garments of mourning and covers her head with ashes and dung, ritually debasing the parts of her body that were normally considered beautiful.

Mordecai's dream is similar to the portents and dreams found in Greek novels, which create a dramatic sense of expectation for the reader. The second set of additions, the two florid rhetorical decrees, may at first appear to be an attempt to lend historical authenticity to the book by giving the exact words of the king, but a literary effect is more likely intended. They serve to set the scene and tone of a palace pronouncement, at the same time that they place the novella as a whole in a world of elegance and literary attainments, a pretension that runs throughout the Greek novels. The first decree, which Haman has placed in the mouth of the king, presents typical anti-Jewish arguments common among Greek-speaking intellectuals in Alexandria, in such a way as to make them sound plausible. These arguments will of course be triumphantly exploded in the second decree, or at least swept away by the goodness of Mordecai, but one senses that the use of such elegant Greek, combined with so exquisite a sense of the opposing arguments, reflects the ambivalence of educated Jews in the greatest Greek city outside of Athens. These two decrees prove that Jewish novellas could enter the orbit of some of the Greek literary conventions; the indigenous style has (in these additions, at any rate) been brought into the intellectual mainstream.

The third addition mentioned above, Esther's ritual debasement of her sexuality, alien as it may seem to us, is paralleled in every one of the Jewish novellas except for Tobit. Whether enacted by the heroine, as in Esther, or imposed upon her, as in Susanna, this motif has evidently become a fixture in the Jewish novella, usually tied to a strongly emotional experience of penance and renewal. Erotic tensions are played out which are a reverse image of the Greek novel: female sexuality is piously repudiated, not channelled (along with male sexuality) through a chaste adolescence into wedlock. It is also in the context of this scene that we find an odd specimen of the bewitching power of love so common in Greek novels. Esther, who has just declared in her prayer her loathing of the king's bed, in the next scene beautifies herself in the finest apparel in order to approach him on behalf of the Jews. Upon seeing him, however, she swoons and faints. The king's heart is immediately melted, not by Eros, but by God, and the king moves quickly to pick her up (15: 7–10). This is not a typical love-match, but the relation of the king and Esther is *stylistically* developed as it would be in romance. The author inflates the emotional intensity of what is at least a *potential* love scene in a way typical of the Greek novel.

The Book of Tobit tells the intertwined stories of Tobit and his kinswoman Sarah, who are each suffering, apparently at the hands of an unjust God. He, though a pious man who has buried the bodies of dead Jews, has been 'rewarded' by God with blindness, and now begs God to deliver him by taking his life. She, in a far away city, also prays to God for release by death, because she has been betrothed seven times, only to see each husband killed by the evil demon Asmodaeus before the wedding can be consummated. It is only a temporary illusion that God has forsaken them, however, as the angel Raphael is sent to restore both of them to happiness at the same time. Posing as a kinsman, Raphael guides Tobit's son Tobias to Sarah's house, where the young man and woman are betrothed. Raphael gives Tobias incense which wards off Asmodaeus, allowing their marriage to be consummated. They then return to Tobit with an ointment Raphael has given them to cure Tobit's blindness.

Whereas the books of Daniel and Esther both derive from developments of the court narrative, Tobit evidences a totally different background. With slight modifications, one can detect the plot structure of the common folk-tale 'The Grateful Dead Man', in which a traveller comes upon the corpse of a man killed by robbers and buries him. Later on in his travels he is befriended by a stranger – the spirit of the dead man – who guides him to the site of a woman whose bridal chamber is cursed. The stranger aids him in marrying the woman and ridding her of the demon. The parallels to Tobit are obvious, but the main actions of the folk-tale's protagonist (burying and marrying) are split between Tobit and his son, and the spirit of the dead man is now found in the figure of Raphael. Many other folk-tale motifs are found in this novella as well, for example, magical ointments from animal parts and the binding of the demon. Still, although this novella is clearly much closer to traditional oral narrative in its structure and motifs than are the other novellas, it is not simply an oral folk-tale committed to writing. The first two-and-a-half chapters, written in the first person, may have been altered or expanded; there is a section of proverbs (Chapter 4) woven into the narrative; and the ending (Chapters 13 and 14) may have been extended as well. The length of the whole certainly comports with the other novellas, as does its emphasis on the extended family and its use of irony and humour. Thus, although it may have arisen from oral traditions, it has been adapted somewhat to its new function as a written novella.

The Book of Judith is one of the longer of the Jewish novellas, yet it is famous for only one scene, Judith's decapitation of the enemy general Holofernes. The rest of the work provides the background for this climactic moment. Nebuchadnezzar, here incorrectly called 'king of the Assyrians', has sent his general Holofernes on a punitive expedition against all of the countries to his west. The battle plans, movements of vast numbers of troops and swift victories of Holofernes occupy the first half of the novella. Judith, a widow in the village of Bethulia, is only introduced in Chapter 8, where she comes forward, first, to reprimand the citizens for their weak will, and second, to initiate a secret plan to undo Holofernes. She puts off her widow's garments, adorns herself in her finest clothes and sets out to the enemy general's camp. She joins the general in his tent and after waiting for him to drink himself into a stupor, chops off his head with his own sword. The first impression upon reading the work is that it is composed of two halves placed side-by-side, much like Daniel. The first half, which does not mention Judith, is a long-winded account of the growing threat of the military campaigns of Nebuchadnezzar's general, Holofernes. The second is the response of the pious Jewish widow, Judith, in insinuating herself into the enemy general's tent and unceremoniously beheading him as he is lying unconscious. In one part, the scope covers the entire ancient Near East; in the other, the dramatic setting is quite limited, covering only the mountain village of Bethulia and the enemy's camp. Yet the two halves are very carefully constructed in a set of parallel, ironic contrasts, which make it clear that the author has quite consciously arranged the narrative in parallel halves (Craven 1983; Alonso-Schökel 1975).

The name Judith means 'Jewess', and her steadfast courage

creates in the work a minor morality play: in the face of an overwhelming threat to the Jewish people, faith in God will triumph. Most would agree that Judith's actions are motivated by the extreme threat, but there has been a consistent reaction in the Christian West since about 1600 *against* Judith, based on her deceit and her violent methods, presumably actions unbecoming a lady. A new age will probably cast off such judgements, and see the story not just as a pious story of the deliverance of Israel, but also as an entertainment about cleverness and the reversal of sexual roles (Jacobus 1986; Stone 1992; Levine 1992).

The Jewish novella that is most similar to Greek novels is *Joseph and Aseneth*, written most likely in the first century CE.[5] *Joseph and Aseneth* spins a tale of considerable length, which enlarges on a single line of scripture (Genesis 41: 45): 'And Pharaoh called Joseph's name Zaphenathpaneah; and he gave him in marriage Aseneth, the daughter of Potiphera priest of On.' It recounts in melodramatic fashion the courtship, marriage and family battles of the Biblical Joseph in Egypt, enlarging the section of the narrative after he had been placed in charge of the collection of food during the seven years of plenty. It begins with his meeting of his future bride, Aseneth. She is a wealthy and haughty Egyptian woman who will look at no man, preferring to reside apart in her private rooms, filled with luxuries and Egyptian idols. Once she has laid eyes on Joseph, however, she is stricken, first with love, then with remorse at ever having spoken unkind words about him. Her father arranges a marriage between them, but Joseph tells her that she must first put away her idols and convert to the one true God. While he leaves once again to oversee the gathering of grain, she undergoes a week-long process of scourging and repentance. The tone of this romance shifts, from the love story of a petulant teenager, to the ordeal of penance of a convert to Judaism. Aseneth repudiates her idols, her riches and her beautiful clothes, and puts on sackcloth and ashes. She weeps and lies on the floor, spent, for a week, and when this period of catharsis is done, she is visited in her room by a 'man from heaven', who participates with her in several mysterious rituals, including eating of a honeycomb. This interlude is dominated by a number of unexplained, and nearly inexplicable symbols, from special garments to multicoloured bees. Despite obvious implications for Jewish mysticism and conversion rituals, there is little scholarly consensus about the actual practices that might be reflected here (Collins 1983: 211–18;

Burchard 1985: 177–200). It is sufficient for us to note that it may reflect the introduction of allegorical levels of meaning into a fairly typical romance storyline, for when this conversion scene is over, Aseneth returns to a nubile state, is married to Joseph, and the romance intrigue resumes. Pharaoh's son, who has pined for Aseneth since the opening chapter, now enlists some of Joseph's brothers in a plot to kill him. Joseph's other brothers come to his aid, saving him and Aseneth. The novella thus ends in a way that is typical of novelistic entertainments, without any hint of mystical allegory.

These five novellas, then, constitute ample evidence of a proliferation of popular Jewish writings which exercised an appeal to Jewish consciousness different from that which was available before. They create a fanciful atmosphere in which historical figures can be recast at will, Jews can become the most powerful officials in the land and the tyrant Nebuchadnezzar is capable of repentance – or of being vanquished. The Jewish novellas, along with all of the other indigenous writings, must be placed in a carefully articulated comparative framework with the Greek and Roman novels. The latter share in all of the new themes that arise in the art and literature of the Graeco-Roman period: eroticism, a baroque aesthetic, domestic values, manipulation of emotion, fascination with the grotesque and unusual (Fowler 1989). Only some of these elements are present in Jewish novellas, however, and in ways often markedly different from their Greek and Roman counterparts. Eroticism, for example, is manifested in almost all of the novelistic writings from antiquity, but Jewish novellas refuse to engage an erotic interest as a positive end in itself. Instead, erotic possibilities are suppressed. The Book of Tobit is very circumspect in describing the wedding night of Tobias and Sarah, preferring to see in it only the establishment of a proper marriage. Judith is portrayed at the same time as a stunningly beautiful woman and also as a proper widow, in continual mourning. Her exaggerated denial of her sexuality (in fact, an imposed celibacy) is contrasted with her provocative seduction of Holofernes, a liminal period in which she flouts accepted restraints to save her people. It should be noted that the author in no way condemns this, nor her obvious lies, as later generations have. Greek Esther sublimates the erotic into a romantic delicacy of sensibilities, as Esther swoons and faints when she beholds the king's power. Susanna places an ambivalent experience before the reader: the lust of the elders as they observe Susanna bathing, and the vulnerability of the female innocent as she prays to God. *Joseph and Aseneth* treats the erotic interest on two levels. It is sublimated into a powerful experience of the 'love-sickness' typical of Greek novels, but the union of the protagonists is described in terms of mystical secrets.

Ultimately, the similarity of Jewish novellas to Greek novels is not proven by the presence of certain themes, such as eroticism or the importance of domestic virtues; it is indicated more by an aspect that is both theme and technique: the manipulation of emotions. Much of the Greek art and literature that remains from the classical period was oriented toward the civic identity and values of the audience, and it has been argued that when this civic identity broke down, with its attendant concern with the extended family ties, the emotions and experiences of the individual – and the love-match of the conjugal couple – were explored more fully. The two motive forces of the Greek novel are love, which draws the two protagonists together, and travel and adventures, which pull them apart. They can be felt almost as palpably as the forces of magnets held a fraction of an inch apart. Identity on a personal level, in this brave new world of individualism, is thus provided in the form of the value of conjugal marriage that is freed from traditional ties. Jewish novellas seem to be betwixt-and-between the older social order of the tribe and temple-state, and the individualism of the new city. Jews in the Greek diaspora found themselves experiencing fully the Greek world (they were, for instance, not confined to a ghetto, but often integrated into civic life), but they evidently still valued the *extended* family ties. Each of the novellas places the extended family relationship centrally in the narrative. Although Tobit is concerned with the uniting in marriage of Tobias and Sarah, it is really the binding in marriage of two wings of the extended family (every character in Tobit, except for the Assyrian kings and the evil demon Asmodeus, is related to Tobit, even the angel Raphael!); Esther is strongly influenced by the arguments of her cousin and adoptive father, Mordecai; Susanna is shamed before her extended family and servants of the household; Judith is devoted to her dead husband's family. The conjugal love-match is only a positive value in the last and most 'Greek' of the novellas, *Joseph and Aseneth*, but even here, Aseneth struggles to become reconciled to her husband's father and brothers.

Thus it becomes clear why the two most noteworthy

characteristics of the Greek novel, love and travel, are lacking in Jewish novellas. The motive forces experienced by the audience are quite different: not conjugal love, threatened by separation, but the extended family ties of Judaism, threatened by evil, especially evil which is directed against the corporate body of Jews. Granting, then, that this is the difference, what is the similarity? If love and travel constituted the essential elements of the Greek novel, the similarities would of course be insignificant. But love and travel are not the constitutive elements of the Greek novel, as important as they often (but not always) are to its very fabric. The constitutive element is the exploration and manipulation of emotion, an element shared in grand proportions by the Jewish novellas. All of the ancient novelistic literature partakes of this, and yet each subcategory will find different vehicles for it. It is the particular attraction of the Jewish novellas that they constitute, relatively speaking, such a large body of novelistic literature, and that they can be more precisely dated and located in a social and historical context than can many of the others. We can also find in their pages a marvellously intimate portrait of the values and wish-fulfilments of wealthier Jews in the Graeco-Roman period.

NOTES

1 Braun 1938. He also compares the style of Artapanus to the *Testament of Joseph*, one of the *Testaments of the Twelve Patriarchs*, and to Josephus' treatment of Joseph and Potiphar's wife in *Antiquities* (2.4.1–5 §§ 39–59). Braun's is the only book-length treatment of the Jewish novelistic literature to appear to date; see, however, Wills (forthcoming), and note the important remarks of Pervo 1987, Hengel 1974: 1.30, 110–12, and Smith 1987: 121–4.

2 It was a genre evidently very popular among Persians and in Persian-controlled lands, on which see Wills 1990: 39–74.

3 Cf. the much older cycle of Elijah and Elisha legends in 1 Kings 17–2 Kings 10.

4 Cf. Ctesias' *Persika*, on which see Bickerman 1967: 169–240, esp. 182–4.

5 One of the strongest arguments to date for treating one of the Jewish novellas as a novel is that of West 1974; cf. more recently Pervo 1991.

BIBLIOGRAPHY

Alonso-Schökel, Luis (1975), *Narrative Structures in the Book of Judith*, Berkeley: Center for Hermeneutical Studies in Hellenistic and Modern Culture.

Berg, Sandra Beth (1979), *The Book of Esther*, Missoula, MT: Scholars.

Bickerman, Elias (1967), *Four Strange Books of the Bible*, New York: Schocken.

Braun, Martin (1938), *History and Romance in Graeco-Oriental Literature*, Oxford: Blackwell.

Burchard, C. (1985), 'Joseph and Aseneth', in James H. Charlesworth (ed.), *The Old Testament Pseudepigrapha*, 2 vols, Garden City: Doubleday.

Clines, David J. A. (1984), *The Esther Scroll*, Sheffield: University of Sheffield Press.

Collins, John J. (1983), *Between Athens and Jerusalem*, New York: Crossroad.

Craven, Toni (1983), *Artistry and Faith in the Book of Judith*, Chico, CA: Scholars.

Flory, Stewart (1987), *The Archaic Smile of Herodotus*, Detroit: Wayne State University Press.

Fowler, Barbara Hughes (1989), *The Hellenistic Aesthetic*, Madison: University of Wisconsin Press.

Fox, Michael V. (1991a), *Character and Ideology in the Book of Esther*, Columbia, SC: University of South Carolina Press.

Fox, Michael V. (1991b), *Redaction in the Books of Esther*, Atlanta: Scholars.

Hengel, Martin (1974), *Judaism and Hellenism*, 2 vols, Philadelphia: Fortress.

Jacobus, Mary (1986), 'Judith, Holofernes, and the phallic woman', in id., *Reading Women: Essays in Feminist Criticism*, New York: Columbia University Press.

Levine, Amy-Jill (1992), 'Sacrifice and salvation: otherness and domestication in the Book of Judith', in James C. Van der Kam (ed.), *'No One Spoke Ill of Her': Essays on Judith*, Atlanta: Scholars.

Loader, J. A. (1978), 'Esther as a novel with different levels of meaning', *Zeitschrift für die alttestamentische Wissenschaft* 90, 417–21.

Nagy, Gregory (1990), *Pindar's Homer*, Baltimore, MD: Johns Hopkins University Press.

Pervo, Richard I. (1987), *Profit With Delight: The Literary Genre of the Acts of the Apostles*, Minneapolis, MN: Fortress.

Pervo, Richard I. (1991), 'Aseneth and her sisters: women in Jewish narrative and in the Greek novels', in Amy-Jill Levine (ed.) *'Women Like This': New Perspectives on Jewish Women in the Greco-Roman World*, Atlanta: Scholars.

Reardon, Bryan (1991), *The Form of Greek Romance*, Princeton: Princeton University Press.

Smith, Morton (1987), *Palestinian Parties and Politics that Shaped the Old Testament*, 2nd edn, London: SCM.

Steussy, Marti J. (1993), *Gardens in Babylon: Narrative and Faith in the Greek Legends of Daniel*, Atlanta: Scholars.

Stone, Nira (1992), 'Judith and Holofernes: some observations on the development of the scene in art', in James C. Van der Kam (ed.), *'No One Spoke Ill of Her': Essays on Judith*, Atlanta: Scholars.

West, S. (1974), '*Joseph and Asenath*: a neglected Greek romance', *Classical Quarterly* 24, 70–81.

Wills, Lawrence M. (1990), *The Jew in the Court of the Foreign King: Ancient Jewish Court Legends*, Minneapolis, MN: Fortress.

Wills, Lawrence M. (forthcoming), *The Poetics of Jewish Novels in the Greco-Roman World*.

14

EARLY CHRISTIAN FICTION

Richard I. Pervo

I NARRATIVE AND FICTION IN ANCIENT CHRISTIANITY

Introduction

Narrative 'fiction' (by which I mean composition rather than concoction), treating Christian subjects and serving religious ends, begins with the formation of stories about Jesus into a coherent narrative plot, continues with the composition of works featuring apostles and issues in stories about holy men and women, a genre that has arguably never died.[1]

Antecedents[2]

Extant models included Jewish and other ('pagan' is an undesirable bin into which to lump all but two or three ancient religions and movements; 'secular' is a category that can only with qualification be applied to antiquity) tales about suffering righteous heroes, lives of great teachers, leaders and sages, and various early representatives of the ancient novel. Scholarly discussions about the possible roles of these antecedents assume roughly the same shape in disputes about the origins of Christian literature as they take in debates about the genesis of the Greek novel. For some critics these questions are fundamental; others regard them as of minimal relevance.

Gospels and Acts

The anonymous author of what is now called 'The Gospel of Mark' apparently produced the first work conforming to the description given above. Its hero, Jesus of Nazareth, embarks upon a career of teaching and wonder-working that excites the authorities to plan his death. When Jesus goes to Jerusalem at the time of a religious festival, tension rises, but his enemies are frustrated until one of his intimates sells him out. Following his trial and execution, women disciples who visit the tomb hear that Jesus has been raised.

The narrator shapes the plot in an ironic fashion: the religio-political establishment wishes Jesus executed for acts of beneficence. They succeed in putting him to death, unaware that by this very act they are conforming to God's plan of redemption. Mark begins and ends abruptly. Matthew and Luke give the story a biographical orientation with stories of Jesus' birth and childhood, then extended it to provide appearances of the risen Christ.

If the canonical gospels have dramatic plots and exciting content of a popular variety, they contain relatively little adventure or melodrama, apart from the Passion story. The third of the evangelists, traditionally called 'Luke', wrote a sequel, now called Acts, focusing upon the travels, deeds and speeches of Christian leaders, especially Paul, the central figure. Acts gives larger scope to adventure than to instruction and has affinities with ancient fiction. Paul covers much of the territory over which the leading figures of Greek novels wander, and his life, too, is marked by intrigue, captivity and narrow escapes from death, including deliverance from shipwreck.

The marcan shape, itself inspired by Jewish stories of the fate of the suffering righteous, predominates in Acts, which gave it a new and enduring vitality. A literary examination of the composition of Gospels and Acts reflects a growing tendency toward the production of coherent, extended narrative. This is quite evident in the work of Luke, whose Gospel constitutes a substantial literary 'improvement' over that of Mark, and whose second volume reflects yet further advances: in place of pithy sayings, distinct anecdotes and brief miracle stories there are set speeches conforming to rhetorical patterns and a wealth of narrative incident.

From the historical perspective the composition of full-scale narrative gospels appears, apart from combinations and abbreviations of the extant works, to have soon subsided. The 'Gospels' of the second and later centuries begin where Mark, so to speak, left off. They are essentially discourses of the glorified, risen Christ. The Gospel of John, with its lengthy addresses (cf. John 13–17), begins to point in this direction. Narrative flourished in the composition of various acts.

II THE MAJOR APOCRYPHAL ACTS

The problem of the category

If the theological term 'canonical' should not be used as a literary or historical category, the adjective 'apocryphal' creates even greater distortions. 'Apocryphal' literally means 'hidden' and thus implies secret books surreptitiously produced by subversive sects. In common parlance 'apocryphal' simply means 'untrue'. The very phrase 'Apocryphal Acts' (hereafter ApocActs) thus suggests a group of works that have failed to pass their exams.

As a widely-held notion would have it: once upon a time there were any number of Gospels and Acts engaged in competition for biblical status, with the role of Paris taken by Christian bishops, who, after suitable scrutiny of the entrants, awarded prizes. This popular belief, that Christian apocrypha simply imitated their canonical antecedents with the goal of inclusion within the Bible, is incorrect. Moreover, having received this disparaging label, the Christian apocrypha found themselves relegated to a collection with all of the typical resultant phenomena: the group becomes an object of distinct and isolated study, with its own handbooks, journals, monographs and clientele. The inclusion of the present chapter within this volume is witness to the contemporary effort to shatter inappropriate barriers and bridge traditional chasms.

If some of the Christian apocrypha do offer alternative pictures to those found in the writings later judged canonical, most of them appear rather to ignore these texts. Nor did they lead a generally shadowy existence. These writings remained a vital source of spiritual nurture and provided artists with so many subjects that they constitute required reading for historians of art. Their concluding sections found a home in the liturgical celebration of the various apostles. Other witnesses to their popularity are the editors who could not or would not repress them but rather adapted their contents to meet changing theological and cultural standards, and those who provided for their translation and adaptation into a number of ancient and medieval languages and cultures.

General observations

There are five major ApocActs dating from the period *c.* 150–250 CE: those of Paul (*APl*), Peter (*APtr*), John (*AJn*), Andrew (*AA*) and Thomas (*AThom*). None survives in original form; all but the *AThom* are incomplete. The last was apparently written in Syriac; all of the others derive from Greek originals. The reconstruction of critical editions and the translation of these into modern languages is an arduous and uncertain task.

It is erroneous to evaluate these works as a corpus, although they were assembled into a body by Manicheans in the fourth century. As in the case of the Greek romances, treatment of the ApocActs as a unit tends to isolate them from other writings and give undue weight to their similarities. The ApocActs are a disparate group, in structure, style and levels of literary accomplishment, as well as in viewpoint.

A superficial survey of these works yields a first impression of monotonous sameness. Credulity seems to rule. The modern reader soon has enough of dreadful demons exposed and banished, speaking animals, raised corpses and long speeches, not to mention temples and marriages left in ruins. To this catalogue Christian readers would add varieties of theological aberration. If Catholic scholars often took offence at the omnipresence of heresy, Protestants possibly more tolerant of such were not likely to swallow the large doses of asceticism and wonder. Talking dogs and balking wives long relegated the ApocActs to the lower shelves of the academic supermarket. Shifts in academic orientation, including changed approaches to early Christianity, interest in social history, interdisciplinary research and feminist studies, have brought renewed interest.

The literary charges against the ApocActs – naive plotting, limited variations upon a small repertory of episodic themes and lack of sophistication – are more or less the same as those traditionally lodged against the Greek romantic novels. These accusations are often overblown, but they do reflect the 'popular' character of the works in question. These writings reflect the interests and beliefs not just of marginal groups but of the more ordinary early Christian believers. Chief among these interests is power, including, of course, the power to remove such misfortunes as hunger, disease and even death with a simple command, as well as the power of women to manage their own lives, and the capacity to resist oppressive officials. Other prominent concerns are the quest for identity, a longing for community and the wish for excitement. If all of these benefits come instantly and often, that means no more than that the ApocActs appeal, so to speak, to the same markets and desires pursued by present-day commercial advertising. The new life proffered by the messengers of this new god comes as quickly and with as far-reaching effects as a certain shampoo, which will not only immediately and permanently banish dandruff but also transform its user into an attractive sexual object. Modern criticism, moreover, projects an excess of positivism upon early readers, who were very probably quite capable of apprehending the symbolic quality of many of the stories they heard and read.

In their surface structures the ApocActs exhibit some features in common. Most of the action revolves about an apostle, upon whom the narrator's camera usually remains fixed. A common approach to launching the story (the openings are often lost) seems to have been an account of the 'apostolic lottery', in which the Twelve, after the manner of senior Roman senators, cast lots to determine their portions of the world mission.

The featured apostle thereupon sets forth – or should set forth – to his designated territory. In the course of their travels to and about these regions, the apostles establish and confirm various communities, do much that is beneficent and remarkable and come into frequent conflicts with authorities. A major source of the last is conversion of women occupying highly-placed beds, whose partners simply cannot reconcile themselves to the perpetual chastity conversion entails and vent their frustrations against missionary, wife or both. These nefarious designs are without avail until the final scene, when martyrdom brings the work to a resounding close. There can be no doubt that these endings are no less happy than they are glorious. This typical plot, like the typical plots of Greek romances, met its readers' expectations. It also left room for much variation.

The question of the genre of the ApocActs and their relation to the romantic novels has long been a subject of discussion. As with the Greek novel, much of the debate has focused upon antecedents. Here also the material comprises a relatively small number of works that imitate one another. One of the major goals of research upon ApocActs has been the construction of the widest possible barrier between these works and the canonical book of Acts. This dam is both high and deep, but it leaks like a sieve. Some of these leaks come from the possession of common ancestors. Since the Christian Gospel story underlies all of the Acts, the possibility of a single prototype is removed before play can begin. The ApocActs happily plunder a number of sources and forms: Jewish and Christian writings, Greek epic, historiography, paradoxography, philosophical biographies of the more popular sort and utopian, historical and romantic novels. Resemblances to the last are quite apparent in the accounts of threatened chastity and its preservation.

The ApocActs are novels not because they share, on balance, sufficient motifs with Chariton and Heliodorus, but because they are novels: the products of an extended narrative designed by an author who has welded various sources and forms into a unified whole. Like most ancient novels they are historical fictions. Their service to a particular group and creed may set them apart, but this could be a somewhat deceiving conclusion. It is easier for a modern reader to envision the social group addressed by the *APl* than it is to put oneself in the place of an Aphrodisian reading *Callirhoe*. Nonetheless, it is rather unlikely that many read the ApocActs for private edification and entertainment without regard for the belief systems they promote.

The ApocActs do belong on the shelves where ancient novels are stored, even if at the bottom, rather nearer to the *Alexander Romance*, *The Life of Aesop*, and Xenophon of Ephesus than to Achilles Tatius, but there is among them much that an admirer of Philostratus' work on Apollonius, or, for that matter, *The Education of Cyrus*, would recognize if not quite fully appreciate.

The individual Acts

(1) The *Acts of Andrew*. These, the worst-preserved of the major ApocActs, appeared in approximately the middle of the second century, possibly at Alexandria. Popular in later western circles, the *AA* encountered the improving hand of the Bishop of Tours, Gregory, who set out late in the sixth century to produce a more accessible Latin edition. He largely eliminated the speeches, made

some structural changes, abbreviated episodes and gave the entire work a more catholic accent.

From the martyrdom, which has a separate history, and various fragments and versions, it is possible to reconstruct a fair amount of the text and its perspectives. There is, in addition, an *Acts of Andrew and Matthias among the Cannibals*, which may be either a separate work or a component of the original *AA*. This text, or segment, was the sort of thing pilloried by Lucian in his *True Story*.

Matthias' portion of the world mission includes Myrmidonia, whose inhabitants practice cannibalism. After their wont, they seize, blind and incarcerate the apostle for a period of fattening-up. Jesus apprises Andrew, to whom Greece has fallen as his lot, of the situation and sends him to the rescue. A flood (cf. the Noah story) falls upon the city. Matthias is rescued, the worst of the cannibals perish, the less reprobate convert and the apostles set out on their journey across Asia Minor into Macedonia and Greece, where Patras will be the centre of Andrew's mission and the locale for his martyrdom.

The text, especially through the interpretative speeches, invites the reader to see the symbolic meaning of the healings, exorcisms and resurrections it narrates. Two textual levels may be present also, for D. MacDonald makes an intriguing case for seeing the *AA* as a Christian retelling of the *Odyssey*. The underlying theology is also sophisticated, for it has explicit links to Middle Platonism, stoic ethics and contemporary Gnosis. The apostle brings a message of redemption through realization of one's true nature. That discovery frees believers from passions and leads them to embrace an ascetic life detached from the pursuit of honour and pleasure. Andrew illustrates these sentiments by delivering from the cross upon which he is being executed a lengthy address on the illusory nature of the phenomenal world. The source of salvation is the one God, who may be called 'Father' or 'Son'. Unorthodox as this may be by traditional standards, the *AA* contain no suggestions that they are presenting an esoteric message known to only a few.

Readers or hearers with less education could certainly enjoy the stories and appreciate the message. In addition to such sensations as a woman condemned to a brothel and a couple who perish together in a bath, there is humour: Maximilla deceives her ardent husband by introducing her maid into his bed, an angel produces female voices to conceal the absence of women from their domestic quarters while attending religious duties and a call of nature removes a proconsul from the scene at a crucial moment.

Its fragmentary state makes the assessment of this work difficult, but comparison to the *Metamorphoses* of Apuleius, which also presents a Platonic understanding of a 'mystery religion' in the form of a story that is often bawdy and boisterous, is quite apt. Modern readers find the tone of a puritanical message in a most non-puritanical form dissonant and suspect that something is wrong. The error probably lies in modern categories.

(2) The *Acts of John*. Censorship and other factors have left the *AJn* in a truncated state. This work, which appears to exploit the association of the Apostle John, identified as the author of the Fourth Gospel, with Ephesus,[3] may have been written in Syria or Alexandria and comes from the late second or even early third century.

The initial section of the book is lost. The story evidently opened in Palestine, with an appearance of the glorified Christ to John, who came in due course to his ultimate base, Ephesus, where the extant text begins. There he raised a woman, Cleopatra, and revived her husband, Lycomedes, who had died out of sorrow. The latter commissioned a portrait of the Apostle, which he venerated. When John discovered this he reproved Lycomedes.[4] The text begins to narrate the public healing of the entire populace of sick, elderly women before breaking off. Following this action John became embroiled with one Andronicus, whose wife, Drusiana, he had converted. Incarceration followed and was resolved with the conversion of Andronicus.

Drusiana was confused by the manifold forms of Christ, who had appeared to her in prison, giving the apostle occasion for an explanation in the form of an embedded 'Gospel', an ultra-johannine exposition that presents a different account of the Last Supper, including the famous 'Hymn of Christ', with its accompanying liturgical dance.[5] This section includes apparent interpolations that move it toward the orbit of Valentinian Gnosticism. The Polymorphy of Christ – a quality also exhibited by the earthly Jesus – exhibits the meaning of the one among its many manifestations.

Following another gap in the text, John wondrously ruins one of the seven wonders of the ancient world: the Temple of Artemis. In the wake of this event he restored the life of a priest who had perished in the collapse. Following this he dealt with the situation of a young man involved in an adulterous affair who had killed his reproving father and then castrated himself out of remorse.

John then set out on travels around Asia Minor. During his absence the faithful Drusiana had died out of despair because of the lust her beauty had aroused in a prominent Ephesian male. Divine intervention thwarted his efforts to achieve his ambition upon her corpse, whereupon this virtuous Ephesian matron could be restored to life. Shortly thereafter John became the only hero of an ApocActs to die a natural death.

The *AJn* coheres literarily and theologically. The episodes, which cannot be found wanting in variety and interest, have been shaped to reinforce the explicit theological message of the several addresses. Resurrection, which is the essential type of healing, is but a symbol of authentic life. Mere revivification accomplishes nothing. Language no less than act is a limited medium for the communication of transcendent reality. This constitutes a profound protest against the unambiguous solutions of 'orthodoxy'. Like the *AA*, then, the *AJn* in its original form was a rather sophisticated work. In this case, however, the project involved less the appropriation of Greek philosophical thought than an intense concentration upon one facet of a particular heritage: johannine Christianity. That orientation, together with some of the ideas it expresses, has given the *AJn* the distinction of receiving more ecclesiastical denunciation than any other of the ApocActs.

(3) The *Acts of Paul*. The early North African lay theologian, Tertullian, had some issues with the *APl*, to which he assigns authorship and provenance: a second-century presbyter in Asia Minor, who, he claims, lost his position because of this publication (*On Baptism*, 17). Two sections of this work have had an independent existence: the martyrdom, as usual, and the famous Acts of Paul and Thecla, retained because of their use in her cult. The addition of modern papyrus discoveries to these texts has made about two-thirds of the ancient Acts available. Not all agreed with Tertullian. The *APl* appears in some lists of biblical texts and long remained an honoured source for church historians. This relative success stems from both interesting content and relatively non-controversial theology.

Only hints and fragments of the opening survive. When his mission brings him to Iconium, Paul's preaching sweeps away a young woman named Thecla, who accepts his message and rejects her fiancé. He, in turn, allies with her mother to have the apostle run out of town and Thecla burned at the stake. Rescued by heaven-sent rain, she joins Paul *en route* to Pisidian Antioch. There her beauty captivates one Alexander, with the predictable results: rejection of him and condemnation of her. The vicious seals assigned to devour her demur, but their pool provides water for a self-administered baptism. Finally convinced by these demonstrations, Paul makes Thecla a missionary. Although these well-known chapters do form a part of the original *APl*, Thecla, rather than the apostle, is their central figure. Paul is a foil against which Thecla's radiance gleams. For earthly protection and support she must turn to women rather than to her mentor.

Paul proceeds on his mission of building churches and ruining marriages. At Ephesus the conversion of an official's wife eventuated in condemnation to the beasts. The lion selected for this task was, however, himself a product of the pauline mission and demurred. Whereas the canonical Acts bring Paul to Rome as a prisoner but leave him alive and all but free, the *APl* recount his arrival as a free person and his death at the behest of Nero.

These Acts play variations upon the theme of opposition arising from a message of renunciation. Their spiritual world breathes some of the atmosphere that would erupt in the rigorous charismatic movement known as Montanism. Constant revision and partition make a literary assessment of the original text difficult, but the *APl* appear to have been a unified composition rather than an amalgamation of diverse traditions.

(4) The *Acts of Peter.* Perhaps two-thirds of this probably late second-century work is still available, the largest portion in a Latin translation of the fourth century or later. Church history (Peter as the 'first Pope') has influenced both the shape and the survival of this text, the extant portions of which centre about Rome. Whereas most of the ApocActs reflect, or at least present, loosely and democratically organized groups with distinctive beliefs and practices, the *APtr* are distinctly ecclesiological, with interests in the conversion of wealthy patrons from the upper strata, solid church organization and the suppression of heresy. *APtr* thus exhibits relatively limited affinity with the conventional sort of Greek novel.

The story presumably opened in Jerusalem and included an encounter between Peter and Simon (negatively characterized as

'Magus', a wizard). The latter evidently withdrew to Rome, where he offered no particular challenge until Paul departed for Spain. Simon then began to attract numerous adherents, including Marcellus, a Roman senator. At this juncture Christ, through a vision, sent Peter to intervene. In the course of the voyage he converted the ship's captain.

Once in Rome, the apostle begins to repair the damage. The core of the extant text relates his extended *agon* (contest) with Simon, which resembles the biblical competition between Moses and Pharaoh's magicians. Simon is no mean craftsman, but Peter repeatedly both reverses and trumps his accomplishments. In the course of these duels a dog and an infant are made to speak, a dried fish comes to life, demons flee and corpses are raised in a public exhibition. Like Apollonius of Tyana (4.20) Peter restores an imperial statue shattered by an expelled demon. The denouement comes when Simon, in his ultimate bid for power, undertakes to fly (cf. Apuleius *Met.*3.21). Brought down by Peter's prayer, he withdraws from Rome and dies of his injuries.

With heresy safely abated, concupiscence may rear its head. The chastity of converted wives and mistresses brings conspiracy and persecution in its wake. Peter sets out on the path of discretion but returns when shamed by an appearance of Christ and suffers crucifixion upside down, delivering a speech from the cross. A vision finally leads Nero to abandon the persecution.

The popular character of these Acts emerges in its approach to theological dissension: rather than refute false teachings, there is a narrative account of resolution through the manifestation of superior power. This approach appalls scholars but has never lacked appeal, as its repristination in more recent novels and cinema indicate.[6] The *Quo Vadis* story (which may have its origins in the *APtr*) is familiar to many who have no notion that it derives from one of the ApocActs. Those who would prefer not to regard the *APtr* as an ancient novel must reckon with its great success as source for modern novels.

(5) The *Acts of Thomas*. As a complete text evidently written in Syriac rather than Greek the *AThom* stands out. This is also the most outstanding representative of the ApocActs by virtue of its literary and intellectual depth. The *AThom* probably derives from the region around Edessa in the early third century, a thriving area with a rich bilingual culture as well as a centre of commerce and

exchange between East and West. The 'normal' Syrian Christianity of that era was, by western standards, rather abnormal. A Greek translation soon appeared. Although there are a number of Syriac manuscripts, the Greek tradition has most faithfully preserved the original character of the *AThom*.

At first sight the initial six 'Acts' of the thirteen sections appear lacking in organization and development, whereas Acts 7–13 centre about the court of King Misdai (Masdaeus) and exhibit considerable literary unity. The driving force behind the first half is not its surface episodes but a thick texture of allusions to biblical stories and texts. For the biblically learned, every reading brings fresh discoveries.

AThom contains two long poems, one of which is the admirable 'Hymn of the Pearl'. Outwardly this is a fairy-tale of some charm. At the symbolic level it summarizes the message of the book. Apuleius' use of the story of Cupid and Psyche provides an extremely apposite analogy. The cohesion of narrative, symbol, allusion and poetic inserts with its philosophy (a dualistic Christianity akin to Gnosis but not related to any of the specific Gnostic systems) makes *AThom* a profound and well-crafted religious novel that can evoke appreciation from readers quite unsympathetic to its worldview.

(6) The *Pseudo-Clementines*. The title refers to a number of writings purporting to relate the autobiography of St Clement of Rome. Since its first appearance, probably in Syria *c.* 250 CE, this work has undergone numerous revisions. Now extant are the *Homilies*, evidently the work of an editor with Arian sympathies, and the *Recognitions*, which survive in Latin and Syriac translations. The theological perspective of the *Ps-Clems* includes elements that frustrate modern constructs, for they are rationalistic, 'Judaeo-Christian', and have affinities with some elements known from Gnosis.

The narrative line follows the fortunes of an aristocratic Roman family. In response to a dream, Clement's mother leaves the city with his older twin brothers. They disappear. The father goes in search of them and fails to return. Meanwhile, Clement is involved in a quest of another sort: for truth. Investigation of the various philosophies fails to satisfy him, so, upon hearing of the appearance of God's son in Judea, he sets out for that place, and meets Peter, who has the answers to his questions. Clement accompanies Peter on his local missionary journeys, one feature of which is confrontation with Simon Magus (whose views are, in fact, pauline).

Those who want their romances brief and action-packed will be disappointed here, for the *Ps-Clems* are richly endowed with examples of Peter's preaching. As the work draws to a close, the several members of the family are discovered, rescued, if need be, from the low estates into which they have fallen, and all happily reunited. If the ApocActs appear to share various motifs and techniques with romantic and other novels, the *Ps-Clems* have apparently devised or appropriated the frame of a novel rather like *Apollonius, Prince of Tyre*. Since similar plots can be found in New Comedy and other genres, it is not necessary to posit the use of an actual novel, although this is far from unlikely. The themes of recognition and quest do unite the story of Clement with those of his family, but the narrator does not particularly exploit this opportunity for parallelism. By contrast, then, the *Ps-Clems* suggest that the ApocActs are not best viewed as works of Christian propaganda that simply imitate Greek novels to enliven their plots.

III CONCLUSION

The composition of new Acts continued for centuries, alongside the revision of the older works discussed above, merging with and influencing the writing of lives of post-New Testament saints. Liturgical practice, especially monastic devotion, required texts that could be heard on a single occasion and thus gave strong impetus to the preservation of those portions recounting apostolic martyrdoms.

These texts considerably expand both the repertory and horizon of the ancient novel. The *floruit* of the Graeco-Roman novels coincides with that of the ApocActs (*c.* 100–250 CE), a fact that is scarcely accidental, for these works respond to similar and evolving tastes and needs. In the case of the Christian texts the social and ideological issues, while varied, are quite clear. This does not constitute a reason for disqualifying them from membership in the academy of ancient fiction, as it were; it may provide those searching for the social and intellectual worlds of the Greek romance with some very useful contingent data. Since the surviving Greek novels tend to represent the more cultivated products of the genre, the ApocActs give indications of the style and contents of more genuinely 'popular' novels. Moreover, these Christian texts provide indirect evidence for the appeal of romantic novels, with some of which they evidently shared potential readers.

Generalizations are both useful and dangerous. Christian fiction, like 'pagan' novels, exhibits substantial fluidity. This was a genre wide enough to hold different viewpoints and a variety of literary and intellectual accomplishment. The present task is both to relate these Christian texts to their wider literary and cultural environments, including Graeco-Roman novels, and to emphasize the particularity and uniqueness of each work. Research on fiction in antiquity, then, is following the same general course, regardless of the body of material under investigation.

ABBREVIATIONS

ABD	*The Anchor Bible Dictionary*, chief ed. D. N. Freedman, New York: Doubleday, 1992.
ANRW	*Aufstieg und Niedergang der römischen Welt*, ed. W. Haase and H. Temporini, Berlin: de Gruyter.
Schneemelcher	Schneemelcher, W. (ed.), *New Testament Apocrypha*, rev. edn, tr. and ed. R. McL. Wilson, Cambridge: James Clarke, 1992.
ApocActs	The Apocryphal Acts of Apostles
AA	The *Acts of Andrew*
AJn	The *Acts of John*
APtr	The *Acts of Peter*
APl	The *Acts of Paul*
AThom	The *Acts of Thomas*

NOTES

1 See the contribution of J. Perkins to this volume (Ch. 15).

2 See the contribution of L. Wills to this volume (Ch. 13).

3 This association formed one of the pillars of the 'orthodox' appropriation of the tradition of the 'Beloved Disciple', an anonymous figure in the Gospel whose authority is, through later additions (John 21) placed behind it.

4 This had a ruinous effect upon the text of *AJn*, for it was condemned at the final council of Nicaea, which rejected Iconoclasm (787).

5 The Hymn is well known through its modern musical setting by Gustav Holst.

6 Henry Sienkiewcz's *Quo Vadis* was reprinted in a new English translation as recently as 1989 and has been put onto the screen at least twice. *The Silver Chalice* by Thomas B. Costain (1952) was a best-seller that became a major film of its era.

BIBLIOGRAPHY

General

For contemporary introductions, translations and bibliographical information see W. Schneemelcher (ed.), *New Testament Apocrypha*, rev. edn, tr. and ed. R. McL. Wilson, Cambridge: James Clarke, 1992, 75–541. See also the articles on the several works in *Aufstieg und Niedergang der römischen Welt*, II.25.6 and the entries in the *Anchor Bible Dictionary*, all listed below.

Editions and translations

The standard edition of the ApocActs is:

R. A. Lipsius and M. Bonnet (eds), *Acta Apostolorum Apocrypha*, 2 vols in 3 pts, 1891–8, repr. Darmstadt: Georg Olms, 1959.

New editions are emerging under the auspices of the *Association pour l'étude de la littérature apocryphe chrétienne*, in the *Corpus Christianorum Series Apocryphorum*. These include introduction, commentary and French translation as well as the texts. Now available are:

E. Junod and J-D. Kaestli, *Acta Johannis*, 2 vols, Turnhout: Brepols, 1983.
M. Prieur, *Acta Andreae*, 2 vols, Turnhout: Brepols, 1989.

Note also:

D. R. MacDonald, *The Acts of Andrew and The Acts of Andrew and Matthias in the City of the Cannibals: Society of Biblical Literature Texts and Translations: Christian Apocrypha Series*, Atlanta: Scholars, 1990.

English translations of the ApocActs are available in Schneemelcher. An old standard, which includes some material not available in Schneemelcher, is:

M. R. James, *The Apocryphal New Testament*, Oxford: Oxford University Press, 1924 (frequently reprinted, with some changes and additions).

New American translations will soon be available in a series of Christian Apocrypha issued by Polebridge Press. K. Elliott is completing a new edition of *The Apocryphal New Testament*.

The current edition of the Greek and Latin texts of the Pseudo-Clementines is:

B. Rehm, *Die Pseudoklementinen I & II: Griechische Christlichen Schriftsteller*, Berlin: Akademie Verlag, 1965–9.

There is no recent edition of the Syriac text and no full English translation. Schneemelcher includes a partial translation. A complete translation will soon appear in the Polebridge series of Christian Apocrypha.

Other

Attridge, H. W., 'Thomas, The Acts of', *ABD* 6, 531–4.
Bovon, F. *et al.*, *Les Actes apocryphes des apôtres*, Geneva: Labor et Fides, 1981.
Bovon, F. *et al.*, 'Les Actes de Philippe', *ANRW* II.25.6, 4431–527.
Bovon, F. *et al.*, 'Philip, The Acts of', *ABD* 5, 312.
Davies, S. L., *The Revolt of the Widows*, Carbondale: Southern Illinois University Press, 1980.
Drijvers, Han J. W., 'The Acts of Thomas', in W. Schneemelcher (ed.), *New Testament Apocrypha*, 2, 322–38.
Irmscher, J. and Strecker, G., 'The Pseudo-Clementines', in Schneemelcher, 2, 483–93.
Jones, F. S., 'Clementines, Pseudo', *ABD* 1, 1061–2.
Junod, E., 'Le dossier des "Actes de Jean": état de la question et perspectives nouvelles', *ANRW* II.25.6, 4293–362.
MacDonald, D. R., 'Andrew and Matthias, Acts of', *ABD* 1, 244.
MacDonald, D. R., *The Legend and the Apostle*, Philadelphia: Westminster Press, 1983.
MacDonald, D. R., *Christianizing Homer* (forthcoming from Oxford University Press).
Pervo, R. I., *Profit with Delight: The Literary Genre of the Acts of the Apostles*, Minneapolis: Fortress, 1987.
Prieur, J-M., 'Andrew, The Acts of', *ABD* 1, 245–7.
Prieur, J-M., 'Les Actes apocryphes de l'Apôtre André: Présentation des diverses traditions apocryphes et état de la question', *ANRW* II.25.6, 4384–414.
Prieur, J-M. and Schneemelcher, W., 'The Acts of Andrew', in Schneemelcher, *New Testament Apocrypha* 2, 101–18.
Poupon, G., 'Les "Actes de Pierre" et leur remaniement', *ANRW* II.25.6, 4363–83.
Schaeferdiek, K., 'The Acts of John', in Schneemelcher, 2, 152–71.
Schneemelcher, W., 'The Acts of Paul', in *New Testament Apocrypha*, 213–37.
Schneemelcher, W., 'The Acts of Peter', in *New Testament Apocrypha*, 271–84.
Schneemelcher, W., Introduction to second and third century Acts of Apostles in *New Testament Apocrypha*, 75–100.
Schneemelcher, W. (ed.), *New Testament Apocrypha*, revised edn, trans. ed. R. McL. Wilson, Cambridge: James Clarke & Co., Ltd., 1992.
Sellew, P., 'Paul, The Acts of', *ABD* 5, 201–2.
Stoops, Jr, R. F., 'Peter, The Acts of', *ABD* 5, 267–8.
Tissot, Y., 'L'encratisme des Actes de Thomas', *ANRW* II.25.6, 4415–30.

15

REPRESENTATION IN GREEK SAINTS' LIVES

Judith Perkins

Hagiographic narratives, accounts of saints' lives, first began to appear in the middle of the fourth century. *Acts of the Martyrs* (mid-second century and later) were popular and subsequent early *Lives* focused on the institutions of eremitism and monasticism. Later saints were discovered in varying milieux from the airy isolation of the Stylites to the social centrality of wealthy women. The quick translation into Latin versions and wide circulation of the earliest example, the *Life of Anthony*, attributed to Athanasius, attest to the genre's immediate popularity – a popularity that continued throughout the Latin middle ages and the Byzantine period. The basic challenge facing students of hagiography, in fact, results from the genre's wide appeal; most of the *Lives* exist in several textual versions (Greek, Latin, Coptic, Syriac, Arabic) and great effort has been expended in establishing both the best and most primitive texts. Jean Bolland began the critical study of hagiography in the seventeenth century with the publication of *Acta Sanctorum*, a collection of texts. His followers, the Jesuit Bollandists, as well as many others, have continued this textual work. Attention has also been directed toward assessing the historicity of the *Saints' Lives* and the usefulness of their historical information.[1] Understanding of the genre and of its context, however, demands exploration of the modes and functions of representation in these narratives.

Current critical theory has drawn attention to the politics of representation. Representation is by its nature partial and selective and inevitably excludes material which might have been represented or represented differently. There is growing recognition that a culture's reality, its sense of the way 'things really are' is a function of its systems of representation, the processes and particularities used to bring its cultural world to consciousness. What gets represented, how and by whom are essential questions not just for making sense of literary texts themselves, but for coming to understand the cultures producing such texts and in turn reproduced through them. Humans come to understand themselves, their roles and their world through the scripts their cultural representations offer them.

Narrative's function in the formation of the self is not a modern notion; the authors of hagiography acknowledge it. The texts of a number of *Saints' Lives* express an acute awareness of the close connection between discourse and self-understanding. Quite explicitly hagiographers write to offer their readers models for human action. In this sense all *Saints' Lives*, whether based on historical figures or otherwise, can be considered 'fictions', fashioned models for emulation rather than historical portraits. The prologue to the *Life of Anthony* (251–356 CE), is clear about the work's purpose:

> Since you have asked me about the career of the blessed Anthony, hoping to learn how he began the discipline (*askesis*), who he was before this, and what sort of death he experienced, and if the things said concerning him are true – so that you might lead yourselves in imitation of him . . .
>
> (Gregg 1980: Intro.)

The *Lives* repeatedly refer to the effect texts have on 'real' lives. Both Anthony and Simeon the Elder (387–459), for example, chose the ascetic life after hearing passages from the Gospels read in church (Gregg 1980: 2; Lent 1917: 112). St Augustine testifies that reading the *Life of Anthony* led some men to abandon their careers and the world. Female saints had female literary models. The *Life of Olympias* (died early fifth century) opens by linking Olympias with Thecla, the female heroine of the second century *Acts of Paul and Thecla*: 'Thecla, a citizen of heaven, a martyr who conquered in many contests. . . . Olympia walked in the footsteps of this saint, Thecla, in every virtue of the divinely inspired way of life' (Clark 1979: Ch. 1). Quite clearly the writers of hagiography would concur with contemporary literary theorists on the important consequences in actual human lives of narrative representation.

Identifying Christianity's representational strategies offers, I suggest, the key to understanding how Christianity acquired power and influence in the ancient world. The so-called 'triumph' of

Christianity was a triumph of representation. But it is difficult for us as heirs to the representational *coup* effected by Christianity not to view the texts of the early Christian period with simplifying hindsight, overlooking their radicalism in the light of its centrality in our own tradition. B. P. Reardon's statement in his recent book, *The Form of Greek Romance*, that the popularity of hagiography put an end to the writing of Greek romance is suggestive (1991: 167). Greek romance's eclipse by hagiography obviously belongs to the far-reaching ideological rearrangements that Christianity accomplished in the Graeco-Roman world. Reardon's comment suggests an avenue for examining the working out of this ideological shift in a limited representational space. Comparing the *Saints' Lives* with the romances they replaced allows them to be historicized, set into their historical situation so that what is distinctive about them can emerge. The representational enterprise of the early Greek *Saints' Lives* was to open up cultural space for the centrality of a new kind of human subject – the subject as sufferer, as poor or sick. Constructing this subject through discourse, Christianity as an institution formed around this subjectivity, not only conceptually, but also actively – collecting funds, acquiring power, administering hospitals and poorhouses to succour various categories of sufferers.

Representation in hagiographic narratives functioned to bring to cultural consciousness a reality quite different from that previously provided in the prose narratives of the Graeco-Roman world and to introduce new actors onto the cultural stage.[2] The specific parameters of this difference can be seen by comparing the *Lives* with the Greek romances. That these two prose narrative forms share similarities of plot and incident has often been noted; trials, travels, adventures, sufferings are features of both. But Elizabeth Clark in her discussion of the *Life of Melania* (385–439) precisely defines the difference between the two forms. Clark notes the close correspondence between the heroines of romance and the saint. Melania, a beautiful adolescent of high birth, kept from her heart's desires by her kin, travels throughout the Mediterranean world, is shipwrecked and beset by pirates (Clark 1984: 155). In spite of these romance conventions Clark maintains that Melania's ascetic lifestyle and the reality of its depiction separate her from the world of romance; in Clark's summation: 'lice are not the stuff from which romances are made' (165). Clark's perception deserves extrapolation, for lice are conspicuously the stuff of hagiography. The

Lives are filled with the specifics of the more wretched aspects of human existence; lice, worms, pus and rotting flesh feature significantly in them. If a culture's reality results from the particularities of human existence represented in the cultural media, *Saints' Lives* functioned to construct a reality radically different from that of the narrative representations of the Greek romances.

The plot of the typical romance begins when two well-born and handsome young people fall in love and somehow become estranged. During their separation, they suffer both because of their unfulfilled love for one another and because of the many misfortunes and dangerous situations they find themselves in, or threatened by – shipwrecks, slavery, prison, pirate attacks, disembowelment, crucifixion, torture. But fundamental to the depiction of suffering in romance is that it is offered as specifically the condition that is to be passed through or avoided in the nick of time. The suffering and trials of romance exist only to provide piquancy for or to delay the happy ending that every reader anticipates. Northrop Frye notes that romance is the genre of social affirmation; the audience's sense of 'this should be' at the reunion or marriage that concludes each narrative is a social judgement affirming the present worth of the human community and its future (1957: 167). Each romance ends with an implicit promise that no more suffering follows and that the hero and heroine return to or commence a life characterized by 'wealth, marriage and luxuriousness' (Achilles Tatius 6.13). In effect, the action of romance entails the flight from a world where poverty, pain and loneliness can touch the protagonists. Romance affirms that their 'real' life, their 'real' community excludes exactly such conditions. The narratives, at times, mark the unreality of suffering for their protagonists by depicting apparent misfortunes as illusory.

Achilles Tatius' heroine, Leucippe, for example, appears to die in the narrative on three different occasions; on one she is apparently disemboweled and her entrails roasted and eaten. The narrative emerging from this scene suggests a certain cultural obsession with pain that also shows up in the *Acts of the Martyrs*, but the episode's real point is that Leucippe has not, in fact, been harmed. The reader later learns that the whole gruesome spectacle had been staged with the aid of an actors' trunk to fool the robbers holding her (3.15–17).

At another point Leucippe is apparently killed, decapitated and thrown from a pirate ship (5.7). The narrative portrays Clitophon sorrowfully gathering up the headless body and burying it. Again the suffering turns out to be an illusion – at least for Leucippe who later explains that another woman, an unfortunate prostitute, was substituted and beheaded in her place (8.16). In this episode the text suggests that the murder is not the tragedy the reader had interpreted it to be because it happened, not to Leucippe, but to a woman of the lower sort. In the narrative representation of romance the second woman's suffering is invisible. The romance betrays here its inherent bias against the lower classes, a bias shared by the rest of Graeco-Roman culture. Achilles Tatius repeatedly represents the lower classes (except for favoured slave companions) as 'other', savage, dangerous and deserving little sympathy (Egger 1990: 148–69). Sailors caught in a storm act cowardly, seizing the lifeboat, abandoning ship and fighting off the passengers with axes and swords (3.3). After the shipwreck Leucippe and Clitophon are attacked by herdsmen/robbers (*boukoloi*), described in the most negative terms; savage, dark, foreign, with shaven heads and thick bodies (3.9).

Chariton's romance shares a similar perspective. In the scene depicting the near-crucifixion of Chaereas and Polycharmus the heroes are saved at the last moment, but their fourteen companions, the other workmen (*ergatoi*) die without any authorial comment or sympathy. In the textual representation of these romances only actions affecting the well-born are expected to elicit readers' sympathy. For these well-born characters, the pain, poverty and suffering are only temporary, alien conditions, as foreign to the real existence of the protagonists as the exotic lands they often travel through before their reunion and return to the authentic human community. The romance functions as part of a cultural script that represents poverty, pain and suffering as unauthentic human conditions estranging those experiencing them from legitimate society. Hagiographic discourse offers a radically different script and works to introduce new categories of subjects into the cultural consciousness. Two groups of *Saints' Lives* demonstrate this thesis – those depicting Stylite saints and women saints.

The Christian cultural script had been initiated by the narrative of the *Acts of the Martyrs*, portraying the torture, suffering and death of Christians (Perkins 1985: 225–9). These popular and widely distributed texts presented the message that to be a Christian was to suffer. The earliest *Saints' Lives*, although focused on the institutions of eremitism and monasticism, continued to depict the physical suffering of the saints and place it in the tradition of the martyrs. Both Pachomius (286–346) and Anthony are beaten by the devil, and Pachomius explicitly compares his mortifications to the martyrs' actions. Sick, he considers eating some healthy food, but determines not to, remembering 'if the martyrs of Christ, having their limbs cut off and being beheaded or burnt, persevered to death in their faith in God, shall I be a coward in a very minor trouble?' (Veilleux Gr. Life 1980: 13) But the *Lives* of the Stylite saints present the message that to be a Christian is to suffer much more forcefully. Stylites were those who chose to take up a position on a pillar (*stylos*), hold it for years, unprotected from the elements, fasting, praying, experiencing extreme physical hardship and achieving immense fame and influence. (Delehaye 1923: *passim*). The earliest Stylites were Syrian, and the rigour of their practice is often explained by the extremism of the Syrian ascetic tradition. This, however, leaves unexplained their wide popularity. Despite their isolation the lives attribute to these saints a wide popularity. Simeon the Elder is visited by numerous pilgrims from as far away as Britain: Daniel the Stylite is consulted by emperors and bishops. Their *Lives* themselves were curiously popular, translated into many languages and circulated widely. The depiction of the Stylites centres on the real physicality of their suffering – this is no illusory pain. What strikes a modern reader of these *Lives* is the brutally graphic delineation of the suffering human body they include. These texts do not avert their gaze from the noisome reality of actual human suffering. These saints attracted so much attention, I suggest, because they were enacting the cultural script that determined that to be a Christian *was* to suffer. Now, however, the suffering was located in the afflicted human body.

Anthony's version of the *Life of Simeon the Elder* contains graphic descriptions of bodily affliction (Harvey 1988: 86–7). Even before Simeon mounts his pillar, he tightly binds a reed cord around himself under his clothes and wears it until his body becomes infected down to the very bones (5). The other monks complain to the archimandrite that Simeon smells and is full of worms – a description that is repeated several times in the early chapters. When the archimandrite discovers that indeed Simeon is rotting, infested with worms, he tries to have the cord unfastened. Hot water is poured over Simeon's body to try and separate the cord from his garments and rotting flesh, but finally doctors have to be summoned to cut apart the putrid mass (8). From the beginning, Anthony emphasizes in all its appalling detail the reality of Simeon's physical sufferings. Nor do these abate when Simeon mounts his pillar; the Syriac text notes, for example, that the ulcers on Simeon's feet (filled with maggots) emitted such a stench that those climbing to see him were distressed when only half-way up the ladder (Lent 1915–17: 156). Disciples put incense and fragrant ointment on their noses so they could ascend to him.

A later episode conveys not only the reality of Simeon's suffering but its worth. A Saracen leader arrives under Simeon's pillar just as a worm falls from the saint's leg. The Saracen catches the worm and blesses himself with it. Simeon shouts down for him not to touch it; it is a stinking worm from stinking flesh (18). His words shock the reader into visualizing the repugnant aspects of the suffering body. But when the Saracen looks into his hand, he finds a pearl, not a worm. In the reversed rhetoric of Christian discourse, suffering in all its horror is transmuted into treasure, and sufferers are honoured. In the same way Christian martyrs had insisted that their torture was victory and their death, life. Nevertheless, for Simeon the worms remain worms; the realism of the scene insures that the loathsomeness of actual physical suffering is explicitly represented. Nor does the narrative displace this suffering on to some 'other', as the romance does, but describes it as the constitutive action of a major Christian cultural hero. Simeon's condition binds him physically with all those who come to him to be healed. Some commentators suggest that the rot and worms act as tropes figuring the saint as already dead to this world (Browning 1981: 126). Perhaps so, but more concretely they convey the similarity between the saint's physical condition and all those others suffering from grievous physical ailments.

The *Life of Simeon* influenced the practice and the portrayal of later equally popular Stylite saints. Daniel the Stylite (409–93), who made himself an imitator of Simeon, was likewise famous and honoured for his ascetic exertions. His depiction shows him actually crippled by his life. Dismounting from his pillar to travel to Constantinople to intercede against the Monophysites, Daniel is described descending 'with difficulty owing to the pain he suffered in his feet' (Dawes and Baynes 1948: 72). In Constantinople a woman throws herself at the saint's feet and the reader shares her view: 'she saw that on one foot the sole had dropped away from the ankle bone and there was nothing left but the shin bone; she was amazed at the man's endurance' (82). Again, the saint is represented as a sufferer; the *Life* portrays a miracle-worker as physically maimed as those he heals.

By the sixth century, the Church was a well-established healing institution. Healing is the central focus of the *Life* of Simeon the Younger (521–92), whose pillar on the 'Wondrous Mountain' attracted a veritable carnival of sufferers. Once again, the *Life* illustrates that this Stylite prodigy, who took up his position on the pillar when only 7 years old, is himself afflicted and crippled by the life he has chosen. Like Simeon the Elder, Simeon the Younger winds a cord around himself with the same result – the offensive odour of rotting flesh (van der Ven 1962: 26). Next he determines to remain in a crouched position for a year. This causes the flesh of his thighs and hams to rot, melting together so that he is unable to straighten out his legs (van der Ven 1962: 26). His crouching deforms his knees, but these are healed by the Lord. The text portrays in detail Simeon's gruesome physical suffering and describes the numbers of those appealing to him for help, for exorcism (in most cases the sufferers' afflictions are ascribed to Satan). This record of so much terrible suffering wearies the modern reader. So many sick – the dropsical, lepers, those with plague, snakebite, haemorrhage – parade through the text. The reader is taken aback by the unflinching realism in the depiction. One woman, for example, who is unable to expel excrement through her anus but only through her feminine organ presents herself. At Simeon's word, the demon who had obstructed her departs and, thereafter, the *Life* notes, she excreted naturally (van der Ven 1962: 114).

One understands from such descriptions why hagiography is such an important source for medical historians (Magoulias 1964: *passim*). With the exception of certain specifically medical writings, hagiographic texts focus as do no others on the particulars of human disease and suffering. The representation of the saint's suffering and that of his clients functions to bring to cultural consciousness in realistic particularity new categories of cultural subjects – the sick and the suffering. This explains the insistent noisome realism of the texts. The texts insist on the presence of these subjects, excluded from earlier literary narratives, and urge their centrality. Romance projected as its goal an ideal human community without suffering. Like the *Acts of the Martyrs* the

Lives construct a human community focused on suffering and made up of sufferers – its goal an escape from all human community to another place. Human life in the *Lives* is defined as a state of suffering.

Women saints' *Lives* contribute to this altered representation. Christians were the first, it seems, to write biographies of women and the choice of subject itself testifies to a new and changed representational world (Meredith 1984: 181). The *Life of Melania* (385–439) offers a developed example of a conventional plot for women saints – the story of a rich woman who reconstitutes herself as a poor person by disposing of all her wealth. The Gospels may assert that the 'poor are always with us', but that was not the situation in the represented world of Graeco-Roman culture. The poor exist outside its focus.

The text of the *Life of Melania* insists on the saint's real poverty. The *Life* describes in detail the tremendous exertions it took for this fabulously rich women to rid herself of her fortune; at times it appears almost fixated on money with its strict accounting: 'They sent money to different regions, through one man 40,000 coins, through another 30,000, by another 20,000, through another 10,000, and the rest they distributed as the Lord helped them do' (15). Some episodes of almsgiving strike the contemporary reader as almost humorous. In Egypt, for example, Melania visits the hermit Hephestion; she is moved by the sight of the holy man's poverty – his sole possessions a mat, a few biscuits and some salt. Since he has already refused gold, she hides some in his salt before leaving his cell. When Hephestion discovers her ruse he chases after her, demands she take the gold back and finally throws it into the river (38). In Christian representation no one willingly accepts the wealth of this world. Hagiography, like the *Acts of the Martyrs*, inverts the values of its contemporary society.

Melania's sacrifice, however, is not humorous but very real. When the devil tempts her to recall the beauty of one of her estates, the pain of her renunciation can be overheard in her description:

> We had an extraordinary piece of property, and on it was a bath that surpassed any wordly splendour. On one side of it was the sea, and on the other, a forest with diverse vegetation in which wild boar, deer, gazelles, and other animals used to graze. From the pool, the bathers could see boats sailing on

one side and the animals in the wood on the other . . . there were sixty-two households around the bath.

(18)

The Devil baits Melania by shifting the discourse from the discipline of poverty to the economics of exchange, enacting a temptation in her own motivation: 'What sort of place is this Kingdom of Heaven that it can be bought with so much money?' (17).

Despite temptation Melania persists in her ascetic choice and rids herself of all her wealth. The genuineness of her poverty is emphasized by real effects. The Empress Serena calls her servants to witness:

> Come, see the woman who four years ago we beheld vigorous in all her worldly rank, who has now grown old in heavenly wisdom . . . She has trod underfoot the softness of her upbringing, the massiveness of her wealth, all the delights of the things of this life.
>
> (12)

Melania lives the life of the very poor, eating only on Saturday and Sunday (and then only mouldy bread), wearing haircloth and during Lent sleeping on sackcloth and ashes. Gerontius quotes her servant: 'At the time of Holy Easter, when the blessed woman emerged from the exceedingly narrow cell, we shook the sack that lay under her and enormous lice fell out' (40). For all that she continues to consort with empresses and receive imperial favours, her poverty remains squalid and real. Arriving in Jerusalem Melania testifies: 'we thought of inscribing ourselves on the church's register and of being fed with the poor from alms'(35).

The *Life* of Melania displays its heroine as belonging to the category of the poor. Nor is this offered as a category of the 'other', or a temporary detour from valid social life, but a subject position anyone can and everyone should occupy.[3] Melania recognizes that her renunciation only equates her with the many others suffering deprivations:

> And again, when I see the Evil One [the devil] suggesting a vainglorious thought to me (for example, that far from linen and numerous dresses of silk, I now wear haircloth), I think myself as very lowly. I bear in mind that there are those who lie in the marketplace naked, or only on mats, freezing in the cold.
>
> (62)

Melania's narrative allows the reader to see those left usually outside the traditional focus of Graeco-Roman representation. Hagiographic narratives often provide such glimpses – the *Lausiac History* (419–20), for example, refers to a cripple without hands or feet lying in the marketplace (21.3) and a poor woman giving birth all alone among the poor sleeping on the church porch in Alexandria (68.3). Just as the Stylite saints' *Lives* show their heroes as afflicted, women saints are poor. Greek hagiography in the Stylites' afflictions and the poverty of saintly women provides new roles for cultural heroes.

Gregory of Nyssa's depiction of his sister Macrina (died 379) similarly strives to express the reality of her poverty. During her last illness, Gregory finds her lying on a board, on the ground. When she dies, he searches for appropriate garments to lay her out in, asking her companion if there isn't something in the storage closets. She answers: 'What closets? You have everything she possessed in your hands. Look at her dress, the covering of her head, her worn sandal. This is her wealth; this her property. There is nothing beyond what you see' (189). Like the lice in Melania's *Life*, the worn sandal embodies the actuality of Macrina's poverty. Neither are the stuff of romance; they are precisely the material of the new cultural representation replacing it.

The highly romanticized story of the Antiochene actress, Saint Pelagia, only emphasizes this change. Pelagia is presented in terms reminiscent of the traditional romantic heroine, the very epitome of worldly desire and wealth (Pavlovskis 1976: 144–5). Pelagia walks through Antioch in a cloud of perfume, naked except for the jewels covering her down to her very toes, accompanied by slaves dressed and collared in gold (Petitmengin 1981: 4–5). Her appearance so shocks a group of bishops that they avert their eyes, all except for bishop Nonnus. He gives her the long and steady gaze that so often in romance ends in love. In this case its eventual result is Pelagia's conversion. The converted Pelagia acts quickly, calling for an accounting of her riches so that she may turn them over to the Church and, as she says, rid herself of the means by which the devil had ensnared her (36–7). Then she disappears from Antioch.

Years later Nonnus asks James the Deacon on his way to Jerusalem to carry greetings to a certain Pelagius. James visits this monk and talks to him through a small window in his cell. He doesn't recognize the once beautiful Pelagia; as he says later, how could he? – her eyes were so sunken and her body so wasted by her violent discipline (45). James returns for a second visit, finds the monk dead and watches the wasted body of the saint being carried out as if it were more precious than gold and precious stones (49). Only as she is prepared for burial do the monks discover she is a woman and James recognizes that the pitiful corpse is Pelagia, once called by all Antioch Margarita, Pearl, on account of her many jewels (30).

In the representational calculus of hagiography, suffering is the new riches; the body wasted by suffering is more desirable than one covered in jewels. We may recall the worm dropping from Simeon transposed into a pearl. This is a root metaphor in Christian representation, stressing the worth of suffering and poverty. In Christian narrative the female heroine is no Leucippe who escapes human suffering and returns to a human community characterized by marriage, wealth and comfort, but a Pelagia who leaves wealth and beauty for poverty and pain and whose story concludes with her escape from the human community altogether. This plot and its ending reject traditional social networks and their heroines and concentrate on a new focus for social unity. By making its protagonists afflicted and poor, hagiography introduces new roles into cultural consciousness. Not to be represented is culturally not to exist. Before Christianity as an institution could grow, it had to create the subject of its concern. Telling the lives of saints, their pain, their terrible ailments, their poverty constructs this subject as a focus of cultural attention.

Not only what gets represented but who gets to represent is also an important factor in a culture's representational system. It is difficult to generalize about the authors of Greek romance, but the authors of the *Saints' Lives* were all clerics or monks. Their interest is manifest, especially in the depiction of poverty offered in the *Saints' Lives*. The narratives make clear that it is not enough for individuals simply to divest themselves of their goods and embrace personal poverty; their money must be directed towards those in need and the institutions caring for them and away from its traditional recipients – family and state. The *Life of Melania* makes this point emphatically. Both Melania's father and her husband's relatives are censured for trying to retain a share in the couple's property. The devil is the source of such misguided thinking:

> For the Devil had led her father to such an extent (as we said before) that he, a man of great virtue, had committed a great sin under the pretext of good. It was suspected that he wanted to take their possessions and give them to the other children because he was eager to hinder them from their heavenly project.
>
> (12)

The text also credits divine providence for saving the couple's wealth from the public treasury when the prefect of the city makes an attempt to confiscate it: 'by divine providence, it happened that the people rebelled against him [the prefect] because of a bread shortage. Consequently he was dragged off and killed in the middle of the city. All the others were afraid and held their peace' (19). Neither the state nor the family are to get Christians' wealth.

Palladius in the *Lausiac History* narrates a sketch that makes a similar case against leaving one's riches to kin. There was a rich virgin in Alexandria who the text laments never gave a cent to 'stranger, virgin, church, or poor man'. Instead this woman adopts a niece and 'night and day without any longing for heaven she kept promising her all her wealth' (6.1). Again this is devil's work: 'For this is one way the devil deceives us . . . in the guise of loving one's relatives' (6.2). Saint Macarius saves the rich virgin by a trick, offering to obtain for her emeralds and hyacinths at a bargain price if she will give him 500 coins. He takes her money and uses it for his hospital. When she inquires about her gems Macarius leads her to the hospital and asks:

> what do you want to see first, the hyacinths or the emeralds? . . . He took her to the upper floor, and pointed out the crippled and inflamed women, and said 'Look, here are your hyacinths!' and he led her back down again and showed her the men: 'Behold your emeralds! If they do not please you, take your money back.'

Once again in the root metaphor of the *Saints' Lives* the poor and sick become treasure, an object of cultural desire. Wealth is no longer for the family or the state but is to be given for these poor and sick, introduced into cultural consciousness through the narration of the *Saints' Lives*. Wealth that will be overseen by clerics and monks.

Hagiography introduced new categories of subjects – the poor, the sick, the suffering, and functioned to reform the cultural notion of the human community. A vignette from a miracle collection demonstrates and metaphorically encapsulates these reforms. A crowd sleeping in the Church of Saints Kosmas and Damian awaits cures (Deubner 1907: 162–4; Magoulias 1964: 150). In a dream the saints instruct a paralysed man to lie with a mute woman. He demurs, but the saints insist. At his touch, the woman screams and the frightened man runs away; the result, the text announces, is that the paralytic who taught the mute woman to speak clearly and the speechless woman who taught the man to run marry. Marriage is the traditional happy ending and reflects the affirmation of the social community. In this example we see that through the work of hagiography, the social community of late antiquity has come to include conceptually the mute and the paralytic.

NOTES

1 The works of Peter Brown (1981, 1988) and E. Patlagean (1983) as well as a number of the essays in Hackel's collection consider the social aspects of the writings of *Saints' Lives*.

2 I have not forgotten Aelius Aristides nor the tragedies of Seneca among other examples representing pain and suffering in the ancient world. But the *Acts of the Martyrs* and hagiographic texts suggest the profit in pain with new emphasis.

3 I disagree with E. Patlagean (1983) who suggests the poor are treated as the 'other' in *Saints' Lives*.

TEXTS AND TRANSLATIONS

Blake, W. E. (ed.) (1938), *Chaereas and Callirhoe*, Oxford: Clarendon.

Blake, W. E. (tr.) (1939), *Chariton's Chaereas and Callirhoe*, Ann Arbor: University of Michigan Press.

Callahan, V. W. (tr.) (1967), *Gregory of Nyssa: Ascetical Works*, Washington: Catholic University of America Press (Fathers of the Church 58).

Clark, E. (tr.) (1979), 'Life of Olympias', in id., *Jerome, Chrysostom and Friends*, New York: Edwin Mellen Press.

Clark, E. (1984), *The Life of Melania the Younger: Introduction, Translation, and Commentary*, New York: Edwin Mellen Press.

Dawes, E. and Baynes, N. H. (tr.) (1948), *Three Byzantine Saints: Contemporary Biographies translated from the Greek*, Oxford: Blackwell (Daniel the Stylite).

Delehaye, H. (1923), *Les Saints stylites*, Brussels: *Subsidia Hagiographia*.

Deubner, Ludwig (ed.) (1907), *Kosmas and Damian: Texte und Einleitzung*, Leipzig: Teubner.

Gaselee, S. (tr.) (1917), *Achilles Tatius: Adventures of Leucippe and Clitophon*, New York: G. P. Putnam.
Gregg, R. (tr.) (1980), *The Life of Anthony and the Letter to Marcellus*, New York: Paulist Press.
Groce, D. (ed.) (1962), *Vie de Sainte Mélanie* (Sources chrétiennes 90), Paris: Editions du Cerf.
Lent, F. (tr.) (1915–17), 'Life of St. Simeon Stylites', *Journal of American Oriental Society*, 35, 103–98.
Lietzmann, H. (ed.) (1908), *Das Leben des Heiligen Symeon Stylites*, Leipzig: Hinrichs.
Maraval, P. (ed.) (1971), *Vie de Sainte Macrine: introduction, texte, critique* (Sources chrétiennes 178), Paris: Editions du Cerf.
Meyer, R. T. (tr.) (1965), *Palladius: The Lausiac History*, New York: Newman Press.
Petitmengin, P. (1981), *Pélagie la penitente: métamorphoses d'une légende*, vol. 1, Paris: *Etudes augustiniennes.*
Price, R. M. (tr.), *Theordoret of Cyrrhus: A History of the Monks of Syria*, Kalamazoo, MI: *Cistercian Studies* 88.
van der Ven, P. (ed.) (1962), *La Vie ancienne de S. Syméon Stylite le Jeune (521–592)*, Brussels: *Subsidia Hagiographia* 32.
Veilleux, A. (tr.) (1980), *Pachomian Koinonia*, Kalamazoo, MI: *Cistercian Studies* 45.

BIBLIOGRAPHY

Aigrain, R. (1953), *L'Hagiographia*, Paris: Bloud & Gay.
Barnes, T. D. (1986), 'Angel of light or mystic initiate? The problem of Anthony', *Journal of Theological Studies*, 37, 53–86.
Brown, P. (1971), 'The rise of the Holy Man in late antiquity', *Journal of Roman Studies* 61, 80–101.
Brown, P. (1981), *The Cult of the Saints*, Chicago: University of Chicago Press.
Brown, P. (1983), 'The saint as exemplar', *Representations* 1, 1–25.
Brown, P. (1988), *The Body and Society: Men, Women and Sexual Renunciation in Early Christianity*, New York: Columbia University Press.
Browning, R. (1981) 'The "Low-Level" Saint's Life in the Early Byzantine World', in S. Hackel (ed.), *The Byzantine Saint*, London: Supplement Sorbornost 5, 117–27.
Cameron, A. (1991), *Christianity and the Rhetoric of Empire*, Berkeley: University of California Press.
Clark, E. (1981), 'Ascetic renunciation and female advancement: a paradox of late antique Christianity', *Anglican Theological Review* 63, 240–57.
Clark, E. (1984), *The Life of Melania the Younger: Introduction, Translation and Commentary*, New York: Edwin Mellen Press.
Cox, P. (1983), *Biography in Late Antiquity: A Quest for the Holy Man*, Berkeley: University of California Press.

Delehaye, H. (1907), *Legends of the Saints*, tr. V. Crawford, London: Longman.
Delehaye, H. (1923), *Les Saints stylites*, Brussels: *Subsidia Hagiographica* 14.
Delehaye, H. (1927), *Sanctus: essai sur le culte des saints dans l'antiquité*, Brussels: *Subsidia Hagiographica* 17.
Egger, B. (1990), 'Woman in the Greek novel: constructing the feminine', unpublished Ph.D thesis, University of California, Irvine.
Eliott, A. G. (1987), *Roads to Paradise: Reading the Lives of the Early Saints*, Hanover, NH: University Press of New England.
Frye, N. (1957), *Anatomy of Criticism*, Princeton: Princeton University Press.
Hackel, S. (ed.) (1981), *The Byzantine Saint*, London: Supplement Sorbornost 5.
Halkin, F. (1957), *Bibliotheca Hagiographica Graeca*, 3rd edn, Brussels: *Subsidia Hagiographica* 8.
Harvey, S. (1981), 'The Politicisation of the Byzantine Saint', in S. Hackel (ed.), *The Byzantine Saint*, London: Supplement Sorbornost 5, 37–42.
Harvey, S. (1988), 'The sense of the Stylite: perspectives on Simeon the Elder', *Vigiliae Christianae* 42, 367–94.
Heffernan, T. (1988), *Sacred Biography*, Oxford: Oxford University Press.
Luck, G. (1984), 'Notes on the Vita Macrinae by Gregory of Nyssa', in A. Spira (ed.), *The Biographical Works of Gregory of Nyssa*, Cambridge, MA: Philadelphia Patristic Foundation, 21–32.
Magoulias, H. J. (1964), 'The lives of the saints as sources for the history of Byzantine medicine in the sixth and seventh centuries', *Byzantinische Zeitschrift* 57, 127–50.
Meredith, A. (1976), 'Asceticism – Christian and Greek', *Journal of Theological Studies* n.s. 27, 312–31.
Meredith, A. (1984), 'A comparison between *Vita S. Macrinae* of Gregory of Nyssa, the *Vita Plotini* of Porphyry and the *De Vita Pythagoria* of Iamblicus', in A. Spira (ed.), *The Biographical Works of Gregory of Nyssa*, Cambridge, MA: Philadelphia Patristic Foundation, 181–95.
Nesbitt, J. W. (1969), 'A geographical and chronological guide to Greek saint lives', *Orientalia Christiana Periodica* 35, 443–89.
Olsen, A. (1980), *De Historiis Sanctorum*: a generic study of hagiography', *Genre* 13, 402–29.
Patlagean, E. (1976), 'L'histoire de la femme deguisée en moine, et l'évolution de la sainteté feminine à Byzance', *Studi Medievali* 17, 595–623.
Patlagean, E. (1983), 'Ancient Byzantine hagiography and social history', tr. J. Hodgkin, in S. Wilson, *Saints and Their Cults*, Cambridge: Cambridge University Press, 101–21; originally in *Annales* 23 (1968), 102–26.
Pavlovskis, Z. (1976), 'The Life of Saint Pelagia the Harlot: hagiographic adaptation of pagan romance,' *Classical Folia* 30, 138–49.
Perkins, J. (1985), 'The Apocryphal Acts of the Apostles and early Christian martyrdom', *Arethusa* 18, 211–30.
Reardon, B. P. (1991), *The Form of Greek Romance*, Princeton: Princeton University Press.

Rousseau, P. (1985), *Pachomius: The Making of a Community in Fourth Century Egypt*, Berkeley: University of California Press.

Scarborough, J. (ed.) (1984), 'Symposium on Byzantine Medicine', *Dumbarton Oaks Papers* 38.

Spira, A. (ed.) (1984), *The Biographical Works of Gregory of Nyssa*, Cambridge, MA: Philadelphia Patristic Foundation.

Vikan, G. (1984), 'Medicine and magic in early Byzantium', in J. Scarborough (ed.), 'Symposium on Byzantine Medicine', *Dumbarton Oaks Papers*, 38, 65–86.

Ward, B. (1987), *Harlots of the Desert*, Kalamazoo, MI: *Cistercian Studies* 106.

Wilson, S. (1983), *Saints and Their Cults*, Cambridge: Cambridge University Press (extensive annotated bibliography).

Part V
AFTERMATH

16

BYZANTINE DEVELOPMENTS

Suzanne MacAlister

In the Byzantine world of twelfth-century Constantinople, eight hundred or so years after the *Aithiopika* of Heliodoros, the novel genre suddenly resurfaces in an artificial revival. The new novels – *Hysmine and Hysminias* by Eustathios Makrembolites, *Rhodanthe and Dosikles* by Theodoros Prodromos, *Drosilla and Charikles* by Niketas Eugenianos and *Aristandros and Kallithea* by Konstantinos Manasses (which survives in fragments only)[1] – are written in a learned literary 'ancient' Greek; *Hysmine and Hysminias* is written in prose and the other three in accentual verse. The revival is the precursor to the Greek vernacular verse romances which were to emerge in the fourteenth century. But, unlike the vernacular works which reveal a certain amount of interaction with the 'courtly love' tradition from the West (Beaton 1989: 132, 151ff.; Cupane 1974, 1978; Jeffreys 1976, 1980), the revival works of the twelfth century derive firmly from the Byzantine Greek tradition, from the culture and literature of its inheritance and from its own still-evolving consciousness.

The new novels seem remarkably similar to their predecessors, following, as they do, the established plot outlines of a young couple's meeting and falling in love, departure from the normal environment, separation, trials and reunion. The alien world-settings of the young lovers' adventures are redolent of the ancient novels: foreign, pagan and controlled by chance. The same literary motifs are used, and even some of the characters' names are familiar.

> After being imprisoned by a band of Parthians, Drosilla and Charikles are taken captive by the chief of the Arabs who makes arrangements to transport them to his homeland:

women prisoners are to travel by carriage and men on foot. *En route*, Drosilla is struck from her carriage by the branch of a tree but, instead of meeting a miserable fate on the rocky seashore below, her fall is arrested and she wanders off.

Charikles learns of Drosilla's fall and, imagining her to have perished in the sea, laments. He and his companion Kleandros, freed by the Arab chief, retrace their steps in the hope of learning something about the dead Drosilla. Drosilla, meanwhile, reaches a remote village and is befriended by a kindly old woman who takes the girl to her home.

That night Drosilla experiences a sweet dream of the god Dionysos which prompts her to ask her hostess to escort her to a certain inn. There they encounter the innkeeper's son who, when asked whether a young man named Charikles is staying there, says he is not. Charikles, however, is inside the inn, unaware of the events outside. Drosilla laments, bewails her false dream and wishes to die.

Such is the main action narrated in Book 6 of Eugenianos' novel, *Drosilla and Charikles*. For the reader who comes to the Byzantine novels with expectations and assumptions about the genre, they can appear as somewhat exaggerated and poor imitations of their predecessors. This was the impression gained by Perry at least, who described them as slavish imitations 'written in the twelfth century by miserable pedants' (Perry 1967: 103). But a close look behind the scenes reveals that the novels of the revival are not attempting a straightforward exercise of reproduction: rather their writers are using the discourse of the ancient novel to voice statements which reflect the specific climate of their own time and place rather than that of antiquity.

The new context of the novel's revival was a very different one from the environment of the late Hellenistic period in which the genre had first flourished and which the subject matter of its novels can be seen to express. What the pagan novels of late antiquity encapsulate is an attitude or symptom of a society where, rather than individuals realizing and living their senses of self through indentification with community values and bonds, the subjects experience themselves as atomized individuals struggling for control over the chaotic external facets of their lives, as potentially passive victims of chance or fate. Twelfth-century Byzantium, on the other hand, was a world of a firmly entrenched Christianity:

for centuries the official religion had satisfied the individual's needs for security, and both the Church and the Byzantine belief in a divinely sanctioned universal empire had provided focus for collective feelings (Kazhdan and Epstein 1985: 167).

But there is evidence that people's perception of stability was being disturbed in twelfth-century Byzantium. In the political sphere, the Byzantines had seen the defeat of their army by the Seljuk Turks at the battle of Manzikert in the east of the Empire in 1071 and, in the same year, in the west of the Empire, the loss of their province of Sicily to the Norman conquest.[2] In the social and cultural sphere, Byzantium was now turning to a new identification with its ancient pagan heritage. Contemporary social and ideological concerns were being subjected to reflection and questioning through the medium of ancient philosophy and literature (Kazhdan and Epstein 1985: 135). Active discussion was taking place on the role of Fate or Chance (Τύχη) in controlling history and human affairs (Kazhdan and Franklin 1984: 181–2). And, at the same time, condemnations for religious and intellectual heresy were seeing an all-time high at the hands of the hundred-year-long Komnenian dynasty (1081–1180) (Browning 1975: 19). In the literary sphere, we witness the writing of serious commentaries and interpretations of ancient texts in relation to contemporary times (Kazhdan and Epstein 1985: 135). From the twelfth century we have the Homeric criticisms of Eustathios of Thessaloniki and the allegorical interpretation of Homeric material by the polymath Tzetzes; both Eustathios and Tzetzes commented upon the tragedies and Aristophanes; and for the first time since late antiquity, certain texts of Aristotle were being subjected to serious exegesis (Browning 1962). Contemporary with, and part of, this whole climate of uncertainty and activity was the creation of a secular fiction indicated by the revival of the Lucianic-style satirical dialogue and, more especially, the novel.

The novel makes its reappearance in the first half of the twelfth century, probably in the thirties or forties.[3] In the intensely Christian environment which had followed the genre's demise, the ancient novels – principally those of Achilles Tatius and Heliodoros – had continued to be known and read and, despite their pagan orientation, had come to be justified as pious. The belief that both Achilles Tatius and Heliodoros were Christian bishops had arisen early on and had become quite widely spread.[4] Later, just before and around the period of the genre's revival, there is evidence to suggest that the ancient novels were subjected to a cautious ethical reinterpretation within the spiritual sphere: their underlying theme of the solitary individual's quest for security and identity through secular human love was interpreted as an allegorical description of the soul's aspiration towards salvation.[5]

The new novels might likewise lend themselves to readings appropriate to Christian ideals. The same sort of allegorical interpretation could be applied; the established convention of the central characters' passivity could be re-evaluated within the spiritual sphere as a turning of the other cheek and the passive suffering a Christian is taught to endure (Beaton 1989: 61–2); revelation and guidance provided by dreams had always been an integral part of Christian belief; and the conventional chastity of the lovers is in keeping with Christian values. The characters are made to follow established ancient novel convention and passively endure storms at sea, attempts on their lives, capture and slavery, and bewail their miserable lot. They are made to experience dreams which offer guidance and revelation. And again, in accordance with established convention, all maintain their chastity despite attempts made upon it.

But – to return now to our earlier suggestion – despite surface impressions, the Byzantine novelists are not attempting a straightforward exercise of imitation. Rather, through their appropriation and manipulation of the ancient discourse, and their integration into it of the voices of other diverse discourses, they create a medium for voicing their own new and special statements which they direct towards a contemporary, twelfth-century, reading of the ancient novel. The revival novels thus provide ideal examples of what Bakhtin articulates in his concept of 'the speech of another' – that is, discourse shaped by, and oriented towards, the perspectives, conceptual systems, value judgements and language of another (Bakhtin 1981: 282). This sort of exercise can also serve a subtle polemic function which is intended to jolt and challenge an audience's taken-for-granted assumptions and to subvert accepted values. So, too, the discourse of the new novels can be seen, at times, to clash with their contemporary audience's subjective belief system and, as well, to express statements which their dominant culture might have found ideologically intolerable.

One of the means by which the twelfth-century novelists confronted their contemporary audience was through their reformulation of those established conventions of the genre which could lend themselves to ethical reinterpretation within the spiritual sphere: for example, the central characters' lack of initiative, and the consequent supernatural guidance and revelation they are offered.[6]

In the new novels, as in their ancient predecessors, the characters' powerlessness and passivity is an essential component: upon it depend the couples' falling in love, their separations and their trials. But in the new novels this feature is exaggerated and indeed can emerge as a virtue. One of the surviving fragments of Manasses' *Aristandros and Kallithea* seems to confirm this reading: when faced with the option of action, a character chooses 'rather to suffer and be damned than act and cause damnation'[7] (cf. Beaton 1989: 62).

Sometimes, however, this essential component is subjected to a twist. The Byzantine writers follow their predecessors and render their characters powerless victims as a consequence of the intrusion of some external force – chance, a dream or a pagan god – but, it transpires, their characters' essential suffering is not always due to the intervention of the conventional external force as it appears on the surface: it is sometimes due to the workings of the individual's own inner reasoning or psychological processes. To see the different ways in which all the complete novels make this same statement, let us consider an example from each of them.

In Prodromos' *Rhodanthe and Dosikles*, the hero Dosikles, after seeing Rhodanthe for the first time, falls in love with her. He describes his psychological state: 'Such were the squalls and adverse winds of my concerns that I was thrown into a state of upheaval, like an unstable ship on a rough sea' (2.316–8). Not even the intervention of an encouraging dream apparently revealing the girl's love for him affords him any hope as it might an ancient novel character; rather he explicitly rejects the intrusion of the external force into his affairs as a fleeting illusion and, assuming the voice of Aristotle, dismisses it as a mere product of his own psychological state:[8]

> For the excessive accumulation of earthly anxieties casts down gloom and, wreaking loathsome despondency, deep blackness and oppressive dark dejection throughout, it muddies reason and is much wont to cause sleep, and even this is not without fears, without terrors. For night-time, moulding inordinate phantoms and shadowy traces of

> daytime problems and utterances, and forging solitary images with deceptive finger, gives rise to hallucinations in sleep.
> (2.322–33)

The revelation offered to Dosikles conforms – on one level – to the conventions of the genre in that it offers the reader a foreshadowing of an eventual union with Rhodanthe. But, as far as Dosikles is concerned, the convention is subjected to an inversion: rather than the character passively accepting the intrusion of the external force and reacting under its control as novel convention dictates, it is precisely Dosikles' *rejection* of it as an illusion that motivates him to act in such a way as to be himself responsible for triggering his subsequent sufferings. His abduction of the girl leads directly to their subjection to the conventional tribulations – pirate attack, imprisonment, war, slavery and threatened sacrifice – which he is made to endure passively, only lamenting his miserable fate. Prodromos, therefore, renders Dosikles the essential powerless sufferer, but as a consequence of his own inner processes of reasoning rather than of some external and incomprehensible power.

Let us now consider the way in which Makrembolites' hero becomes the powerless victim of love. At the beginning of the novel, Hysminias is openly contemptuous of love; he is totally preoccupied with his appointment as herald to the religious festival of the Diasia. But normal courses of events are to be disrupted when the hero meets Hysmine and the following night the god Eros appears to him in his sleep and betrothes him to the maiden. On the surface this might all seem quite in accordance with established novel convention: Hysminias does subsequently become subject to Eros and fall in love with Hysmine, and it is his love which leads to all the sufferings which he must endure. But, as we shall see, Hysminias' love is not the conventional love-at-first-sight, nor is it a direct consequence of Eros' intrusion: rather his love is generated in stages through his own inner psychological processes (Alexiou 1977).

First, in order to see how Makrembolites integrates the conventional intrusion of the external force and yet, at the same time, renders it redundant to inner processes, we must turn back to the very beginning of the narrative and view some of the actions of the heroine, Hysmine, while her family is entertaining the newly appointed herald:

> She stood beside me and, with her hand, placed the drinking cup in my hand and, with her eyes, she held my eyes. I reached out my hand for the cup and she pressed my finger, and when she pressed it she sighed, and exhaled a light breath as if from her heart. . . . And the maiden Hysmine crouched down on her heels and, taking hold of my feet, began to wash them with the water. . . . She kept on holding them – restraining, embracing, squeezing, silently fondling – and she stole a secret kiss. And finally, she ran her fingernails across them and tickled me.
>
> (1.11–12)

There is no doubt that the description of Hysmine's behaviour would clash with the expectations of an audience familiar with novel conventions relating to the central characters' lack of initiative and, as well, confront the contemporary reader's taken-for-granted ideals and values relating to sexual behaviour. The episode might be explained, then, as a provocative, but comic, reversal of the conventional ancient novel hero and his essential passivity. We can, however, look beyond the notion of parody and view it in terms of a different sort of challenge to the audience's apperceptive background, and consider it more in the light of what is to follow Hysminias' narrative.

The maiden's unwelcome behaviour is not forgotten by Hysminias: he discusses it later with his friend Kratisthenes and indeed the disturbance it arouses in him is presented as one of the causes of an uneasy dream of the all-powerful god Eros betrothing him to the girl (referred to above) which he is to experience as he sleeps that night. After his dream he lies sleepless for a long time, inwardly pondering the girl's daytime advances and now allowing himself to fantasize about his own responses – reversing his and the girl's daytime roles. While he lets his mind wander freely in this psychological state, Hysminias drops off to sleep again, this time to experience a physically erotic dream (that is, what we might call a 'wet dream') the contents of which directly reflect the contents of his waking fantasies:

> I touch her hand, but she attempts to draw it back and hide it in her dress; but, in this too, I conquer. I draw her hand to my lips, I kiss it and I nibble it, but she pulls it back again and shrinks away from me. I embrace her around her neck, I press my lips to her lips and fill them with kisses,

> and I let my desire pour over her. She makes a play of closing her mouth but nips me on my lip in an erotic way and steals a secret kiss. I kissed her eyes and let my soul flood with utter passion – for the eye is the source of eros. I occupy myself with the girl's breasts as well; she resists in a truly noble way and pulls away from me, using her whole body as a fortress for her bosom, like a fortress protects a city – with her hands, her neck, her chin, she defends and encloses her breasts. And she draws up her knees from below, and she casts tears from her head like missiles from a fortress, all but saying, 'if you love me, be softened by my tears; if you don't love me, refrain from war'. But I feel more shame at defeat, and I hold out more forcefully, and just manage victory. But in winning I am defeated, and my aggression completely goes; for the moment my hand encircled the girl's breast, impotence completely engulfed my heart. I felt pain, my passion slackened, I trembled with a strange trembling, my sight became dim, my spirit softened, my strength subsided, my body grew heavy, my breathing was hindered, my heart beat rapidly, and a sweet pain ran right through my limbs as if it was tickling them. And an indescribable, unutterable, ineffable feeling possessed me and, by Eros, the feeling I experienced I had never felt before. So, the girl flew from my arms, or, to put it more correctly, my arms fell heavily and weakly from her. And sleep straightaway fled from my eyes and, by Eros, I was annoyed at losing so lovely a dream and being severed from my dear Hysmine.
>
> (3.7)

In this way Hysminias' own psychologically generated physical state provides the impulse for his newly born erotic love. He ends the description of his dream with the statement, 'I began to seek the same sort of erotic experience that I had had in my dream' (3.7). Makrembolites thus renders the intrusion of the all-powerful Eros redundant, and instrumental in generating Hysminias' love (and consequent suffering) only in so far as it provided the impetus for his own self-generated, free-floating fantasies.

But taking the raw events of Hysminias' conversion to love as they stand without regard to the psychological processes, his subjugation to the all-powerful god is very like the sort of conversion to Christianity described in hagiography. In stories of the saints, a dream of the all-powerful Christian god or his angels is frequently the instrument of a future saint's or martyr's conversion. The similarity between this kind of spiritual conversion and Hysminias' conversion seems close enough to suggest Makrembolites' deliberate (and provocative) embedding of the discourse of spirituality within the appropriated discourse of the ancient novel. Indeed, that Makrembolites intended his audience to make this parallel is suggested by a statement in Hysminias' narrative, 'but, in this too, I conquer':[9] an allusion to the well-known and much-debated divine imperative 'in this, conquer'[10] which appeared illuminated in the heavens as a sign to Constantine the Great and his army in the battlefield and which, together with a dream of Christ, instigated Constantine's conversion to Christianity.[11]

In the sub-plot of *Drosilla and Charikles* which runs parallel to the story's main action, the heroine, Kalligone, like Hysminias in Makrembolites' novel, had felt no love for Kleandros prior to the intervention of the god Eros. Kleandros narrates:

> I went forward, found and saw the girl, and she, by way of opening conversation with me, said, 'Greetings, o bridegroom of my dream. Eros stood over me in my sleep the other night and joined you in marriage with me, Kleandros, after paying attention to the tears you were shedding. You must find a way, Kleandros, yes, you must find a sure way of somehow tending to our affairs. For neither fire, nor sea, nor the sword would I fear if it meant having Kleandros. For those whom the god has united, who will put asunder?' When I heard these words I said in response, 'My greetings to you too, Kalligone. Come with me, come with me to the nearby harbour so that we may sail away together from Lesbos. Glory be to Eros the tyrant.'
>
> (3.2–17)

A contemporary audience would have had no problem recognizing in Kalligone's rhetorical question 'For those whom the god has united, who will put asunder?'[12] the New Testament 'What God has joined together, let man not put asunder'[13] (Kazhdan 1967: 116) and the liturgical formula in Kleandros' response: 'Glory be to Eros the tyrant'[14] (Beaton 1989: 55).

Once Kalligone has been converted to love, the couple is subjected to its sufferings. Without further ado they elope from their homeland on board a ship, are subjected to a Parthian attack and are separated. Kalligone is to escape but Kleandros is to endure imprisonment at the hands of the Parthians and captivity by the Arabs until he receives chance news that Kalligone has been killed by bandits. At this point Kleandros, rather than passively suffering and bewailing the loss of his loved one in accordance with novel convention, reacts in such a way as to cause his own death: he now becomes the victim of the processes of his own psyche, passively submitting himself to 'a pain of mind which in its sharpness exceeds the power of a sword' (8.312–3) and which, in its power, kills him. Eros' revelation to Kalligone of the couple's future union – although proven false when ancient novel convention demands such predictions prove true – could be regarded as being paradoxically fulfilled: the couple does, after all, become united in death.

The conversion, tribulations and ultimate union in death of the two lovers might lend itself to an interpretation of the episode as allegory of a Christian's quest for salvation and ultimate union with Christ in death. We might even conclude, through the use of the language of Christianity in Kleandros' description of Kalligone's conversion, that such an interpretation was intended by Eugenianos. But Kleandros' death – although suffered with the submissiveness of a Christian martyr – is, in the final analysis, brought about by himself and could thus be seen to confront contemporary ideals relating to the essential passive endurance of trials in this earthly life.

In their focus on the individual's passivity and powerlessness the twelfth-century novels are maintaining what had become an established convention in the ancient novel. The present analysis has attempted to show, however, that all three of the complete extant novels share in reformulating the established convention in such ways as to make it function as a medium for a fundamentally humanist questioning of issues to do with control and responsibility: when are external forces responsible for controlling an individual's destiny and when are purely human processes responsible? The novelists might thus be seen as contributing to the contemporary discussion about the role of Fate in shaping history and human destiny.

But we might also see that the new novels' specific use of Christian metaphor and language would have been provocative to a pious audience – especially when applied in an erotic context

(Makrembolites) or to the patronage of a pagan god (Eugenianos). But if moral sanctions had been brought to bear against them, their own contemporary environment could supply several ready-made defences. The Christian imagination had always experienced difficulties in drawing distinctions between the experience of spiritual and physical love – an ambiguity witnessed by the interweaving of piety and sexual imagery and the exploitation of the symbolism of the Song of Songs throughout the Byzantine tradition. And, parallel to, and part of, this line of argument is, of course, the Byzantines' own reading of the ancient novel's secular experience as allegory within the spiritual sphere.

NOTES

1 No English translations have been made of these novels. The Greek texts used for this paper are: for *Hysmine and Hysminias*, Hirschig 1856: 533–97; for *Drosilla and Charikles*, Hirschig 1856: 1–69; for *Rhodanthe and Dosikles*, Hercher 1859: 289–434; for *Aristandros and Kallithea*, Mazal 1969.

2 For a discussion of the effects of these events in the context of the novel's revival see Beaton 1989: 51.

3 Precise dates for the writing of the novels has been a matter of controversy, see Beaton 1989: 77f., MacAlister 1991, Poljakova 1971: 104–8.

4 In the fifth century Heliodoros was said to have been received into the monastery of Eusebonas when he was 3 years of age (Theod. *Hist.rel.MPG*82.1468) and to have later become bishop of Trikka in Thessaly (Sok. *Hist.ecc.*V.22). The belief that he became a bishop is found expressed again in the ninth century by Photios (*Bibl.*cod.73 (de Iamblichio)); a fourteenth-century remark on a manuscript says that it was expressed in the eleventh century by Georgios Kedrenos (*Schol. Vat.gr.*157) and it is again encountered in the fourteenth century expressed by Nikephoros Kallistos (*Hist.ecc.*XII.34,*MPG*146.860). In the *Souda*, Achilles Tatius too was said to have been a bishop (sv. Achilles Statios).

5 Dyck, in his edition of the eleventh-century Psellos' essay on Heliodoros and Achilles Tatius, suggests that the allegorization of the novel was primarily intended to defend it against moral sanctions – the exercises betray the existence of critics who found it morally dangerous for the young (Dyck 1986: 85). Around the period of the novel revival there appears a defence of Heliodoros written by a certain Philip-Philagathos of Cerami in Sicily which, after praising the novel's didacticism and characterization, discusses its allegorical aspect and symbolism in spiritual terms. The full text of Philip's defence is found edited in Colonna 1938: 336–70.

6 I have attempted to demonstrate the new novels' reformulation of the ancient novel's conventions relating to supernatural revelation in a

separate paper. In the ancient novel, dreams served as a non-human counter-force to the workings of Fate or Chance. In the Byzantine revival, dreams are also introduced apparently to serve the same function but the revelation which they offer is constantly made irrelevant; it either emerges as redundant or is negated somehow by human action, or is rendered as a secondary consideration in the face of human reason or initiative (MacAlister 1994).

7 μᾶλλον παθὼν καὶ κολασθεὶς ἢ δράσας καὶ κολάσας, *AK* Fr.33,1.2

8 The theory that dreams are mere remnants of sensory perceptions and reflections of daytime preoccupations was reasonably widespread in the ancient world but clearly brought together by Aristotle in his treatise *de Insomniis* in the *Parva Naturalia* (459b–461a). Theories from the *Parva Naturalia* are appropriated throughout both Prodromos' and Makrembolites' novels (MacAlister 1990).

9 ἀλλ' ὅμως κἂν τούτῳ νικῶ *HH* 3.7.

10 τούτῳ νίκα Eusebius *de Vita Constantini* 1.28.

11 This allusion has been pointed out by Beaton (1989: 53) and is surely correct given the military metaphor used in Hysminias' description.

12 οὓς γὰρ θεὸς συνῆψε, τίς διασπάσει; *DC* 3.12, cf.*DC* 7.265.

13 ὃ οὖν ὁ Θεὸς συνέζευξεν, ἄνθρωπος μὴ χωριζέτω Mark 10.9, cf. Matthew 19.6.

14 "Ερωτι δόξαν τῷ τυράννῳ *DC* 3.17.

BIBLIOGRAPHY

Alexiou, M. (1977), 'A critical reappraisal of Eustathios Makrembolites' *Hysmine and Hysminias*', *Byzantine and Modern Greek Studies* 3, 23–43.

Bakhtin, M. M. (1981), 'Discourse in the novel', in id., *The Dialogic Imagination* (English translation, first published in Russian as *Voprosy literatury i estetiki*, 1975), Austin, TX, 259–422.

Beaton, R. (1989), *The Medieval Greek Romance*, Cambridge: Cambridge University Press.

Browning, R. (1962), 'An unpublished funeral oration on Anna Comnena', *Proceedings of the Cambridge Philological Society* 118 (8), 1–12.

Browning, R. (1975), 'Enlightenment and repression in Byzantium in the eleventh and twelfth centuries', *Past and Present* 69, 3–23.

Colonna, A. (ed.) (1938), *Heliodori Aethiopica*, Rome.

Cupane, C. (1974), ' "Ερως Βασιλεύς": la figure di Eros nel romanzo bizantino d'amore', *Atti del Accademia di Arti di Palermo*, serie 4, 33(2), 243–97.

Cupane, C. (1978), 'Il motivo del castello nella narrativa tardo-bizantina: evoluzione di un'allegoria', *Jahrbuch der Österreichischen Byzantinistik* 27, 229–67.

Dyck, A. (ed. and comm.) (1986), *Michael Psellus – The Essays on Euripides and George of Pisidia and on Heliodorus and Achilles Tatius*, Vienna.

Hercher, R. (ed.) (1859), *Scriptores Erotici Graeci II*, Leipzig.

Hirschig, G. A. (ed.) (1856), *Erotici Scriptores*, Paris.

Jeffreys, E. (1976), 'The manuscripts and sources of the War of Troy', *Actes du XIVe Congrès International des Etudes Byzantines* (Bucarest 1971), Bucharest, 91–4.

Jeffreys, E. (1980), 'The Comnenian background to the *romans d'antiquité*', *Byzantion* 10, 455–86.

Kazhdan, A. P. (1967), 'Bemerkungen zu Niketas Eugenianos', *Jahrbuch der Österreichischen Byzantinischen Gesellschaft* 16, 101–17.

Kazhdan, A. P. and Epstein, A. W. (1985), *Change in Byzantine Culture in the Eleventh and Twelfth Centuries*, Berkeley, Los Angeles and London: University of California Press.

Kazhdan, A. and Franklin, S. (1984), *Studies on Byzantine Literature of the Eleventh and Twelfth Centuries*, Cambridge and Paris.

MacAlister, S. (1990), 'Aristotle on the dream: a twelfth-century romance revival', *Byzantion* 60, 195–212.

MacAlister, S. (1991), 'Byzantine twelfth-century romances: a relative chronology', *Byzantine and Modern Greek Studies* 15, 175–210.

MacAlister, S. (1994), 'Ancient and contemporary in Byzantine novels', in J. Tatum (ed.), *The Search for the Ancient Novel*, Baltimore: Johns Hopkins University Press, 308–22.

Mazal, O. (ed.) (1969), *Der Roman des Konstantinos Manasses*, Vienna: Wiener Byzantinische Studien Band IV.

Perry, B. E. (1967), *The Ancient Romances: A Literary-Historical Account of their Origins*, Berkeley and Los Angeles: University of California Press.

Poljakova, S. V. (1971), 'O chronologiceskoj posledovatelnosti romanov Evmatija Makrembolita i Fedora Prodroma', *Vizantijskij Vremennik* 32, 104–8.

INDEX

Note. Contributors vary in their transliteration of some proper names, e.g. Aseneth/Asenath, Onchsheshonqy/Onkhsheshonk. The choices made in this index are arbitrary, but should occasion no difficulty to the user.